First World War
and Army of Occupation
War Diary
France, Belgium and Germany

37 DIVISION
Divisional Troops
Royal Army Medical Corps
48 Field Ambulance
28 July 1915 - 17 April 1919

WO95/2525/1

The Naval & Military Press Ltd
www.nmarchive.com
Published in association with The National Archives

Published by

The Naval & Military Press Ltd

Unit 10 Ridgewood Industrial Park,

Uckfield, East Sussex,

TN22 5QE England

Tel: +44 (0) 1825 749494

www.naval-military-press.com

www.nmarchive.com

This diary has been reprinted in facsimile from the original. Any imperfections are inevitably reproduced and the quality may fall short of modern type and cartographic standards.

© **Crown Copyright**
Images reproduced by permission of The National Archives, London, England, 2015.

Contents

Document type	Place/Title	Date From	Date To
Heading	WO95/2525/1 48 Field Ambulance RAMC 37 Div Jul 1915-Apr 1919		
Heading	37th Division 48th Field Ambulance Vol. I July 28th-31st 1915		
Heading	War Diary of 48th Field Ambulance R.A.M.C. From 28th July 1915 to 31st July 1915		
War Diary	S.S. Inventor	28/07/1915	28/07/1915
War Diary	No 5 Camp Havre	29/07/1915	29/07/1915
War Diary	Chateau Moulle	31/07/1915	01/08/1915
Heading	37th Division 48th Field Ambulance Vol. II From 1-28.8.15		
Heading	War Diary of 48th Field Ambulance R.A.M.C. August 1915		
War Diary	Moulle The Chateau	01/08/1915	03/08/1915
War Diary	Chateau At Ebblinghem	04/08/1915	04/08/1915
War Diary	Eecke	08/08/1915	20/08/1915
War Diary	Mondicourt	28/08/1915	28/08/1915
War Diary	37th Division 48th Field Ambulance Vol III Sept 15		
War Diary	Pas	07/09/1915	30/09/1915
War Diary			
Heading	37th Division 48th Field Ambulance Vol 4 Oct 15		
Heading	War Diary of 48th Field Ambulance From 1st October 1915 to 31st October 1915		
War Diary	Pas	31/10/1915	31/10/1915
Heading	37th Division 48th F.A. Vol.5 Nov 15		
Heading	War Diary of 48th Field Ambulance November 1915		
War Diary	Humbercamp	06/11/1915	30/11/1915
Heading	37th Div 48th F.A. Vol. 6 December 1915		
Heading	War Diary of 48th Field Ambulance for December 1915		
War Diary	Humbercamp	09/12/1915	25/12/1915
Heading	37th Div 48th F.A. Vol. 7 Jan 1916		
Heading	War Diary of 48th Field Ambulance R.A.M.C. For Month Ending 31 January 1916		
War Diary	Humbercamp	31/01/1916	31/01/1916
Heading	48th Fld. Ambulance Feb 1916		
Heading	48. Field Amb. 37th Div Vol.8		
War Diary	Humbercamp	03/02/1916	17/03/1916
War Diary	Le. Souich	21/03/1916	31/03/1916
Heading	37th Div War Diary of 48th Field Ambulance April 1916 Vol 24		
War Diary	Le Souich	03/04/1916	26/04/1916
War Diary	Lucheux	27/04/1916	28/04/1916
Heading	37th Div No 48 F. Amb. May 1916		
War Diary	Lucheux	30/04/1916	30/04/1916
War Diary	Humbercamp	02/05/1916	05/05/1916
War Diary	Couturelle	06/05/1916	30/05/1916
Heading	War Diary of 48 Field Ambulance, R.A.M.C. From 1 June 1916 to 30 June 1916 48 Amb. Vol 12		
War Diary	Couturelle	03/06/1916	28/06/1916

Type	Location	Date From	Date To
Heading	War Diary Of 48th Field Ambulance From 1st July 1916 To 31st July 1916 48 Amb Vol 13		
War Diary	Couturelle	02/07/1916	02/07/1916
War Diary	Gaudiempre	04/07/1916	15/07/1916
War Diary	Houvineul	15/07/1916	15/07/1916
War Diary	Chelers	16/07/1916	17/07/1916
War Diary	Fresnicourt	18/07/1916	27/07/1916
War Diary	Grand Servins	28/07/1916	30/07/1916
Heading	War Diary of 48th Field Ambulance for the month of August 1916 Vol 14		
War Diary	Gd Servins	01/08/1916	13/08/1916
War Diary	Fresnicourt	14/08/1916	31/08/1916
Heading	War Diary Of 48th Field Ambulance From 1st September To 30th September 1916 Vol. XIV		
War Diary	Fresnicourt	01/09/1916	18/09/1916
War Diary	Fosse. 10. Sains	19/09/1916	28/09/1916
Heading	War Diary Of 48th Field Ambulance From 1st October To 31st October 1916 (Volume XV)		
War Diary	Fosse. 10. Sains	01/10/1916	15/10/1916
War Diary	Barlin	17/10/1916	17/10/1916
War Diary	Monchy Breton	18/10/1916	19/10/1916
War Diary	Gouy-En-Ternois	20/10/1916	20/10/1916
War Diary	Beauval	21/10/1916	21/10/1916
War Diary	Puchevillers	22/10/1916	22/10/1916
War Diary	Varennes	23/10/1916	28/10/1916
War Diary	Longuevillette	31/10/1916	31/10/1916
Heading	War Diary of 48 Field Ambulance From 1st November to 30th November 1916. Vol 17		
Miscellaneous	A.D.M.S. 37 Division	30/11/1916	30/11/1916
War Diary	Longuevillette	01/11/1916	10/11/1916
War Diary	Puchevillers	11/11/1916	12/11/1916
War Diary	Varennes	13/11/1916	26/11/1916
War Diary	Puchevillers	27/11/1916	30/11/1916
Heading	War Diary of 48 Field Ambulance From 1st December to 31st December 1916 Vol 17		
War Diary	Puchevillers	01/12/1916	04/12/1916
War Diary	Beauval	06/12/1916	11/12/1916
War Diary	Wavans	14/12/1916	14/12/1916
War Diary	Framecourt	15/12/1916	15/12/1916
War Diary	Bergueneuse	16/12/1916	16/12/1916
War Diary	Lierette	17/12/1916	17/12/1916
War Diary	Marquois	18/12/1916	18/12/1916
War Diary	Zelobes	20/12/1916	31/12/1916
Heading	War Diary of 48 Field Ambulance From 1st January to 31st January 1917. (Volume 18)		
War Diary	Zelobes	01/01/1917	31/01/1917
Heading	War Diary of 48 Field Ambulance from 1st February to 28th February 1917. (Volume XIX)		
War Diary	Zelobes	01/02/1917	12/02/1917
War Diary	Bracquemont	13/02/1917	27/02/1917
Heading	War Diary Of 48 Field Ambulance From 1st March To 31st March 1917. (Volume XX)		
War Diary	Braquemont	02/03/1917	02/03/1917
War Diary	Bethune	03/03/1917	03/03/1917
War Diary	Rombly	04/03/1917	08/03/1917
War Diary	Pernes	09/03/1917	09/03/1917

War Diary	Ternas	10/03/1917	30/03/1917
Heading	War Diary Of 48 Field Ambulance From 1st April To 30 April 1917. (Volume 21)		
Miscellaneous	Summary Of Medical War Diaries Of 48th F.A. 37th Div		
War Diary	Moves	05/04/1917	07/04/1917
War Diary	Medical Arrangements	08/04/1917	08/04/1917
War Diary	Moves Detachment	08/04/1917	08/04/1917
War Diary	Operations R.A.M.C.	09/04/1917	09/04/1917
War Diary	Medical Arrangements Transport	09/04/1917	09/04/1917
War Diary	Medical Arrangements Assistance	10/04/1917	10/04/1917
War Diary	Operations	10/04/1917	10/04/1917
War Diary	Medical Arrangements	11/04/1917	11/04/1917
War Diary	Evacuation	11/04/1917	11/04/1917
War Diary	Military Situation	12/04/1917	12/04/1917
War Diary	Casualties R.A.M.C.	12/04/1917	12/04/1917
War Diary	Moves & Transfer	14/04/1917	14/04/1917
War Diary	Transfer	14/04/1917	14/04/1917
War Diary	Medical Arrangements Accomodation	15/04/1917	15/04/1917
War Diary	Moves	19/04/1917	19/04/1917
War Diary	Transfer	19/04/1917	19/04/1917
War Diary	Moves Medical Arrangements. Moves Detachment	21/04/1917	21/04/1917
War Diary	Moves and Transport	22/04/1917	22/04/1917
War Diary	Movest Detachment	22/04/1917	22/04/1917
War Diary	Casualties	23/04/1917	23/04/1917
War Diary	Evacuation	23/04/1917	23/04/1917
War Diary	Casualties. Casualties Gas	24/04/1917	24/04/1917
War Diary	Casualties Med. Arr.	25/04/1917	25/04/1917
War Diary	Casualties	26/04/1917	26/04/1917
War Diary	Operations	28/04/1917	28/04/1917
War Diary	Casualties	28/04/1917	28/04/1917
War Diary	Moves	30/04/1917	30/04/1917
War Diary	Transfer	30/04/1917	30/04/1917
War Diary	Moves	05/04/1917	07/04/1917
War Diary	Medical Arrangements	08/04/1917	08/04/1917
War Diary	Moves Detachment	08/04/1917	08/04/1917
War Diary	Operation R.A.M.C.	09/04/1917	09/04/1917
War Diary	Medical Arrangements Transport	09/04/1917	09/04/1917
War Diary	Medical Arrangements Assistance	10/04/1917	10/04/1917
War Diary	Operation	10/04/1917	10/04/1917
War Diary	Medical Arrangements Moves Detachment	10/04/1917	10/04/1917
War Diary	Medical Arrangements	10/04/1917	10/04/1917
War Diary	Evacuation	10/04/1917	10/04/1917
War Diary	Medical Arrangements	11/04/1917	11/04/1917
War Diary	Evacuation	11/04/1917	11/04/1917
War Diary	Military Situation	12/04/1917	12/04/1917
War Diary	Casualties R.A.M.C.	12/04/1917	12/04/1917
War Diary	Moves & Transfer	14/04/1917	14/04/1917
War Diary	Transfer	19/04/1917	19/04/1917
War Diary	Moves Medical Arrangements Moves Detachment	21/04/1917	21/04/1917
War Diary	Moves and Transport	22/04/1917	22/04/1917
War Diary	Moves Detachment	22/04/1917	22/04/1917
War Diary	Casualties	23/04/1917	23/04/1917
War Diary	Evacuation	23/04/1917	23/04/1917
War Diary	Casualties Casualties Gas	24/04/1917	24/04/1917
War Diary	Casualties Med. Arr	25/04/1917	25/04/1917

War Diary	Casualties	26/04/1917	26/04/1917
War Diary	Operations	28/04/1917	28/04/1917
War Diary	Casualties	28/04/1917	28/04/1917
War Diary	Moves	30/04/1917	30/04/1917
War Diary	Transfer	30/04/1917	30/04/1917
War Diary	Ternas	01/04/1917	04/04/1917
War Diary	Manin	05/04/1917	06/04/1917
War Diary	Duisans	07/04/1917	13/04/1917
War Diary	Ambrines	14/04/1917	18/04/1917
War Diary	Agnes-Lez-Duisans	19/04/1917	20/04/1917
War Diary	Haute. Avesnes	21/04/1917	30/04/1917
Heading	War Diary of 48 Field Ambulance From 1st May To 31st May 1917 (Volume XXII)		
Miscellaneous	Summary of Medical War Diaries of 48th F.A. 37th Div		
War Diary	Moves Detachment	02/05/1917	02/05/1917
War Diary	Operation R.A.M.C.	03/05/1917	18/05/1917
War Diary	Transfer	18/05/1917	18/05/1917
War Diary	Moves	18/05/1917	18/05/1917
War Diary	Moves Med. Arrangements Accommodation	19/05/1917	19/05/1917
War Diary	Operations	20/05/1917	20/05/1917
War Diary	Casualties	20/05/1917	20/05/1917
War Diary	Moves Detachment	22/05/1917	22/05/1917
War Diary	Operations Enemy	24/05/1917	24/05/1917
War Diary	Decorations	25/05/1917	25/05/1917
War Diary	Operations Enemy	26/05/1917	26/05/1917
War Diary	Casualties	26/05/1917	26/05/1917
War Diary	Casualties R.A.M.C.	26/05/1917	26/05/1917
War Diary	Military Situation	28/05/1917	28/05/1917
War Diary	Medical Arrangements	28/05/1917	28/05/1917
War Diary	Operations	30/05/1917	31/05/1917
War Diary	Casualties	30/05/1917	31/05/1917
War Diary	Transfer	18/05/1917	18/05/1917
War Diary	Moves	18/05/1917	18/05/1917
War Diary	Moves Med. Arrangements Accommodation	19/05/1917	19/05/1917
War Diary	Operations	20/05/1917	20/05/1917
War Diary	Casualties	20/05/1917	20/05/1917
War Diary	Moves Detachment	22/05/1917	22/05/1917
War Diary	Operation Enemy	24/05/1917	24/05/1917
War Diary	Decoration	25/05/1917	25/05/1917
War Diary	Operations Enemy	26/05/1917	26/05/1917
War Diary	Casualties	26/05/1917	26/05/1917
War Diary	Casualties R.A.M.C.	26/05/1917	26/05/1917
War Diary	Military Situation	28/05/1917	28/05/1917
Miscellaneous	Medical Arrangements	28/05/1917	28/05/1917
War Diary	Operations	30/05/1917	30/05/1917
War Diary	Casualties	31/05/1917	31/05/1917
War Diary	Lignereuil	01/05/1917	17/05/1917
War Diary	Berneville	18/05/1917	18/05/1917
War Diary	Tilloy-Les-Mafflaines	19/05/1917	31/05/1917
Heading	War Diary for 48 Field Ambulance from 1st June to 30th June 1917 (Volume XXIII)		
War Diary	Tilloy-Les-Mafflaines	31/05/1917	01/06/1917
War Diary	Arras	02/06/1917	02/06/1917
War Diary	Ambaines	03/06/1917	03/06/1917
War Diary	Liencourt	04/06/1917	06/06/1917
War Diary	Fiefs	07/06/1917	07/06/1917

War Diary	Erny St Julien	07/06/1917	23/06/1917
War Diary	Guarbecque	24/06/1917	24/06/1917
War Diary	Kreule	25/06/1917	25/06/1917
War Diary	Lochre	26/06/1917	28/06/1917
War Diary	Keersebrom	29/06/1917	30/06/1917
Heading	War Diary of 48th Field Ambulance From. 1st July to 31st July 1917 (Volume XXIV)		
War Diary	Keersebrom	01/07/1917	31/07/1917
Heading	War Diary of 48 Field Ambulance From 1st August to 31st August 1917. (Volume XXV)		
War Diary	Keersebrom	01/08/1917	07/08/1917
War Diary	Kemmel	08/08/1917	11/09/1917
War Diary	Tyrone Farm Dranoutre M36a 9.4	12/09/1917	13/09/1917
War Diary	Dranoutre	14/09/1917	26/09/1917
War Diary	Keersebrom	27/09/1917	30/09/1917
Heading	War Diary of 48th Field Ambulance Vol. 27 From 1st Oct 1917 to 31st Oct 1917		
War Diary	Keersebrom	01/10/1917	03/10/1917
War Diary	Voormezeele	04/10/1917	08/10/1917
War Diary	Larch Wood Hill 60 1.29.c.2.7	08/10/1917	09/10/1917
War Diary	Larch Wood	09/10/1917	10/10/1917
War Diary	Larch Wood Hill 60	10/10/1917	10/10/1917
War Diary	Larch Wood	11/10/1917	13/10/1917
War Diary	Mcgilligan Camp Bailleul	14/10/1917	17/10/1917
War Diary	Mcgilligan Camp	18/10/1917	31/10/1917
War Diary	Mcgilligan Camp Bailleul	01/11/1917	07/11/1917
War Diary	Mcgilligan Camp	07/11/1917	08/11/1917
War Diary	Kemmel	08/11/1917	11/11/1917
War Diary	Kemmel And Voormezeele	12/11/1917	13/11/1917
War Diary	Voormezeele	14/11/1917	30/11/1917
Heading	War Diary of 48th Field Ambulance From 1st Dec 1917 to 31st Dec 1917 Volume 29		
War Diary	Voormezeele	01/12/1917	31/12/1917
Heading	War Diary 48th Field Ambulance from 1st January 1918 to 31st January 1918. Volume 30		
War Diary	Voormezeele	01/01/1918	12/01/1918
War Diary	Bandringhem	13/01/1918	31/01/1918
Heading	War Diary 48th Field Ambulance From 1st February 1918 to 28th February 1918 Volume 31		
War Diary	Bandringhem	01/02/1918	15/02/1918
War Diary	Waratah Camp G 15.c.2.9	15/02/1918	15/02/1918
War Diary	Waratah Camp	16/02/1918	16/02/1918
War Diary	Waratah Camp G 15.c.2.9	17/02/1918	27/02/1918
War Diary	Waratah Camp	28/02/1918	28/02/1918
Heading	War Diary of 48th. Field Ambulance. From 1st. March 1918 to 31st March 1918 Volume 32		
War Diary	Waratah Camp G 15.c.2.9	01/03/1918	03/03/1918
War Diary	Waratah Camp	04/03/1918	27/03/1918
War Diary	Caestre	28/03/1918	29/03/1918
War Diary	Toutencourt	30/03/1918	30/03/1918
Heading	War Diary of 48th Field Ambulance From 1st April 1918 To 30th April 1918 Volume 33		
War Diary	Authie	01/04/1918	01/04/1918
War Diary	Couin	02/04/1918	16/04/1918
War Diary	Autie St Ledger	17/04/1918	23/04/1918
War Diary	Souastre	24/04/1918	30/04/1918

Heading	War Diary For 48th Field Ambulance From 1st May 1918 To 31st May 1918 Volume 34		
War Diary	Souastre	01/05/1918	17/05/1918
War Diary	Marieux	17/05/1918	31/05/1918
Heading	War Diary Of 48th Field Ambulance From 1st June 1918 To 30th June 18 Volume 35		
War Diary	Marieux	01/06/1918	05/06/1918
War Diary	Dreuil Les Molliens	06/06/1918	10/06/1918
War Diary	L'Hortoy	11/06/1918	13/06/1918
War Diary	Vers	14/06/1918	20/06/1918
War Diary	Creuse	21/06/1918	21/06/1918
War Diary	Terramesnil	22/03/1918	24/03/1918
War Diary	Pas	25/03/1918	30/03/1918
Heading	War Diary of 48th Field Ambulance from 1st July 1918 to 31st July 1918 Vol 37		
War Diary	Pas	01/07/1918	31/07/1918
Heading	War Diary Of 48th Field Ambulance From 1st August 1918 To 31st Augt 1918 Volume 37		
War Diary	Pas	01/08/1918	21/08/1918
War Diary	Henu	22/08/1918	22/08/1918
War Diary	Bienvillers	23/08/1918	23/08/1918
War Diary	Bucquoy	24/08/1918	31/08/1918
Heading	War Diary Of 48th Field Ambulance From 1st Sept 1918 30th Sept 1918 Volume 39		
War Diary	Bucquoy F26.c.7.7	01/09/1918	02/09/1918
War Diary	Achiet-Le-Grand	03/09/1918	18/09/1918
War Diary	Logeast Wood	19/09/1918	25/09/1918
War Diary	Le Barque	26/09/1918	29/09/1918
War Diary	Metz	30/09/1918	30/09/1918
War Diary	Metzen Couture Sheet 57.c	30/09/1918	30/09/1918
Heading	War Diary of 48th Field Ambulance From 1st October 1918 to 31st October 1918 Volume 39		
War Diary	Gouzeaucourt	01/10/1918	06/10/1918
War Diary	Vaucelles	07/10/1918	09/10/1918
War Diary	Esnes	09/10/1918	09/10/1918
War Diary	Caudry	10/10/1918	11/10/1918
War Diary	Beaumont	12/10/1918	12/10/1918
War Diary	Caudry	13/10/1918	22/10/1918
War Diary	Viesly	23/10/1918	31/10/1918
Heading	War Diary of 48th Field Ambulance from 1st to 30th Novr-1918 Volume 40		
War Diary	Viesly	01/11/1918	02/11/1918
War Diary	Solesmes	03/11/1918	06/11/1918
War Diary	Beavrain	07/11/1918	08/11/1918
War Diary	Briastre	09/11/1918	30/11/1918
Heading	War Diary of 48th Field Ambulance From 1st Decr 1918 to 31st Decr 1918. Volume 41		
War Diary	Briastre	01/12/1918	06/12/1918
War Diary	Bavai	07/12/1918	19/12/1918
War Diary	Lodelinsart	20/12/1918	31/12/1918
Heading	War Diary of 48th Field Ambulance From 1st to 31st January 1919 Volume 42		
War Diary	Lodelinsart	01/01/1919	31/01/1919
Heading	No 48. Field Ambulance Feb. 1919		
War Diary	Lodelinsart	01/02/1919	21/02/1919
War Diary	Gosselies	22/02/1919	28/02/1919

Heading	48th F.A. Mar 1919		
War Diary	Gosselies	01/03/1919	31/03/1919
Heading	No. 48 F.A. Apr. 1919		
War Diary	Gosselies	01/04/1919	16/04/1919
War Diary	Antrench	17/04/1919	17/04/1919

WO95/2525-1

48 Field Ambulance RAMC

37 Div

Jul 1915 – Apr 1919

12/6343

37th Division

48th Field Ambulance

Vol. I

July 28th – 31st 1915

Confidential

War Diary
of
48th Field Ambulance R.A.M.C

from 28th July 1915 to 31st July 1915.

WAR DIARY
or
INTELLIGENCE SUMMARY
(Erase heading not required.)

Army Form C. 2118

Place	Date	Hour	Summary of Events and Information	Remarks and references to Appendices
S.S. Inventor	28th July 1915	5 pm	The 48th Field Ambulance left Camp at Tidworth Park on the night of 27th–28th July in 2 parties, the 1st, consisting of A section & bearers of C. section with two F.S. wagons, left Camp at 12.20 A.M. The 2nd party, consisting of the remainder 2 hour later. The 1st trainload commenced to entrain at 1.50 AM, left Tidworth at 2.50 AM and arrived at Southampton about 4 AM. Here the transport was subdivided, the C.O. & Quartermaster with 3½ sec. & men & the transport proceeding on S.S. Inventor, the remainder on another ship. The same procedure was carried out with the 2nd trainload, which was not encountered at Southampton.	
No 5 Camp. Havre	29th July	8 pm.	All the detachments arrived in Havre by 11 A.M. and marched under [guidance] to No 5. Rest Camp. which was reached at 1.30 pm., except by the transport of the 2nd trainload, which was disembarked last and reached Camp at 6.45 pm.	
Chateau Proville	30th July	10 a.m.	Started to entrain at the Gare des Marchandises, Havre, at 0.0. on the night 29th/30th. and left at 4.15. A.M. the whole F.A. together with 2 Officers and 125 men of the N. Staffords, with transport, occupying one train.	

Army Form C. 2118

WAR DIARY
or
INTELLIGENCE SUMMARY
(Erase heading not required.)

Place	Date	Hour	Summary of Events and Information	Remarks and references to Appendices
Chateau Morielle	31st July 1915	2 p.m.	The Ambulance detrained at St Omers at 10.30 p.m. on the 30th and marched out to Morielle where they billeted, all being settled in by 3.30 A.M. on the 31st. All the personnel of NCOs & men are billeted at the Chateau, here they occupy lofts and wagon houses, the transport being parked in the home paddock. All Officers are billeted in neighbouring houses. The men's billets are clean & sufficiently commodious. Thrashing floors & two rooms at the Chateau have been allotted provisionally for the treatment of sick of the Division, which is to be carried out by "A" section. The office is also established in the Chateau. Reveille was at 7 A.M. Orders issued at 11.30 A.M. including strict prohibition of smoking in mens quarters.	
Chateau Morielle	1st Aug			

S/Ldr Moore
O.C. 48th Field Ambulance

121/6607

37th Division

48th Field Ambulance
Vol. II
From 1- 26. 8. 15

August '15

War Diary of
48th Field Ambulance
R. A. M. C

August 1915

Army Form C. 2118

WAR DIARY
or
INTELLIGENCE SUMMARY
(Erase heading not required.)

Instructions regarding War Diaries and Intelligence Summaries are contained in F.S. Regs, Part II. and the Staff Manual respectively. Title Pages will be prepared in manuscript.

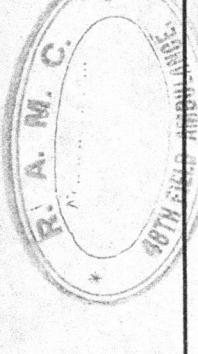

Place	Date	Hour	Summary of Events and Information	Remarks and references to Appendices
Nouelle The Chateau	1st Aug 1915	3 pm	Four motor ambulances were yesterday attached to the F.A. for evacuation of sick of the division. They proceeded to the refilling points of the Div. at 10 AM in two parties, each under an officer. Only two cases were brought in, making a total of five admissions for the day. Of these, two were evacuated to 20. Clearing hospital at St Omer. Information was received from the French Chief Medical Officer that our cases could not be treated in the Chateau. Accordingly, it was arranged with the Maire to use the Schoolrooms as a hospital, these being situated close to the Chateau. The men were sent for a route march from 10 AM to 1 PM.	
"	2nd Aug	5 pm	Capt Alcock Name detailed as M.O. to Divisional Cyclist Coy. at Sergues. Admissions 5. Evacuated 2. Ambulance convoy working as before. Men employed on fatigues & parades.	
"	3rd Aug	3 pm	Admissions to Hospital #7. Evacuated 6. Remaining 6. Lt Godfrey Name detailed in temp charge of 289th Coy A.T.C. and Ammunition Park, both at Nouelle.	

Army Form C. 2118

WAR DIARY
or
INTELLIGENCE SUMMARY

(Erase heading not required.)

Instructions regarding War Diaries and Intelligence Summaries are contained in F.S. Regs., Part II. and the Staff Manual respectively. Title Pages will be prepared in manuscript.

Place	Date	Hour	Summary of Events and Information	Remarks and references to Appendices
~~Bailleu~~ Chateauvert Estlinghem	4.8.15	9 p.m.	The F.A. left Morbe with the 110th Bgde this morning and reached billets here about 6 p.m. 2 of the attached motor ambulances proceeded back to the rear of the Division at Lostralt and then all four came on in rear of the Division to pick up casualties. Twenty two cases were kept for treatment in the F.A.	
Secke.	8.4.8.15	6.30 p.m	Twenty Cases were evacuated back to St. Omes when the F.A. left Estlinghem at 8.30 A.M. this morning. The F.A. marched with the 110th Inf Bgde via Hazebrouck to Secke arrived into Billets on the outskirts of the town in two adjacent farms. The day was very hot and the three ambulance wagons were filled with men fallen out. On arrival all except five wagons were sent back to their units, including two brought on from Estlinghem. These five cases detained are the only ones being treated in the F.A. A Section only is opened up.	
Secke	9.8.15	4 p.m.	We remain in billets here. The 110th Inf Bgde having left for instruction at the front. The F.A. receives cases from Divisional troops only. The motor wagons have been received and are undergoing structural alteration. 600 doses of antitetanic serum and six syringes were received from the Advanced Medical Stores at Hazebrouck on the 9th	

1875 Wt. W593/826 1,000,000 4/15 J.B.C. & A. A.D.S.S./Forms/C. 2118.

Army Form C. 2118

WAR DIARY
or
INTELLIGENCE SUMMARY

(Erase heading not required.)

R.A.M.C.
48TH FIELD AMBULANCE

Place	Date	Hour	Summary of Events and Information	Remarks and references to Appendices
Eecke	20.8.15		The officers, sergeant major and 12 n.c.o's and 60 men of the FA have been sent on three lorries to the 84th (T) Field Ambulance, forming a Divisional Rest Camp at Boescheepe & dressing station at Dranoutre, in order to experience the conditions of the medical service at the actual front. There have been five cases of dysenteric diarrhoea in B and C sections yesterday and today.	
Mondicourt 2888			The Ambulance marched yesterday to Cassel & entrained there, reaching Mondicourt at 10 p.m. & settling into bivouacs in two fields by 12.30 A.M.	

S.P.Wharton

37/Kitwein

121/6923

48th Field Ambulance
Vol III.
Sep 1. 15.

Sept 1/15

Army Form C. 2118

WAR DIARY
or
INTELLIGENCE SUMMARY
(Erase heading not required.)

Instructions regarding War Diaries and Intelligence Summaries are contained in F. S. Regs., Part II. and the Staff Manual respectively. Title Pages will be prepared in manuscript.

Place	Date	Hour	Summary of Events and Information	Remarks and references to Appendices
Pas.	7.9.15		The Field Ambulance marched to Pas yesterday taking over two school buildings from a French Ambulance for use as a hospital. The men are split up in four billets in the town. The hospital and billets were all in an extremely dirty condition, and the sanitary arrangements at the hospital were very bad.	
"	9.9.15		A Divisional Rest Station was opened today about ½ mile away on the Famechon road. A camp for 200 men is pitched with the tents of 48 + 50 F.As. Capt Evans is in charge, with personnel from 3 F.B. teet.	
"	13.9.15		The Divisional Rest Camp was inspected by the D.M.S. 3rd Army on the 11th and the site pronounced unsuitable, as being too exposed. A new site has been found at Mondicourt where the Rest Station is being transferred today.	
"	30.9.15		The Divisional bathing establishment was started working yesterday. It is found 80 men can be given hot bath every ¾ hr. No laundry work is yet started as the F.A. is kept ready to move at short notice.	

D. Phelan Major
O.C. 48 F.A.

121/7430

48th Field Ambulance
Vol 4
Oct 15

<u>Confidential</u>

War Diary
of
48th Field Ambulance

from 1st October 1915
to 31st October 1915

Army Form C. 2118

WAR DIARY
or
INTELLIGENCE SUMMARY
(Erase heading not required.)

Place	Date	Hour	Summary of Events and Information	Remarks and references to Appendices
Pao.	31.10.15		The Field Ambulance has remained stationary during the past month, maintaining the hospital for H.Q. troops at Pao. Rest Station at Mudros & the Div. Bathing establishment at Pao. The structural alterations for the Laundry are not quite complete. The F.A. has already begun to exchange details with No. 48 F.A. with which they are changing over on the 5th Nov.	

A Watson Maj
Major, R.A.M.C.,
O.C. 48th Field Ambulance.

37 R. F. Nurseron

48: 7.a.
Oct: 5

121/7624

Nov 19P

Nov 15.

Confidential

War Diary
of
48th Field Ambulance

November 1915

O.C. 48th Field Ambulance.

Army Form C. 2118

WAR DIARY
or
INTELLIGENCE SUMMARY
(Erase heading not required.)

Instructions regarding War Diaries and Intelligence Summaries are contained in F.S. Regs., Part II. and the Staff Manual respectively. Title Pages will be prepared in manuscript.

[Stamp: 48th FIELD AMBULANCE, 30 NOV 1915, R.A.M.C.]

Place	Date	Hour	Summary of Events and Information	Remarks and references to Appendices
HUMBERCAMP		6ᵃ hrs	This field Ambulance has now changed places with the 49th. The change was effected piecemeal and completed yesterday, when the men formed the 7.A. marched from PAS to HUMBERCAMP. The advanced dressing stations at BERLES-AU-BOIS and BIENVILLERS are retained. The first case of "Trench-foot" was admitted yesterday.	
"	15th Nov		The available accommodation is kept pretty well occupied, the average daily number of patients being somewhere near sixty. The wounded average 2 or 3 daily. The weather during the past week has been extremely wet and cases of "Trench-foot" are on the increase. A hut is being erected, providing additional accommodation for 50 cases. The average number of CHds under treatment lately has been about 90.	
"	30th Nov		Mostly cases of Myalgia and Influenza. During the past week, with the advent of drier weather cases of "Trench foot" have ceased to come in. Lt. F.D. Maclean having been transferred as Regimental M.O., the Ambulance is short of one officer.	

J.W. Odom Major
R.A.M.C. F.Amb.

48th J.a.
vol. 6

1798/51

Confidential

War Diary of
48th Field Ambulance.

for December 1915.

Army Form C. 2118

WAR DIARY
or
INTELLIGENCE SUMMARY

(Erase heading not required.)

Instructions regarding War Diaries and Intelligence Summaries are contained in F.S. Regs., Part II. and the Staff Manual respectively. Title Pages will be prepared in manuscript.

Place	Date	Hour	Summary of Events and Information	Remarks and references to Appendices
HUMBERCAMP	9.12.15		Capt. A.A. Fyffe RAMC (S.R.) transferred to 30th Div. for duty with Field Ambulance.	
"	10.12.15		Lt. J. Dewar RAMC (Temporary) arrived for duty in place of Capt Fyffe. The weather for the past 10 days has been extremely wet. A few cases of trench foot are admitted daily. C.H. Alcock RAMC (S.R.) has been detached for duty with Corps Troops.	
"	16.12.15		One Ford Ambulance Car has been stationed at HANNESCAMPS and five men of the Ft. Amb. attached for duty at the Regimental aid Posts there.	
"	17.12.15		Lt. Hindley RAMC reported that during heavy shell fire at HANNESCAMPS Pte Burke RAMC 48 F.A. displayed great heroism rendering aid and bringing in wounded.	

Army Form C. 2118

WAR DIARY
or
INTELLIGENCE SUMMARY
(Erase heading not required.)

Place	Date	Hour	Summary of Events and Information	Remarks and references to Appendices
HUMBERCAMP	22.12.15		Lieut W.A. Rogerson RAMC (Temp) Joined for duty from the Base.	
"	23.12.15		Advanced dressing station at Bienvillers was struck by a shell, which did no material damage.	
"	24.12.15		Capt. S. Wickenden RAMC (S.R.) Transferred to 32nd Div. for duty.	
"	25.12.15		Lieut: R. Ingram RAMC (Temp) arrived for duty from 32nd Div. Ammunns for Trench foot have practically ceased, and the numbers treated in the ambulance generally have diminished.	

J.A. Wilson Major
O.C. 48th Fd Amb.

37

48ste J.J.
tot: 7

31.K.Dw

F/19 1/2

Jan. 1916

Confidential

War Diary of

48th Field Ambulance R.A.M.C.

for month ending 31 January 1916.

Army Form C. 2118

WAR DIARY
or
INTELLIGENCE SUMMARY

(Erase heading not required.)

Place	Date	Hour	Summary of Events and Information	Remarks and references to Appendices
HUMBERCAMP	31.1.16		The Ambulance has continued doing duty at HUMBERCAMP. No events worthy of record have happened, except that the first case of Cerebro-Spinal Fever in the Division was admitted to the F.A. on 28.1.16. The Ambulance was brought up to strength by reinforcements this month. Number of wounded during the month 127.	

H. Naton.
Lt. Col. R.A.M.C.,
O.C. 48th Field Ambulance.

48th Fld. Ambulance.

Feb 1916

48. Field
Amb.
37th Div

Vol. 8.

Army Form C. 2118

WAR DIARY
or
INTELLIGENCE SUMMARY
(Erase heading not required.)

Place	Date	Hour	Summary of Events and Information	Remarks, and references to Appendices
HUMBERCAMP	Feb 3rd		Lt. George Deivas Rame was killed by a shell while doing duty at the advanced dressing station at BERLES. The shell burst among the crowd listening to the Divisional Band, killing about 20 and wounding the same number. 17 wounded were admitted to the Field Ambulance spelm 3 died there.	
	5th		O.C. Field Ambulance is also carrying out the duties of Town Major	
	19th		The second case of anthrax was admitted	
	21st		3 Reinforcements were posted, bringing the ambulance to 4 below full strength	
	23rd		Lt. J.J. Robertson Rame was posted	
	26th		Lt. P.D. Little Rame who posted, bringing the officers 1 over strength	
	29th		Lt. On Mackie Cornell appointed Town Major of HUMBERCAMP, vice OC 485 F.Amb. Few cases of sick or wounded are coming to the ambulance	

J. Antoon Lt-Col.
Lt. 485 Ft. Amb.

Army Form C. 2118

WAR DIARY
or
INTELLIGENCE SUMMARY
(Erase heading not required.)

48 Field Ambulance

Place	Date	Hour	Summary of Events and Information	Remarks and references to Appendices
HUMBERCAMP	6.3.16		Lt. J.D. Robertson was sent sick to 50th F.Amb.	
	7.3.16		Lt. D.W. Daniels posted for duty.	
	8.3.16		Lt. P.W. Little left, posted M.O. 6th Bn. Warwicks	
	14.3.16		Lt. R.A.b. Proctor R.a.m.c. posted to the Ambulance for duty.	
	17.3.16		Lt. Renwick, 1 nco + 6 men sent this advanced party to Le Souich, within the Ambulance is move on the 21st inst., & take over from the 10th F.A.	
LE. SOUICH	21.3.16		The Ambulance marched at 9. A.M. yesterday by GAUDIEMPRE and LUCHEUX reaching LE SOUICH at 2.30. P.M. The hospital accommodation consists of a french wooden hut capable of taking 60 patients and which building that will take 30. The Hospital is being run by B. Section. The men are billetted in farms. A course of thorough training of the unit is being instituted at once.	
"	23.3.16		Lt. Ingram R.a.m.c. relieved to join the 2nd F.amb. for duty.	

AWATSN Spith
Rowe R.A.M.C.,
O.C. 48th Field Ambulance.

Army Form C. 2118

WAR DIARY
or
INTELLIGENCE SUMMARY
(Erase heading not required.)

48 Field Ambulance

Place	Date	Hour	Summary of Events and Information	Remarks and references to Appendices
LE SOUICH	29.3.16		L. Russell R.A.M.C. from 47th F.Amb. attached for 14 days duty & course of Equitation.	
"	31.3.16		Training according to Syllabus Continues	

S Whitton Lt. Col.
R.A.M.C.,
O.C. 48th Field Ambulance.

48 Amb
Vol 10

34th Div

Confidential

War Diary of
 48th Field Ambulance

April 1916

Army Form C. 2118

WAR DIARY
or
INTELLIGENCE SUMMARY

48 Field Ambulance

(Erase heading not required.)

Instructions regarding War Diaries and Intelligence Summaries are contained in F.S. Regs., Part II. and the Staff Manual respectively. Title Pages will be prepared in manuscript.

Place	Date	Hour	Summary of Events and Information	Remarks and references to Appendices
LE SOUICH	3.4.16		Lt. R.A.W. Proctor R.A.M.C. left, being posted as M.O. 13th R. Fusiliers	
	9.4.16		Capt. J.S. Cook R.A.M.C. joined the Ambulance for duty. Also Lt. A.F. Smith from 50th F. Amb.	
	10.4.16		2/Lt. J.D. Robertson is struck off the strength, having been invalided to England. Lt. A.F. Johns posted to the Amb. from 20th Div.	
"	12.4.16		Lt. Johns sent for temporary duty with 8th Worcesters	
"	14.4.16		Capt. J.S. Cook has been evacuated to 34 F.Amb & transferred to No 19 C.C.S.	
"	26.4.16		A party of 2 Officers and 35 N.C.Os and men of C. Section proceeded to LUCHEUX to form a hospital in the Chateau	
LUCHEUX	27.4.16		The remainder of the Ambulance marched to LUCHEUX, and are billeted in huts.	
"	28.4.16		The C.O. proceeded to England on 8 days leave, handing over to Capt. Nicholson R.A.M.C.	

Moreton Lt.Col.
R.A.M.C.,
O.C. 48th Field Ambulance.

31st Div

No. 148 F. Amb.

May 1916.

WAR DIARY
or
INTELLIGENCE SUMMARY

Army Form C. 2118

48 Field Ambulance Vol II

Place	Date	Hour	Summary of Events and Information	Remarks and references to Appendices
LUCHEUX	30.4.16		Lt Elliot posted to 9th York Staff Regt for temporary duty. Field Ambulance won the Football Challenge Cup presented by Major General Count Gleichen, beating the 9th Leicesters. Lt Godfrey returned from 44 Cas Clearing Station. Sick parade to 124th Bde field amb.	
HUMBERCAMPS	2.5.16.		Lt Godfrey for temporary duty with 124th Brigade RFA for temporary duty. The ambulance left LUCHEUX at 10 AM this morning and marched to HUMBERCAMPS where the sick were accommodated in 2 huts and 2 marquees in an orchard. The personnel being billeted in barns near here.	
"	4.5.16.		The ambulance took over the Divisional Rest Station from 58th Fd Ambulance and accommodated the Rest in tents.	
"	5.5.16.		Lt Johns posted to 6th Batt Leicester Regt permanently.	
COUTURELLE	6.5.16.		The Ambulance left HUMBERCAMPS this morning at 10 AM and marched to COUTURELLE where they took over the outbuildings of the château for hospital purposes. Two rooms in the château itself were taken over for use as our wards for officers. From marquees were pitched in the grounds of the château for the accommodation of the 37th Divisional Rest Station.	

Chas Nicholson Capt RAMC
for OC 48th Field Ambulance.

Army Form C. 2118

WAR DIARY
or
INTELLIGENCE SUMMARY
(Erase heading not required.)

48 FIELD AMBULANCE

Place	Date	Hour	Summary of Events and Information	Remarks and references to Appendices
COUTURELLE	17.5.16		The C.O. of the F.A. returned from leave. Lt. Col. W. G. N. CARNELL RAMC appointed 2nd i/c. Lt. ROGERSON RAMC posted temporarily i/c 7th Leicesters.	
"	11.5.16		Lt. A. F. ELLIOTT RAMC posted temporarily as 2nd O. i/c 11th Ry. Hussars.	
"	20.5.16		Capt. G. A. FENWICK RAMC posted temporarily as no. 9/c Div. Ammunition Column.	
"	21.5.16		Lt. A. F. ELLIOTT returned to duty.	
"	23.5.16		Capt. ROGERSON returned to duty with the F.A.	
			Instructions received from ADMS 37th Div. that establishment is to be reduced by:-	
			1 Sgt. A.S.C. (H.T.)	
			1 Driver A.S.C. (H.T.)	
			1 Riding horse	
			1 Draught horse	
			1 Heavy Draught horse.	
			Sergt A.S.C. is to be retained until a warrant officer A.S.C. is posted. Reduction carried out accordingly by Butter.	
"	29.5.16		Lt. E. S. MASSIAH RAMC posted to the ambulance for duty.	
			Lt & Qr Mr G. N. CARNELL proceeded on 10 days leave, Lt ELLIOTT acting Qr Mr perhaps.	
"	30.5.16		Capt W. A. ROGERSON left for 4 days instruction at Divisional Gas School.	
			The weather during May has on the whole been fine and warm with some heavy rain at intervals.	
			Admissions are principally for "French fever", but very few cases are hospitalized outside the Div. Rest Station.	
				J. Horton Lt. Col. R.A.M.C 48 F. Amb.

48 F Amb.   Vol 12 June

Confidential

War Diary of

<u>48 Field Ambulance, R.A.M.C.</u>

<u>From</u> 1 June 1916
<u>To</u>   30 June 1916.

WAR DIARY or INTELLIGENCE SUMMARY

48 FIELD AMBULANCE

Army Form C. 2118

Place	Date	Hour	Summary of Events and Information	Remarks and references to Appendices
COUTURELLE	3.6.16		Capt. ROGERSON returned from the Divisional Gas School. He will carry out a course of lectures and practical instruction in the use of gas helmets to all the personnel of the F. Amb.	
"	5.6.16		Lt. GODFREY proceeded on 14 days special leave. A canteen is being run by the Ambulance under Capt NICHOLSON. The profits are being expended on comforts for the personnel - principally on fresh vegetables procured at DOULLENS. 1 N.C.O. and 30 men sent to BIENVILLERS to dig dugout for 49 F.A. Adv. Post.	
"	10.6.16		Lt. & Qr.Mr. CARNELL returned from leave.	
"	11.6.16		Lt. ELLIOTT was posted to 8th E.LANCS. for temporary duty as Regt. M.O.	
"	12.6.16		Capt. RENWICK proceeded on 14 days special leave. The members in the Div. Rest Station for the past week have averaged over 120. A large number being convalescent from "Influenza" so-called. Capt. H.W.EVANS RAMC sent for temporary duty with 126 Bgde R.F.A. Sergt. Major BENNETT. A.S.C. was posted to the Ambulance yesterday for duty with the transport.	
"	21.6.16		Under instructions from A.D.M.S. 37th Div. the Ambulance is to be evacuated with during the next 6 days with the exception of 1 officer & 50 men & remain in the Div. Rest Station, to be retained to feeding trains at the C.C.S.	

War Diary

Army Form C. 2118 — 48 Field Ambulance

Place	Date	Hour	Summary of Events and Information	Remarks and references to Appendices
COUTURELLE	26.6.16		1 N.C.O. and 30 men returned from duty at HANNESCAMPS. Three aeroplane bombs were dropped in the environs of the Chateau this morning. Two exploded harmlessly. The third killed an ASC driver and wounded four horses.	
"	26.6.16		Sergt Collins detached for detective service under A.P.M. The Ambulance is acting as reserve ambulance in the operations now proceeding.	
"	27.6.16		Capt. G.A. KENWICK returned to duty from leave. Lt D.W. DANIELS 1 N.C.O. and 8 men proceeded to No. 20 C.C.S. for duty. Lt A.F. ELLIOTT. Struck off the strength on appointment as M.O. 5th battalion.	
"	28th		Two N.C.Os and 18 men proceeded to HANNESCAMPS for duty at the Advanced Aid Post of the 49th F.A. The remaining 50 men in DRS. transferred to 20 CCS for bearing duties. The F.A. is now being kept practically empty, a few slight cases likely to recover in 3 days only being admitted to Divn. Rest Station.	

A.P. Watson Lt.Col
O.C. 48th F.Amb.

Confidential

War Diary of 48th Field Ambulance

from 1st July 1916 to 31st July 1916

COMMITTEE FOR THE
MEDICAL HISTORY OF THE WAR

Date   5-SEP 916

Army Form C. 2118

WAR DIARY
or
INTELLIGENCE SUMMARY
(Erase heading not required.)

48 FIELD AMBULANCE

Place	Date	Hour	Summary of Events and Information	Remarks and references to Appendices
COUTURELLE	2.7.16		Secret orders received from A.D.M.S. 37th Div. to be ready to move at short notice. Ambulance standing to. 8 patients only remain in the D.R.S. who will be moved if the Ambulance moves.	
GAUDIEMPRE	4.7.16		The Ambulance marched this morning to GAUDIEMPRE and took over a camp of huts from the 1st & 3rd N. MIDLAND F. Ambulances of the 46th Div. The 55th F.A. also occupies part of the same camp. The 48th F. Ambulance is dealing with all the sick of the Division	
"	5.7.16		Two N.C.Os + 20 men returned yesterday evening from HANNESCAMPS where they were doing duty with the 49th F.A. The sick are being cleared to No 43 C.C.S. less than two miles away; so that evacuation can be speedily carried out. The party attached to 3rd Army School has returned (thirty today). This Division is prepared to move at 3 hours notice.	
"	7.7.16.		The Division having been split up, and the infantry brigades sent to other divisions there is now no prospect of an early move. Our triples are now 63, 102, + 103. Capt. H. ALCOCK returned yesterday to this unit for duty, having been detached since December '15 in charge of Corps troops.	
"	11.7.16.		Capts. RENWICK and ROGERSON with 25 R.C.O.S. men proceeded to BIENVILLERS to take over the Advanced Dressing Station from the 2nd N. Midland F.A., the 83rd B.g.R. relieving troops of the 46th Div. in the trenches.	

Army Form C. 2118

WAR DIARY
or
INTELLIGENCE SUMMARY
(Erase heading not required.)

48 Field Ambulance

Place	Date	Hour	Summary of Events and Information	Remarks and references to Appendices
GAUDIEMPRE	14.7.16		Orders received this morning from A.D.M.S. 37th Div for the movement of the Ambulance tomorrow morning to the VIth Corps, accompanying the 63rd Bgde, at present in the trenches. All cases unable to march are being evacuated to no 43 C.C.S. This C.C.S. is only two miles away and the Cars of the Ambulance are used for evacuation. Capts RENNIER and ROGERSON with the personnel of the A.D.S. returned from BIENVILLERS this evening.	
	15.7.16 6 p.m.		The Ambulance left GAUDIEMPRÉ at 8.20 A.M. without hanking over to another unit, and marched in rear of the 63rd Bgde, via SAULTY – SOMBRIN – LIENCOURT – BERLENCOURT and MAGNICOURT to HOUVIGNEUL arriving at 5.30 p.m. & billeting. The three horse ambulance wagons were detached to accompany the Bgde. Two motor Ambulances to accompany 124 + 125 Bgdes RFA and the remaining motor ambulances followed in rear of 63rd Bgde to bring on stragglers.	
HOUVINEUL				
CHELERS	16.7.16 6 p.m.		The ambulance left HOUVINEUL at 9.30 A.M. marching in rear of 63rd Bgde together by MAGNICOURT – MAIZIERES – AVERDOINGT and TINQUES to CHELERS where it went into billets at 3.30 p.m. Similar arrangements to yesterday were made with the ambulance wagons and cars. Six cases were evacuated from HOUVINEUL to No 6 Stationary Hospital FREVENT in the morning before starting.	

Army Form C. 2118

WAR DIARY
or
INTELLIGENCE SUMMARY
(Erase heading not required.)

22 **48 FIELD AMBULANCE**

Place	Date	Hour	Summary of Events and Information	Remarks and references to Appendices
CHELERS	17/7/16	6 p.m.	The Ambulance has remained here today & has cleared the 63rd Bgde area, proceeding to AUBIGNY.	
FRESNICOURT	18/7/16	7 a.m.	Orders to march were received at 5 A.M. and the Ambulance marched at 9.30 a.m. following the rear battalion of the Bgde by VILLERS-BRULIN - MINGOVAL - CAMBLIGNEUL to MAISNIL-BOUCHÉ, where they went into billets soon after 1 p.m. At 3.45. Orders were received to move to FRESNICOURT to take over from the 6th F.Amb. The ambulance arrived at 5.45. The Officers going into billets and other ranks into a large hut. No patients were carried, the only three collected in the morning being evacuated from MAISNIL to BRUAY.	
"	26/7/16		Capt ALCOCK. 1 NCO. and 12 men proceeded to the Advanced dressing station at ABLAIN ST. NAZAIRE to take over, relieving half the personnel of the VIth LONDON F.A. there. The A.D.S. is in a ruined house, the personnel sleeping in dugouts and cellars. Clearing from the Regimental aid post in the Quarry on the slopes of VIMY ridge, a mile and a half further on can only be effected by dark, the whole place being overlooked by the German lines.	
"	27/7/16		CAPT. RENWICK, 1 NCO. and 7 men proceeded to the A.D.S. relieving the other half of personnel of VIth LONDON. F.A. CAPT. EVANS and personnel of B. section proceeded to GRAND SERVIN. F.A. following tomorrow to take over from VIth LONDON. F.A.	

Army Form C. 2118

WAR DIARY
or
INTELLIGENCE SUMMARY
(Erase heading not required.)

48 Field Ambulance

Place	Date	Hour	Summary of Events and Information	Remarks and references to Appendices
GRAND SERVINS	28.7.16		The Ambulance moved to Gd. SERVINS this afternoon and took over the huts site left by the VI* LONDON. F.A. There are 5 large and 2 smaller huts, and some outhouses.	
"	29.7.16		All Scabies cases are to be treated here, the R.A.M.C. personnel that was occupying one of the huts is turned out into bell tents, of which 12 have been brought from those taken over at FRESNICOURT, the remainder being handed over to the S. AFRICAN. F. Amb., which took over there from the 48th F.Amb.	
"	30.7.16		Two cases of wounded were admitted last night, the only casualties that have come thro' the A.D.S. up to date.	

F Morton Lt Col
O.C. 48th F. Amb.

37th Div.
/48th Amb.

Vol 14

Confidential

War Diary of

48th Field Ambulance

for the month of

August 1916.

Aug 1916.

Army Form C. 2118

WAR DIARY
or
INTELLIGENCE SUMMARY

(Erase heading not required.)

2¼ 48 FIELD AMBULANCE

Place	Date	Hour	Summary of Events and Information	Remarks and references to Appendices
GD. SERVINS.	1.8.16.		The Ambulance is clearing the 102nd Bgde Area. This Bgde held the left sector of the CARENCY. Sector of the line. The problem of clearing large numbers of wounded from this sector shoved the need arise, appears to be a very difficult one. At this end of the line wounded can only be brought down straight by the "DUCKWALK" through SOUCHY. The "DUCKWALK" is a gangway of French boards in bad repair, the ground on either side being practically impassable by reason of shellholes and natural irregularities. An alternative route is via CABARET ROUGE and "HOSPITAL CORNER" CARENCY. This involves a carry of 3 or 4 miles, mostly thro' communication trenches. In the QUARRY at the left of the sector is indifferent dugout accommodation for some 60 men. It appears this place would be a death trap in the event of an attack. The solution of the difficulty appears to be the construction of new dugouts in the ridge, preferably in alley 130 near "KINGS CROSS."	
	3.8.16.		One hut is set aside for the treatment of Scabies. A hut is being constructed at the end of it. Fleas are being brought up from ABLAIN for the floor.	
	7.8.16		1 Officer and 4 men were admitted this morning for wounds. The result of a bombing accident. All belonged to 8th Black Watch. The Officer & one inspires were very grave, was sent onto No 6. C.C.S. at BARLIN, in charge of an M.O.	

Army Form C. 2118

WAR DIARY
or
INTELLIGENCE SUMMARY
(Erase heading not required.)

25 / **48 FIELD AMBULANCE**

Place	Date	Hour	Summary of Events and Information	Remarks and references to Appendices
GD SERVINS	8.8.16		Very few Casualties are occurring in our sector of the line, and for those few the present clearing arrangements are working satisfactorily.	
"	11.8.16		Capt. ALCOCK and 12 men returned from the ADS having been relieved by a party from the 2/8 F.Amb., who are taking over from us.	
"	13.8.16		Capt. RENWICK and the remainder of the ADS detachment returned. An advance party of 1t + Q.M. CARNELL and 6 O.R. proceeded this afternoon to FRESNICOURT to take over from the S. AFRICAN. F.A.	
FRESNICOURT	14.8.16	2 p.m.	The Ambulance marched here this morning, arriving at 10.45 A.M., and taking up the same quarters that it vacated on 28th July. The patients were transported in the motor ambulances. The Beaver Division is to be held in readiness to move at short notice on receipt of orders from D.M.S. 1st Army.	
"	19.8.16		The Ambulance is clearing 63rd & 102nd Bgde. areas. Capt. EVANS. left for duty at IVth Corps School at PERNES.	
"	20.8.16		Lieut. MASSIAH left for temp. duty with 23rd Bn. N. Fusiliers at FREVILLERS	

Army Form C. 2118

WAR DIARY
or
INTELLIGENCE SUMMARY
(Erase heading not required.)

48 FIELD AMBULANCE

Place	Date	Hour	Summary of Events and Information	Remarks and references to Appendices
FRESNICOURT	21.8.16		Capt. J.E. COOK, who was evacuated sick on 14th April is struck off the strength of the unit.	
"	23.8.16		Capt. H.M. GODFREY transferred for duty with 13th Bn. Rifle Bgde. The 102nd Bgde has now left this area.	
"	26.8.16		The DDMS Capt. H. ALCOCK left to 14 days duty with 9th Bn. N. Stafford.	
"	31.8.16		Rubble is being drawn for the construction of horse standings here. The ambulance remains here clearing sick from 63rd Bgde. only.	

A.P. Paton Lt. Col.
OC 48th F. Amb.

Confidential

War Diary
of
48th Field Ambulance

From 1st September to 30th September

1916.

Vol: XIV

Army Form C. 2118

WAR DIARY
or
INTELLIGENCE SUMMARY
(Erase heading not required.)

27 / **48 Field Ambulance**

Place	Date	Hour	Summary of Events and Information	Remarks and references to Appendices
FRESNICOURT	1.9.16		Capt. PROCTER. R.A.M.C. attached to the F.A. temporarily for duty.	
"	"		Lt. MASSIAH " returned to the F.A. for duty.	
"	2.9.16		112th Bgde returned to 37th Div. and their sick as well as those of the 63rd Bgde are to be cleared by the F.A. 112th Bgde are situated in BEUGIN. LA COMPTÉ and DIEVAL.	
"	4.9.16		Lt. & Qr. Mr. E. HAYNES. arrived for duty with the F.A. vice Lt. & Qr. Mr. G.W. CARNEL transferred to ETAPLES.	
"	5.9.16		Sergt. Major. H.J. POWER. left on transfer to No. 20. Gen. Hosp. ETAPLES. Sergt. Major L.J. BRAIN. Takes over the duties of Sergt Major of the unit.	
"	9.9.16		Capt. PROCTER left on 14 days special leave.	
"	14.9.16		Capt. ALCOCK returned to duty with the F.A.	
"	17.9.16		Sudden orders were received this morning to take over from F.Ambulances of 63rd Div. Extract from Operation Order by Colonel R.W. WRIGHT. A.M.S. A.D.M.S. 37th Div:— 1. The 37th Division will relieve the 63rd Division in the SOUCHEZ, ANGRES & CALONNE Sections immediately. the relief will be completed by 10 A.M. on Sept. 20th. 2. The Field Ambulances will move as follows:— 48th Field Ambulance. Sept. 17th Take over from 3rd Field Ambulance the Advanced Dressing Station at PONT GRENAY. (4.0. p.m.)	

Army Form C. 2118

WAR DIARY
or
INTELLIGENCE SUMMARY
(Erase heading not required.)

48 FIELD AMBULANCE

Place	Date	Hour	Summary of Events and Information	Remarks and references to Appendices
FRESNICOURT	17.9.16		Sept. 18th. Take over from No I. Field Ambulance the Advanced Dressing Station at AIX NOULETTE. — Advanced party at 4.p.m. on 17th Sept. Take over from No II. Field Ambulance the Advanced Dressing Station at BULLY GRENAY. (morning) Sept 19th. Take over from No II. Field Ambulance — MAIN DRESSING STATION at School of mines. FOSSE. 10. (morning) No I. Field Ambulance (63rd Division) will take over from 48th Field Ambulance at FRESNICOURT. (Advanced party on evening of 17th Sept.) At 2.p.m. Capt. RENWICK, 1 N.C.O. + 12 men left for the A.D.S. at PONT GRENAY, and Capt. ROGERSON, 1 N.C.O. and 3 men for that at AIX NOULETTE.	
"	18.9.16		At 7.30 A.M. Capt. ALCOCK and 33. O.Rs left to take over the A.D.S. at BULLY GRENAY, with personnel to bring that at PONT GRENAY to 1 Officer & 24. O.Rs. and at AIX NOULETTE to 1 Officer and 38. O.Rs. The 1st F. Amb. arrived here at 5.p.m. The remaining personnel of this unit have moved into one of the hospital huts thus relieving their billets for the 1st F.A.	
FOSSE. 10. SAINS.	19.9.16		The remaining personnel with the transport of the F.A. marched from FRESNICOURT at 8.30. A.M. arriving at FOSSE. 10. at 11. A.M.	

WAR DIARY or INTELLIGENCE SUMMARY

Army Form C. 2118

48. Field Ambulance

Place	Date	Hour	Summary of Events and Information	Remarks and references to Appendices
FOSSE 10 SAINS	20.9.16		The clearing arrangements for the line are as follows:— The two battalions holding the SOUCHEZ sector are cleared by means of relay posts, the first being situated at the R.A.P. of the Right battalion, to AIX NOULETTE, which place are also cleared cases from the Right battalion of the ANGRES sector. The Left battalion of the ANGRES sector is cleared by means of relays to BULLY GRENAY. In the COLONNE SECTOR. There is an advanced post of 1 N.C.O. and 11 men in CALONNE where all the R.A.P.s of the Left Brigade are, and cases are carried directly back to PONT. GRENAY without relays. The main dressing station is situated in 3 blocks of school buildings, which lend themselves admirably to hospital purposes and are capable of accommodating 350 cases. Large open spaces separate the blocks, providing parade grounds or ground for parking transport or pitching tent accommodation. The personnel are billeted in excellent lofts in the hospital blocks.	
"	21.9.16		LT. G.T. SYMONS. R.A.M.C. was posted for duty with the F.A. CAPT. F.S. GILLESPIE. R.A.M.C. of the 49th F.A. was sent for temporary duty to the A.D.S. at AIX NOULETTE, and CAPT. M.F. WAY. of the 50th F.A. to that at PONT. GRENAY. CAPT. H. ALLCOCK. is posted to the 11th Rop. Warwicks. for duty, and has been relieved at BULLY GRENAY by Lt. E.S. MASSIAH.	

Army Form C. 2118

WAR DIARY
or
INTELLIGENCE SUMMARY

(Erase heading not required.)

48 FIELD AMBULANCE

Place	Date	Hour	Summary of Events and Information	Remarks and references to Appendices
FOSSE.10. SAINS	22.9.16		The first case of "Trench Foot" was admitted today. He came from the AIX.NOULETTE section of the line, where there is about a foot of water in parts of the fire trench, left from the recent heavy rain.	
"	24.9.16		Capt. PROCTER. R.A.M.C. returned from leave and is posted for duty with the 13th Bn. Ry. Fusiliers. One slight case of trench foot admitted from the ANGRES. section.	
"	25.9.16		The A.D.S. at AIX. NOULETTE is to be handed over to 49th F.A. A/Ds with 8th Clear the cases from there to FOSSE. 10. Half their personnel proceeded to AIX today to relieve half the personnel of the 48th F.A. there.	
"	26.9.16		The handing over of the A.D.S. at AIX NOULETTE was completed today. Capt. ROGERSON returned to the main dressing station.	
"	28.9.16		Lt SYMONS relieved Capt RENWICK at the A.D.S. at PONT GRENAY. Capt RENWICK reported to O.C. 13th K.R.R. for temporary duty.	

HPWatson.

Confidential

War Diary

of

48th Field Ambulance

from 1st October to 31st October

1916.

(Volume XV)

Army Form C. 2118

WAR DIARY
or
INTELLIGENCE SUMMARY

(Erase heading not required.)

31. 48 FIELD AMBULANCE

Place	Date	Hour	Summary of Events and Information	Remarks and references to Appendices
FOSSE.10. SAINS.	1.10.16		Lt. Col. D.P. WATSON proceeded on leave; temporary command of the Ambulance taken over by Capt. C. NICHOLSON. Capt. W.A. ROGERSON relieved Lt. E.S. MASSIAH at the Advanced Dressing Station at BULLY GRENAY; the latter was admitted to hospital and evacuated sick to no 22 Casualty Clearing Station. Capt. C.J.B. WAY returned from the Advanced Dressing Station at PONT GRENAY In duty at the Main Dressing Station leaving Lt. G.Y. SYMONS in sole charge.	Cr.
"	2.10.16	3 p.m.	Under orders from A.D.M.S. 37th division Lt. D.W. DANIELS relieved Lt. G.T. SYMONS at the Advanced Dressing Station at PONT GRENAY; the latter proceeded to report to D.D.M.S. XVII Corps In duty with 9th Division and is struck off the strength, Capt. C.J.B. WAY returned to 50th Field Ambulance.	Cr.
		8 p.m.	Capt. H.R. SOUPER from 49th Field Ambulance reported for temporary duty with this Field Ambulance.	Cr.
"	2.10.16	9 a.m.	Capt. H.R. SOUPER took over charge of the Advanced Dressing Station at PONT GRENAY. Lt. D.W. DANIELS returned for duty at Main Dressing Station.	Cr.
		2 p.m.	Lieut. J.C. MACKWOOD and Lieut J.A.S. BURGES arrived for duty from 24th Division, Lieut BURGES relieved Capt. SOUPER at the Advanced Dressing Station at PONT GRENAY; the latter returned to 49th Field Ambulance	Cr.

WAR DIARY
INTELLIGENCE SUMMARY

48th FIELD AMBULANCE

Army Form C. 2118

Place	Date	Hour	Summary of Events and Information	Remarks and references to Appendices
FOSSE 10. SAINS.	8.10.16		Extract from Order by A.D.M.S. 37th Division:— "On 9th instant the Division will extend its left as far as M.4.c.5 7½. 48th Field Ambulance will take over the Advanced Dressing Station in MOROCCO SOUTH, at present found by 135 Field Ambulance of 40th Division by 3 p.m. on 9th instant." Lieut J.C. MACKWOOD and a party of 1 N.C.O. and 14 men proceeded this morning at 11 a.m. in accordance with above order S.	(i) (i)
"	9.10.16			
"	10.10.16		Lt-Col D.P. WATSON returned from leave.	SPN
"	12.10.16		Capt. ANDREW. was brought back from MAROC S. to PONT. BRENAY. and 1 N.C.O. and 8 men left at MAROC S. as an advanced post.	SPN
"	13.10.16		Extr. from Operation orders by A.D.M.S. 37th Div. 1. The 37th Div. will hand over the line to the 2nd Canadian Division and go into First Army Reserve. 2. Field Ambulances will move and billet under the orders of the Infantry Brigades to which they are affiliated, they will arrange ambulance transport for the Brigades in direct communication with Brigade H.Q. and will clear the Brigade areas.	SPN

Army Form C. 2118

WAR DIARY
or
INTELLIGENCE SUMMARY

(Erase heading not required.)

33 **48 Field Ambulance**

Place	Date	Hour	Summary of Events and Information	Remarks and references to Appendices
FOSSE 10 SAINS	13.10.16		On the 18th inst 48th F.A. will clear the area CAMBLAIN-CHATELAIN, MARSET, BOIRS, MONNEVILLE occupied by the Divisional R.A. on the 17th inst, and the 69th N. Staffords at La Comté. 3. Movement of the Field Ambulances will take place as follows:— 48th F.A. to CITE 90 9. on 17th inst. with M.a Infantry Brigade moving into the area BARLIN, HERSIN, MAISNIL-LES-RUITZ. 4. The 5th Canadian F.A. will relieve the 48th F.A. at FOSSE 10. on morning of the 17th inst., Advanced Dressing Station party on 15th inst. The 4th Canadian F.A. will relieve the 48th F.A. at CITE no 9. on the 18th inst.	
"	14.10.16		Capt. ANDREW returned to 50th F.A.	JPN
"	15.10.16		Lt. MACKWOOD proceeded on 14 days special leave. Lt. BURGES proceeded to 49th F.A. for duty. Capt. EVANS and Capt. RENWICK returned to the F.A. for duty. The personnel from the Advanced dressing station was relieved by the 5th Canadian F.A. and returned to the main dressing station. All cases are being evacuated	JPN JPN.

Army Form C. 2118

WAR DIARY
or
~~INTELLIGENCE SUMMARY~~
(Erase heading not required.)

34A 48 FIELD AMBULANCE

Place	Date	Hour	Summary of Events and Information	Remarks and references to Appendices
BARLIN.	17.10.16	9.30 P.M.	The Ambulance marched from FOSSE 10. SAINS. and is billeted in BARLIN. Orders from 111th Bgde received to march at 9.45 A.M. tomorrow to MONCHY BRETON. via RANCHICOURT and LA COMPTE. The following areas have to be cleared. HERSIN. BARLIN. MAISNIL LES RUITZ. CAMBLAIN - CHATELAIN. MAREST. BOURS. MONNEVILLE. This will be done by Moto Ambulances before moving.	SPN
MONCHY BRETON	18.10.16	5 p.m.	The Ambulance marched in rear of the 111th Bgde via RANCHICOURT and LA COMPTE to MONCHY BRETON. arriving at 2.30 & going into billets. The motor ambulance cars left 4½ hours after the ambulance and following the same route, arrived immediately after it. 4 cases of sick collected from the HERSIN (Bgde) area were collected before moving and evacuated to No 6 C.C.S BARLIN. 3 cases from the CAMBLAIN - CHATELAIN (Div Artillery) area were collected after the Ambulance had marched, brought to MONCHY BRETON and evacuated to No 12 Stationary Hospital ST. POL. There is fair hospital accommodation for some 12 cases here.	
	19.10.16	9 A.M.	Notice received from 111th Bgde that the Bgde does not move today.	SPN

WAR DIARY or INTELLIGENCE SUMMARY

Army Form C. 2118

48 Field Ambulance

Place	Date	Hour	Summary of Events and Information	Remarks and references to Appendices
GOUY-EN-TERNOIS	20.10.16	2pm	The ambulance marched at 9.45 A.M. in rear of 111th Bgde. via BAILLEUL, AUX-ORMAUX and AVERDOIGNT to GOUY. EN. TERNOIS, where it went into billets at 12.30 P.M. Before leaving MONCHY BRETON, the 111th Bgde. and Divisional artillery areas were cleared and the sick (1 officer and 11 men) evacuated to No.12 Stationary Hospital, ST. POL.	J.P.N.
BEAUVAL	21.10.16	6 pm	The ambulance marched in rear of 111th Bgde. leaving GOUY at 8 A.M. and arriving at BEAUVAL at 4.30 pm. Where it went into billets. The motor cars remained behind the Ambulance at GOUY and cleared the 111th Bgde & Div. Artillery areas and then proceeded under Lt. DANIELS to BEAUVAL via FREVENT, where the sick were evacuated to No 6 Stationary Hospital.	J.P.N.
PUCHEVILLERS	22.10.16	12 pm	The ambulance marched from BEAUVAL at 6 A.M. And went into billets here. At 11.30. A.M. The 111th Bgde area was cleared by the cars at 7 A.M. and the sick were evacuated to No 47 C.C.S. BEAUVAL.	J.P.N.
"	"	8 p.m.	Orders received from A.D.M.S. 37th Div. to relieve 3rd F.A. (R.M.D) at VARENNES tomorrow after 10. A.M. advanced party to be there by 7.30. A.M.	J.P.N.
VARENNES	23.10.16	4.30 pm	The ambulance left PUCHEVILLERS at 8.30 A.M. & marched by TOUTENCOURT and HARPONVILLERS. Short of the latter place the Ambulance was halted off the road from 10. A.M. to 3. A.M. as Capt RENWICK who was with the advanced party, thought that	J.P.N.

WAR DIARY
or
INTELLIGENCE SUMMARY
(Erase heading not required.)

Army Form C. 2118

36. 48 FIELD AMBULANCE

Place	Date	Hour	Summary of Events and Information	Remarks and references to Appendices
VARENNES	23.10.16	4.30 pm	The 3rd F.A. was not expecting to be relieved. Went in search of the A.D.M.S. 37th Div & with him to the A.D.M.S. VII Corps. From whom it was ascertained that the F.A. was to proceed near 3rd F.A. This was done at 4 p.m.	JPW
"	24.6.16	10.30	Lt. DANIELS, 5 N.C.Os and 31 men were attached this morning to the 3rd F.A. to form a Main Dressing Station in VARENNES	JPW
"	"	6 pm	Capt. WAY with one bearer section from 50th F.A. and Capt. BROUGH & Lt. BURGES of 49th F.A. with the bearer division of 49th F.A. arrived here at 5/6 pm. Orders received from A.D.M.S. this morning that the Combined bearer division, less 2 sections of 50th F.A. will be under command of Lt. Col. D.R. WATSON. Owing to shortage of Officers one bearer section from each ambulance still be commanded by a Sergeant.	JPW
"	25.10.16	10 AM	The above parties that arrived last night moved at 9 A.M. to ACHEUX, where there is better accommodation for them.	JPW
"	"	6 pm	Lt. E.S. MASSIAH having been invalided sick to England is struck off the strength.	JPW
"	"	6 pm	Lt. Col. D.R. WATSON accompanied the A.D.M.S. 37th Div to office of A.D.M.S. 63rd Div. where arrangements for clearing the battlefield were formulated. Capt. R.C. POYSER and Lt. A.A. MURISON reported for duty with the F.A.	JPW
"	26.10.16		The accommodation at ACHEUX being required for other troops the bearers from 49th & 50th F.A. have returned to their respective units	JPW

Army Form C. 2118

WAR DIARY or INTELLIGENCE SUMMARY

(Erase heading not required.)

37 / 48 FIELD AMBULANCE

Place	Date	Hour	Summary of Events and Information	Remarks and references to Appendices
VARENNES.	27.10.16		Three Officers and 100 O.R. of the Divisional Bearer Coy are employed daily on road drainage. The weather since the burial of the war at VARENNES has been vile, with rain every day.	JPN
"	28.10.16		Operation orders received from A.D.M.S. 37th Div. Disposition of 48th F.A. personnel in the event of an attack. 1 Officer + 38 O.R. at main Dressing Station VARENNES. Bearer division combined with bearers from 49th & 150th F.As under Lt Col HARVEY. Two Sections (B + C of 48 F.A.) in reserve at COOKERS. 1 " (49th F.A.) " " MESNIL Two " (49th F.A.) - to accompany 63rd Inf. Bgde. Two " (A Inf. 48 F.A. + from 50 F.A.) " " 111th " " The hours subdivision with Inf. Bgdes to be detached by the Bgdes.	
LONGUEVILLETTE	31.10.16	9 A.M.	Orders were received from A.D.M.S. 37th Div at 1.30 p.m. yesterday for the ambulance to move with the 111th Bgde. to LONGUEVILLETTE, a previous warning having been received at 11.30 A.M. The C.O. of the ambulance, who was making a reconnaissance, was not found until 2.30 p.m. Surplus rations, dressings etc. were vouchered off to the 1st F.A. (CN.D) and the ambulance left VARENNES at 4 p.m. and marched via LEALVILLERS	JPN

1875 Wt: W593/826 1,000,000 4/15 J.B.C. & A. A.D.S.S./Forms/C. 2118.

WAR DIARY
or
INTELLIGENCE SUMMARY

Army Form C. 2118

38 48 FIELD AMBULANCE

Place	Date	Hour	Summary of Events and Information	Remarks and references to Appendices
LONGUEVILLETTE	31.10.16		RANCHIVAL, BEAUQUESNE, and CANDAS, going into billets about midnight last night at LONGUEVILLETTE, where they are to clear the M.E Ryle. Capt. Mackwood returned from leave this morning	JPN

J.H. Moore A/Col.
Comdg. 48th F.A.

Confidential.

War Diary.

of

48 Field Ambulance.

From 1st November to 30th November.

1916.

(Volume ~~VI~~)

A.D.M.S.
37 Division.

Herewith War Diary
of 48 Field Ambulance
for the month of
November 1916.
Kindly acknowledge
receipt.

30/11/16.

T P Watson
Lt Col R.A.M.C.,
Comdg 48th Field Ambulance.

WAR DIARY
or
INTELLIGENCE SUMMARY
(Erase heading not required.)

Army Form C. 2118

48 FIELD AMBULANCE

Place	Date	Hour	Summary of Events and Information	Remarks and references to Appendices
LONGUEVILLETTE	1.11.16		CAPT. POYSER. left for duty with the 29th F.A.	J.P.M.
"	3.11.16		An expected move today, indicated yesterday by A.D.M.S. 37th Div. has been postponed	J.P.M.
"	8.11.16		The weather has been extremely bad with frequent rain. Information was received last night from Mth Pyle that "2" army is indefinitely postponed. Arrangements are being made to intvine a service of pack-mules in the Ambulance. The bearer division is being employed in stretcher exercises.	J.P.M.
"	10.11.16	5pm	Intimation received from A.D.M.S. 37th that today is W day. In accordance with orders received from 111th Inf. Bgde. the Ambulance will march tomorrow to PUCHEVILLERS via Fm. du ROSEL and VAL de MAISON, leaving cross roads one S of L in LONGUEVILLETTE at 8.15 a.m. One horsed Ambulance to accompany 13th R.B. from LONGUEVILLETTE and one Fm. 10 to R.F. from HEM.	J.P.M.
PUCHEVILLERS	11.11.16	6pm	The Ambulance received orders to stand fast this morning, and at 11.20 AM received orders to start at 11. AM. The Ambulance left LONGUEVILLETTE at 11.25 am, arrived here at 4.30 pm. going into billets	J.P.M.
"	12.11.16		Orders received from Mth Pyle to march at 4.15 to VARENNES via TOTTENCOURT and HARPONVILLE.	J.P.M.

Army Form C. 2118

WAR DIARY
or
INTELLIGENCE SUMMARY
(Erase heading not required.)

48 Field Ambulance

Place	Date	Hour	Summary of Events and Information	Remarks and references to Appendices
VARENNES	13.11.16		The ambulance arrived here at 7.30 pm last night and went into billets. A cycle orderly was detached to Signals for direct communication with 111th Bde. at 11 pm. Orders were received from A.D.M.S. for Lt. MURISON to proceed to 37th Div. Amm. Col. forthwith the C.O.s at once. Also for two bearer subdivisions to stand fast in readiness to proceed with the 111th Bde. A & B bearer subdivisions under Capt. EVANS & Sergt. COLLINS are standing fast for this purpose. This is "Z" day, and the attack commenced early this morning.	SPh
"	13/14.11.16	2 pm	Lt. DANIELS and 6 nursing orderlies have been sent temporarily to 1st F.A. from nursing station here.	SPh
"	"	9 pm	111th Bde having moved up to the battle area, orders were received at 9.30 pm. for two bearer subdivisions to join the A.D.S. of 63rd Div. A section bearers under Capt. EVANS to MESNIL, and B. section bearers under Capt. ROGERSON, was also sent to 1st F.A. to help temporarily.	
		11 pm	Orders were received at 11 pm. for six cars to be sent to 63rd Div. Collecting Station. These have been sent.	SPh
		3 pm	One Ford car was sent away yesterday in exchange for a Siddeley-Deasy.	

Army Form C. 2118

WAR DIARY or INTELLIGENCE SUMMARY

48 Field Ambulance

(Erase heading not required.)

Place	Date	Hour	Summary of Events and Information	Remarks and references to Appendices
VARENNES	14.11.16	4 p.m.	C. Section Bearers under Capt. RENWICK. Left at 11 A.M. in G.S. Wagons & reported South end of STATION Rd. Capt. ROGERSON, Capt. MACHWOOD and five men left in motor ambulances to assist in the work at the A.D.S. at COOKERS. Report received from CAPT. EVANS that Lieut. GAZE and seven men were wounded this morning at HAMEL. All available officers are & have been assisting in the work at the main dressing station of 1st F.A. (R.N.D.) at VARENNES.	JPh.
"	15.11.16 5 p.m.		Under orders from the A.D.M.S. 37th Div. Capt. NICHOLSON, Lt. DANIELS, 5 N.C.O.s & 31 men were sent to main dressing station 1st F.A. to form a combined main dressing station, with a view to taking over from the 1st F.A. at an early date. A.D.M.S. ordained from dressing station returns for the 37th Div. are being rendered by this unit. It is reported that Pte A.J. BETTS, died of wounds yesterday.	JPh.
"	16.11.16 6 A.M.		Instructions received from A.D.M.S. to send 13 more O.Rs. to COOKERS, bringing the personnel there up to a complete tent subdivision. Also that the handing over of medical arrangements of 63rd Div. to 37th Div. will take place as soon as possible.	JPh.

Army Form C. 2118

WAR DIARY
or
INTELLIGENCE SUMMARY
(Erase heading not required.)

42 48 FIELD AMBULANCE

Place	Date	Hour	Summary of Events and Information	Remarks and references to Appendices
VARENNES	17/11/16	6 p.m.	The F.A. took over the main dressing station here from the 72nd F.A. this morning. They marched out at 1 p.m. There are two tent subdivisions with two officers only. But two other officers have been attached by D.D.M.S. 5th Corps — Lt AUSTIN and Lt CLARKE. The Ambulance is clearing today to PUCHEVILLERS. Up to the present there have been very few Casualties. The two Bearer + two tent subdivisions from C.R.S. acts as reserves. M.D.S. Six motor cars of this Ambulance with six from 50th F.A. are stationed, two at each A.D.S. at COOKERS and MESNIL and the remainder forming the (Divisional Exhaust) at NORTHUMBERLAND AVENUE.	JPW
"	18/11/16	5 p.m.	A bearer subdivision from 50th F.A. was sent up to the Car of this Ambulance early this morning to ENGLEBELMER to advance from there with the 12th Inf Bgde. Comparatively few casualties have passed thro' the main dressing station today, roughly about 60 only. Orders received from A.D.M.S. 37th Div. to detail an officer to visit the sick of 37th Div. train at LEALVILLERS daily from the 20th. Capt NICHOLSON is detailed. The car water from COOKERS is changed to HAMEL — MESNIL — ENGLEBELMER — HEDAUVILLE	JPW

1875 Wt. W593/826 1,000,000 4/15 J.B.C. & A. A.D.S.S./Forms/C. 2118.

WAR DIARY or INTELLIGENCE SUMMARY

Army Form C. 2118

48 FIELD AMBULANCE

Place	Date	Hour	Summary of Events and Information	Remarks and references to Appendices
VARENNES	18.11.16	6/pm	The weather changed this morning from hard frost, with snow in the night, to a thaw with rain, which persisted throughout the day. A Bearer subdivision to the Entrips early tomorrow morning by the cars of this ambulance to the ADS at the COOKERS n HAMEL. Capt Rogerson his orders to change the site of the ADS. bright from the COOKERS to HAMEL itself. 3 huts have been erected by the R.E. for this purpose. Tarpaulins were sent up by the their evening to sleet shelters for the personnel	APB
"	19.11.16	6pm	The A.D.S. moved this morning from COOKERS to place close to HAMEL. Comparatively few casualties are coming in – 8 officers 24 OSR & 8 germans in the last 24 hrs.	APB
"	20.11.16	8.30pm	Operation order No. 20. R.A.M.C. 37th Div. received. Extracts:– 111th Bgde will be relieved on night 20/21st Nov...... Two bearer subdivisions of 48th Field Ambulance will take over accompany the 111th Bgde and on arrival of the Bgde at ENGLEBELMER will return to their unit.	APB
"	21.11.16	Noon	Information received from Capt RENNIER that after carrying cases up till midnight A+C Section bearers were bivouaced for the night at COOKERS, and transport was asked for them as they were exhausted. 37th Div have undertaken to send up 3 motor lorries for them.	APB

Army Form C. 2118

WAR DIARY
or
INTELLIGENCE SUMMARY
(Erase heading not required.)

44 **48 Field Ambulance**

Instructions regarding War Diaries and Intelligence Summaries are contained in F.S. Regs., Part II. and the Staff Manual respectively. Title Pages will be prepared in manuscript.

Place	Date	Hour	Summary of Events and Information	Remarks and references to Appendices
VARENNES.	22/1/16	4.p.m.	Capt. RENNICK and the bearers of A & C sections returned to the main dressing station with the exception of 14 bearers unfit to march, who will be returned in small parties by motor ambulance. The men are considerably exhausted after a week of bearing under fire and with no shelter.	App 1
"	23/1/16		The 33rd F.A. having taken over the huts at HAMEL. Capt ROBERSON is helping the A.D.S. at the COOKERS.	App 1
"	23/1/16	5 p.m.	The Divisional Cab rank at NORTHUMBERLAND AVENUE is done away with. Six Cars remain at the COOKERS. The Wolseley Cars of the ambulance have been replaced by 'Siddeley Deasy'. Under instructions from A.D.M.S. 37th Div. all surplus stretchers, medical materials etc at the COOKERS are being returned to Corps Collecting Station at ACHEUX.	App 1
"	24/1/16	9 a.m.	Operation Order No 21 received from A.D.M.S. District. — 48th Field Ambulance will join 111th Inf. Bgde. Group on 26th inst. and will march with the Brigade. The party originally detailed for duty at the main dressing station, VARENNES, will remain there until further orders. The M.A.C. is now calling nice daily by at main dressing station.	App 1

WAR DIARY or INTELLIGENCE SUMMARY

Army Form C. 2118

48 Field Ambulance

Place	Date	Hour	Summary of Events and Information	Remarks and references to Appendices
VARENNES	25.11.16	9 A.M.	Capt EVANS and the bearers of B section returned to the main dressing station yesterday evening. All bearers have now returned. Casualties among the bearers division are as follows:—	
			Killed. No. 39322. Pte BETTS.	
			Wounded No. 37531. Sergt GAZE. No. 52225. Pte CHANDLEY. No. 27839. Pte FRANKS. " 37483. Pte HOOPER. " 106677. " BARWOOD. " 39328. " BRINDLE. " 39586. " FOLEY. " 73476. " BAKEWELL. " 76717. " CROSSLEY. " 39327. " BOYLES. " 36325. " BROWN. " 47341. " O'CONNELL.	JPN
"	26.11.16		Capt. ROGERSON and half the personnel from A.D.S. at COOPERS. returned to the main dressing station. The remainder will return tomorrow morning when the 63rd & 112th Bdes. are clear of the line. Orders from 111th Bde. for Ambulance to march tomorrow at 9.15 A.M. to PUCHEVILLERS via LEAVILLERS. ARQUEVES. RAINCHEVAL.	JPN
PUCHEVILLERS	27.11.16		The Ambulance marched from VARENNES at 9.30 A.M. and reached PUCHEVILLERS at 12.30 yesterday. The last of the A.D.S. party returned to VARENNES about 4. p.m. and came on to PUCHEVILLERS by the motor ambulances, a party for loading blankets being left behind. The ambulance is close billetted, & there is no suitable place for treating sick.	JPN

WAR DIARY

Army Form C. 2118

48 Field Ambulance

Place	Date	Hour	Summary of Events and Information	Remarks and references to Appendices
PUCHEVILLERS	27.11.16		Lt. DANIELS proceeded on 14 days Special leave.	APH
"	28.11.16		Capt MACNWOOD appointed in charge of Divisional baths and laundry.	8 ORs
"	30.11.16		The Ambulance remains at PUCHEVILLERS. All sick have to be sent away. A limited number are kept on the books and treated at No 49 C.C.S. Beauval. The remainder are evacuated to C.C.S's at PUCHEVILLERS. A draft of 12 O.Rs arrived this morning	APH

J.D. Watson Lt. Col.
Commanding 48 F.A.

Confidential.

War Diary

of

48 Field Ambulance.

From 1st December to 31st December.

1916.

(Volume 17)

Army Form C. 2118

WAR DIARY
or
INTELLIGENCE SUMMARY
(Erase heading not required.)

48 Field Ambulance

Instructions regarding War Diaries and Intelligence Summaries are contained in F.S. Regs, Part II. and the Staff Manual respectively. Title Pages will be prepared in manuscript.

Place	Date	Hour	Summary of Events and Information	Remarks and references to Appendices
PUCHEVILLERS	1.12.16		A fatigue party was detached (10 men) to work under C.R.E. at R.E. Store MARIEUX. Capt. R.V. MACDONNELL R.A.M.C. reported for duty with the F.A. yesterday.	APW.
"	3.12.16		A course of training including lectures to Officers and men was commenced today. It follows a weekly programme drawn up by the ADMS 57th Div. Sergt COLLINS and 37 bearers were attached to No 11 C.C.S. yesterday for temporary duty.	APW.
"	4.12.16		Lt. Dr. Mr HAYNES proceeded on 11 days leave.	APW.
BEAUVAL	6.12.16		The Ambulance marched to BEAUVAL arriving at 2 p.m. to take over buildings etc. from 47th C.C.S. and form a Corps rest station. 78 Convalescent cases were taken on the books of the ambulance.	DPW.
"	7.12.16		The C.C.S. have not moved out yet & will not be clear for several days. The ambulance has entirely taken over the girls school and the eastern part of the premises at the Jute factory.	APW.
"	9.12.16		The 47th C.C.S. has also moved out & all buildings and annexes occupied by them have been taken over by the F.A. Some Red Cross stores were received today for equipping the ECOLE DE GARCONS as an Officers' Hospital. Three G.S. Wagons required daily to work at cutting wood near ZOUDES.	APW.

1875 Wt. W593/826 1,000,000 4/15 J.B.C. & A. A.D.S.S./Forms/C/2118.

WAR DIARY or INTELLIGENCE SUMMARY

Army Form C. 2118

48 Field Ambulance

Place	Date	Hour	Summary of Events and Information	Remarks and references to Appendices
BEAUVAL	10.12.16		The Corps Rest Station is opened from 9 A.M. today to receive the Mild Cases of Sickness from the three Divisions of the Corps. The FLORE DE FILLES is to be used for the Cases that require some nursing, and will accommodate 80 to 100 patients. The Marquees are reserved for Skin Cases and those who are able to take heavy exercise. The Big Hall at the Tobacco Factory being kept for Cases of Intermediate Severity.	SPM
"	11.12.16	3.30 pm	Secret instructions received from A.D.M.S. 39th Div. to be prepared to move at a moment's notice. Orders issued accordingly.	ATM
NAVANS.	14.12.16	6 pm	The 1st Corps Rest Station was handed over to the 58th F.A. yesterday, and the F.A. marched with the 112th Bgde via DOULLENS to NAVANS arriving at 2.30 pm & going into billets. Capt. RENWICK followed the infantry of the Bgde with Capt MACKWOOD. Two horsed wagons & dumped Cases at BOUQUEMAISON. Followed several hours after with the motor ambulances and motor lorries and picked up any stragglers. 36 were carried on. The similar arrangement will be carried out tomorrow, tho' as the infantry are marching by two separate routes it must be present modified. 6 Cases are being evacuated to DOULLENS this evening.	

Army Form C. 2118

WAR DIARY
or
INTELLIGENCE SUMMARY

(Erase heading not required.)

48 Field Ambulance

Place	Date	Hour	Summary of Events and Information	Remarks and references to Appendices
FRAMECOURT	15/12/16	5 pm	The ambulance marched from WAVANS at 10.15 this morning via VILLERS L'HOPITAL, BONNIERES, FREVENT to FRAMECOURT, where it went into billets at 8.30 p.m. The Bgde area was cleared at 9 p.m. and sick + those unable to march were collected at BONNIERES, when 19 sick were evacuated to No 6 Stationary Hospital FREVENT. The cars returned thence to BONNIERES and subsequently followed up the two columns of infantry of the brigade to pick up stragglers.	AMcN
BERGUENEUSE	16/12/16	4 pm	The ambulance marched at 8.10 AM via CROISETTE, BEAUVOIS, WAVRANS, ANGIN, to BERGUENEUSE, where it went into billets at 2 p.m. The brigade area was cleared at 7.30 A.M. and cases brought to BERGUENEUSE, whence 1 Officer and 37 O.R. were evacuated to FREVENT. The cars then followed the two infantry columns of the Bgde to BOURS and EPS, BOYAVAL district.	AMcN
LIERETTE	17/12/16	5 pm	The ambulance marched from BERGUENEUSE at 8.30 A.M. and joining the Bgde Column at BOYAVAL marched by SAINS-les-PERNES, FIEFS, NEDONCHELLE to LIERETTE, where it went into billets at 2.30 p.m. The motor ambulance cars cleared the Bgde area of sick, who were evacuated to LOZINGHEM, and then following the Bgde to pick up stragglers.	AMcN

Army Form C. 2118

WAR DIARY
or
INTELLIGENCE SUMMARY
(Erase heading not required.)

50 48 FIELD AMBULANCE

Instructions regarding War Diaries and Intelligence Summaries are contained in F. S. Regs., Part II. and the Staff Manual respectively. Title Pages will be prepared in manuscript.

Place	Date	Hour	Summary of Events and Information	Remarks and references to Appendices
MARQUOIS.	16.12.16	5 p.m.	The Ambulance marched from LIERETTE at 9.35 A.M. and went into billets at MARQUOIS at 2.30 p.m. The motor cars collected sick. Also were evacuated to the W. Riding C.C.S. at LILLERS, & then followed up the Bgde picking up stragglers. CAPT. FINDLATER R.A.M.C. joined the F.A. for duty.	APh
ZELOBES	20.12.16	4 p.m.	The Ambulance marched from MARQUOIS at 9.30 A.M. moving independently and went into billets at ZELOBES at noon. We have taken over a Field Ambulance site, which was not, however, at the time in occupation by a F.A. The hospital buildings comprise a mueline and huts. The Ambulance is to clear the Reserve Bgde. of the Division and is not forming any advanced dressing stations. A good deal of work requires to be done. The men's billets are good, tho' rather scattered.	APh.
"	23.12.16		on the three. Centre-divisional work is being carried out in hospital and billets	APh.
"	24.12.16		Lt. MURISON struck off the strength of the unit.	
"	28.12.16		CAPT. FINDLATER left for temporary duty with the 11th By WARWICKS.	
"	31.12.16		CAPT. EVANS left for temporary duty with D.A.C. CAPT. NICHOLSON returned from leave. The Postmann in Res. Clearing reserve Bgde H.Q.	APh.

1875 Wt. W593/826 1,000,000 4/15 J.B.C. & A. A.D.S.S./Forms/C. 2118.

Confidential.

War Diary.

of

48. Field Ambulance.

From 1st January To. 31st January.

1917.

(Volume 18)

COMMITTEE FOR THE MEDICAL HISTORY OF THE WAR
Date 13 MAR. 1917

Army Form C. 2118

WAR DIARY
or
INTELLIGENCE SUMMARY

(Erase heading not required.)

48 Field Ambulance

Place	Date	Hour	Summary of Events and Information	Remarks and references to Appendices
ZELOBES	1.1.17		Capt. R.V. McDONNELL left the F.A. for duty with the 8th Bn Somerset L. Infantry Regt.	D.S.W.
"	2.1.17		Capt. G.H. RUSSELL joined the F.A. for duty	G.P.D
			63rd Bgde is going into the left sector of the line and the M.A. Bgde taking their place in reserve and now be cleared by the F.A.	
"	6.1.17		Capt. ROGERSON proceeded on 10 days leave to England	G.P.D
"	8.1.17		The Rev. A.A. COUTTS. C.F. left the Ambulance for duty in L.J.C.	
			No 74584 Pte KEEN. W. of the ambulance proceeded to a parade at MERVILLE to receive from the Corps Commander the ribbon of the Military Medal awarded for conspicuous gallantry and devotion to duty in the operations on the ANCRE.	D.Fl.S.
			Sergt Maj. L.J. BRAIN proceeded to the same parade to receive the ribbon of the Meritorious Service Medal. Revd Capt BOOTT C.F. attached to the F.A. for the division.	
"	9.1.17		Lt-Col. WATTON commenced to officiate for A.D.M.S. 37th Div. who has proceeded on indulgence	D.F.D.
"	10.1.17		S.S.M. BENNETT. returned to duty from vans replaced by A.S.M. BLAKE.	
			Two NISSEN huts have now been erected for the use of patients. One is being used as a billet for R.A.M.C. personnel until required for patients.	G.P.A
"	11.1.17		Cover & screens for the big horse standing are now complete. The small standing remains to be covered. Step is being drawn daily for improving the ground in hospital area and horse lines	G.P.B

Army Form C. 2118

WAR DIARY or INTELLIGENCE SUMMARY

(Erase heading not required.)

52 **48 FIELD AMBULANCE**

Place	Date	Hour	Summary of Events and Information	Remarks and references to Appendices
ZELOBES.	12.1.17		Instruction + drill with box respirators (mines 28.12.16) is being proceeded with	APP1
"	13.1.17		Capt EVANS returned to F.A. On duty and is detailed to hold MO sick inspection daily at the 111th Bgde P.Chool	APP1
"	14.1.17		The Divisional Commander inspected the F.A. expressed himself as very well satisfied with everything in connection with the Hospital	APP2
"	16.1.17		Capt RENWICK detailed for temporary duty with 49 F.A.	APP2
"	18.1.17		Capt FINDLATER returned to the F.A. from Temporary Charge of 4th NORFOLKS. The weather is severe with frost.	APP3
"	19.1.17		Capt RENWICK returned to the F.A. for duty	APP2
"	22nd		Capt ROBERSON is detailed for permanent duty with the 53rd H.A.G. north west of the sheep ff of the F.A.	APP1
"	24th		Capt HODGSON reported for duty with the F.A. Capt FINDLATER detailed for temporary duty with the 8th Armourers. The weather continues very severe, but fine.	APP1
"	26th		Capt RENNICK left for temporary duty with 13th R.B. Capt EVANS left for England on 10 days leave. Two of my parties, 40 in all, are going daily to work under C.R.E. at ST MAAT. The cost of the snow & hose standing is now completed. The hard weather continues.	APP1
"	29th			
"	31st		Very severe weather still continues. The ambulance remains here Serving the reserve Brigade area	APP1

D.P. Watson Lt Col
48 F.A.

Confidential

War Diary

of

48 Field Ambulance

COMMITTEE FOR THE MEDICAL HISTORY OF THE WAR
Date 4— APR. 1917

From 1st February To. 28th February

1917.

(Volume XIX)

WAR DIARY or INTELLIGENCE SUMMARY

48 FIELD AMBULANCE

Army Form C. 2118

Place	Date	Hour	Summary of Events and Information	Remarks and references to Appendices
ZELOBES.	1.2.17		Operation orders by A.D.M.S. 37th Div. No. 93. received at 10 p.m. yesterday. Extracts :- 1. The 37th Div. will be withdrawn from the line into G.H.Q. Reserve ----- 4. The 112th Inf. Bgde. will remain in its present area. 7. 48th F.A. will be attached to 112th Inf. Bgde. Operation order No. 92 by G.O.C. 112th Inf. Bgde. received at same time. Set. from daylight 3rd Feb. all units will hold themselves in readiness to move at 6 hours' notice. Instructions received from A.D.M.S. 37th Div. that on movement of 112th Inf. Bgde. a party from 15th F.A. will take over from this unit at ZELOBES.	AMh.
"	2.2.17		CAPT. RENWICK returned to duty & takes over command of C. Section. CAPT. E.A. PEARSON joined the F.A. for duty, and takes over duties of transport officer.	
"	3.2.17		CAPT. FINDLATER is transferred to 13th RRR Corps for permanent duty as M.O. CAPT. HODGSON left for duty at the Base, having been reported only A.D.M.S. 37th Div. as physically unfit for duty at the front.	SPh.
"	4.2.17		Instructions received from A.D.M.S. 37th Div. that the Div. is to be ready to move at 24 hrs notice, units will probably receive 21 hrs notice. Advised O.C. 15th F.A. & arranged about the return to their units of cases from this F.A. belonging to this Division	SPh.

WAR DIARY or INTELLIGENCE SUMMARY

Army Form C. 2118

54 48 FIELD AMBULANCE

Place	Date	Hour	Summary of Events and Information	Remarks and references to Appendices
ZELOBES	5.2.17.		The weather continues the very hard. The number of admissions is falling considerably.	JPh.
"	7.2.17.		The personnel and transport of the Ambulance was inspected by the Divisional Commander, who expressed his satisfaction at the condition of men & transport.	JPh.
"	8.2.17.		Information received from ADMS. that the Division is to go into the line in the Loos salient. The Ambulance is to take over from 73rd F.A. having their dressing Station at NOEUX LES MINES & ADs at PHILOSOPHE (PUITS 2 & ST PATRICK (LOOS) and ST. GEORGE.	JPh.
"	9.2.17.		The O.C. with Capts EVANS & RENICK motored to NOEUX LES MINES & the hos later went on to ADSs at ST PATRICK and ST. GEORGE. Respectively. The OC inspected the main dressing Station & ADs at PHILOSOPHE.	JPh.
"	10.2.17.		Capt RENNICK with 53 OR left to spend the night at NOEUX LES MINES and proceed tomorrow to ADSs at ST PATRICK & ST GEORGE.	JPh.
"	11.2.17.		Capt EVANS & Capt GODFREY left with 3 cars & 6 other ranks for the MDS at PHILOSOPHE. They are to be joined there by 1 officer and 20 OR. from 49th F.A. Capt GODFREY will remain in charge of ADS at PHILOSOPHE. Capt RENNICK at ST PATRICK. Capt EVANS at ST. GEORGE.	JPh.

Army Form C. 2118.

WAR DIARY
or
INTELLIGENCE SUMMARY.
(Erase heading not required.)

48 FIELD AMBULANCE

Place	Date	Hour	Summary of Events and Information	Remarks and references to Appendices
ZELOBES.	12.2.17		The C.O. visited A.D.S. at PHILOSOPHE and main dummy Station of 73rd F.A. at BRACQUE-MONT. Capt. RUSSELL and 30 O.Rs. with 1 section Equipment moved to BRACQUEMONT in the afternoon to take over in the morning of the 13th. Pte. MARSHALL of the F.A. was killed last night by a shell at ST GEORGES. The remainder of the F.A. marched from ZELOBES at 9 a.m. reached BRACQUEMONT at 1 p.m. The 73rd F.A. was not clear until after 2 p.m. 56 cases were taken over from them.	D.W.
BRACQUEMONT	13.2.17			D.W.
"	14.2.17		The C.O. visited A.D.S. at ST PATRICKS and the R.A.Ps. from which patients are cleared. Capt. GODFREY relieved Capt. EVANS at ST PATRICKS and Capt. Wilkes. EVANS took over charge at PHILOSOPHE. The A.D.S. at ST PATRICKS cleans cases from a regimental aid posts in LOOS. The accommodation is for 30 lying cases. Cases are cleared by Ford Car to PHILOSOPHE after dark, only urgent cases being sent during the day. An additional keep dugout in course of construction, giving 288 sq feet of accommodation.	D.W.
"	15.2.17		The C.O. visited A.D.S. at ST GEORGES, bearer posts and R.A.Ps. The accommodation at the A.D.S. is very poor, only for 10 lying cases at the outside. Walking cases are cleared by foot and cross country tracks to PHILOSOPHE. Lying cases by Trolley to PHILOSOPHE via half way house where a reserve relay of M.D.S. clears from two battalions in the line, the one the in support	D.W.

WAR DIARY
or
INTELLIGENCE SUMMARY.

Army Form C. 2118.

48 Field Ambulance

Place	Date	Hour	Summary of Events and Information	Remarks and references to Appendices
BRACQUEMONT	16.2.17		There is a bearer post at CHALK PITS, for conveying cases by wheeled stretcher to Bay horse from the most southerly R.A.P. situated close by. There are also four relay posts situated between the other R.A.P.s and the M.D.S. Capt. RUSSELL R.A.M.C. was admitted to hospital. Lieut. PIGGOTT R.A.M.C. from 49 F.A. was posted for temporary duty.	ADMS
"	19.2.17		The D.D.M.S. 1st Corps accompanied by two officers of the French Medical Service visited the A.D.Ss at PHILOSOPHE and LOOS and the main dressing station	ADMS
"	19.2.17		D.D.M.S. 1st Corps inspected the main dressing station and subsequently expressed his satisfaction with all he saw.	ADMS
"	20.2.17		The C.O. visited all three A.D.Ss. The personnel of A.D.Ss is being relieved piece-meal as far as the numbers available allow. Capt. MENCE. 49th F.A. relieved Capt BROUGH at PHILOSOPHE.	ADMS
"	21.2.17		The C.O. proceeds on 10 days leave tonight; leaving Capt. NICHOLSON in command.	ADMS
"	22.2.17		Lt. BURGES from 149th Field Ambulance was posted for temporary duty.	C.
"	23.2.17		Capt. RUSSELL R.A.M.C. was evacuated to C.C.S. today.	C.
"	27.2.17		Operation order No. 25 received from A.D.M.S. at 7 p.m. this evening. The following retreat can made from it: —	

Army Form C. 2118.

WAR DIARY
or
INTELLIGENCE SUMMARY.
(Erase heading not required.)

48 FIELD AMBULANCE

Place	Date	Hour	Summary of Events and Information	Remarks and references to Appendices
BRADGEMONT	27.2.16		The 37th Division will be relieved in the line by the 6th Division and will move with the ST HILAIRE area. On 2nd March the 16th Field Ambulance (6th Division) will relieve the Advanced Dressing Station and R.A.P.(C. Posts) of the 48th Field Ambulance. On 3rd March 3rd Field Ambulance 1st Canadian Division will relieve the Main Dressing Station of 46th Field Ambulance. On relief the 48th Field Ambulance will move to BETHUNE where it will come under the orders of G.O.C. 111th Brigade for movements and billeting.	A.

Arth Nicholson
Capt. D.A.M.S.
for Lt Col Condy 48th Field Ambulance

Confidential

War Diary

of

48 Field Ambulance.

From 1st March to 31st March

1917.

(Volume XX)

Army Form C. 2118.

WAR DIARY
or
INTELLIGENCE SUMMARY.
(Erase heading not required.)

58   48 FIELD AMBULANCE

Instructions regarding War Diaries and Intelligence Summaries are contained in F. S. Regs., Part II. and the Staff Manual respectively. Title pages will be prepared in manuscript.

Place	Date	Hour	Summary of Events and Information	Remarks and references to Appendices
BLAQUEMONT	2.3.17		Parties from Advanced Dressing Station returned to Headquarters to day having been relieved by parties of 18th Field Ambulance. Patients remaining in hospital were evacuated to CCS. with the exception of 4 cases which go to Expo Nuit Station in the morning. Lt PIGGOT RAMC. returned to duty with the 49th Field Ambulance.	Ci.
BETHUNE	3.3.17	6 p.m.	The main Dressing Station at BLAQUEMONT was taken over this morning by a section of 3rd Canadian Field Ambulance at 10 a.m. and 48th Field Ambulance moved out marching my VERQUIN to BETHUNE, a motor lorry necessary owing to the state of the roads, and went into billets in BIBLIOTHEQUE ARCHIVES, PLACE BARTHOLOME. Billets and food not crowded. Orders were received from 111th Brigade to move to tomorrow to ROMBLY.	Ci.
ROMBLY	4.3.17		The Ambulance moved off from BETHUNE this morning at 8.45. and marched to ROMBLY by CHOCQUES, LILLERS, ST. HILAIRE, arriving at 3 p.m. and going into billets in Various. Advanced Headquarters are at NORRENT FONTES.	Ci.
"	6.3.17		Lt.Col. WATSON returned from leave. The Ambulance remains in billets here clearing the sick from 111th Bgde. groups. Sick are all evacuated at once to next being C.C.S. LILLERS, there being no accommodation P.M for their treatment here.	

WAR DIARY
or
INTELLIGENCE SUMMARY

Army Form C. 2118.

48 Field Ambulance

Place	Date	Hour	Summary of Events and Information	Remarks and references to Appendices
ROMBLY	8.3.17		Operation order no 26 by A.D.M.S. 37th Div received. Extracts :- 1. The Division will march to the ROELLECOURT area on transfer to the W.Flank Third Army. Move to be completed on 10th inst. 2. Field Ambulances will march under the orders of the Bgde. to which they are affiliated. Operation Order no 102 with march tables received from 111th Inf. Bgde.	(App.)
PERNES	9.3.17		The Ambulance marched with 111th Inf. Bgde. to PERNES by FEEFAY and FLORINGHEM and billeted in the Convent	(App.)
TERNAS.	10.3.17		The Ambulance marched with 111th Inf. Bgde. to TERNAS by VALHUON, BRIAS, OSTREVILLE, ROELLECOURT and went into billets. Accommodation for sick is extremely limited and bad, consisting of one Nissen hut and a barn. Capacities taken altogether 30 cases. Men's billets are fair, but nothing exists in the way of cookhouses. There is absolutely nothing in the way of a prepared F.A. position.	(App.)
"	12.3.17		The Ambulance is clearing the sick from 111th Inf. Bgde and Div. Artillery. The personnel, particularly bearer division are going thro' a course of training.	(App.)
"	16.3.17		Capt. NICHOLSON attended a medical conference at Corps H.Q. yesterday, in the absence of Lt. Col. WATSON, who was sick.	(App.)
"	17.3.17		The C.O. with Capts. NICHOLSON and EVANS attended a conference at the office of A.D.M.S. 37th Div. when medical arrangements	(App.)

Army Form C. 2118.

WAR DIARY
or
INTELLIGENCE SUMMARY.
(Erase heading not required.)

48 FIELD AMBULANCE

Instructions regarding War Diaries and Intelligence Summaries are contained in F. S. Regs., Part II. and the Staff Manual respectively. Title pages will be prepared in manuscript.

Place	Date	Hour	Summary of Events and Information	Remarks and references to Appendices
TERNAS.	17/3/17		The forthcoming operations were briefly explained. A second Nissen hut has been handed over to us by the 13th R.R.R. for messroom &c.	A.P.W.
"	18/3/17		Capt PEARSON was sent yesterday for 'duty' in temporary medical charge of the Details Company at POELLECOURT. Capt RENWICK was evacuated yesterday suffering from German measles.	A.P.W.
"	19/3/17		Lt Col J.P.Watson accompanied the A.D.M.S. 37th Div. to ARRAS. to view the medical arrangements in connection with forthcoming operations.	A.P.W.
"	20/3/17	10 A.M.	Instructions received from 110th Infy Bgde that the Bgde is to make its first jump in short moves to move at short notice.	A.P.W.
"	"	11 A.M.	Instructions in above sense received from A.D.M.S. 37th Div. The majority of cases under treatment are being evacuated. No more will be detained than can be cleared more jumps of the motor ambulances.	A.P.W.
"	23/3/17		Notification received that Capt. G.H.H.RUSSELL. was evacuated to England on 5th inst. 6 struck off the strength accordingly. Capt NICHOLSON and 2/Lt. OTR marched to a ceremonial parade at HOUVAIN. HOUVAINEVILLE. For presentation of medals by G.O.C. 3rd Army. Park saddle Carriage is being organised in the ambulance.	A.P.W.

A5834. Wt. W.4973/M687 750,000 8/16 D.D. & L. Ltd. Forms/C.2118/13.

Army Form C. 2118.

WAR DIARY
or
INTELLIGENCE SUMMARY
(Erase heading not required.)

48 FIELD AMBULANCE

61

Place	Date	Hour	Summary of Events and Information	Remarks and references to Appendices
TERNAS.	24.3.17		Capt. RENWICK returned to duty today.	
"	25.3.17		Conference at ADMS' Office of O.C. Field Ambulances with regard to forthcoming operations. 48th FA will find two bearer sub-divisions to advance in touch with 111th Inf. Bgde. one being held in reserve. Two tent sub-divisions will be held in readiness to advance with pack transport and open an advanced dressing station at FEUCHY.	SPN SPN
"	27.3.17.		Capt. C. NICHOLSON left for duty as M.O. i/c 13th Rifle Brigade. Capt. EVANS exchanged in (unreadable) demonstration of Thomas & other splints by Surgical Specialist at HOUVAIN HOUVAINEVILLE.	SPN
"	28.3.17		Capt. FINDLATER RAMC. reported for duty to-day & was posted to A Section. Retiral arrangements 37th Div. Operations No 27. received from ADMS. Exts:- "Bg. Zero plus 3 hours the 27th Div. will be closed up on the line DAINVILLE WAGONLIEU ST. AUBIN - - - - 111th Brigade on the left. Here the Brigades will be joined by their Bearer sub-divisions. The Brigades will move forward through ARRAS by the routes shown on the attached map (noted to Field Ambulances only) to the areas of assembly where they will halt and meal will be taken. - - - - - - There are three existing Advanced Dressing Stations which will be used by the 37th Division - these are shown on the attached map. - - - ."	SPN SPN

Army Form C. 2118.

WAR DIARY
or
INTELLIGENCE SUMMARY.
(Erase heading not required.)

48 Field Ambulance

Place	Date	Hour	Summary of Events and Information	Remarks and references to Appendices
TERNAS.	28.3.17		"From these Advanced Dressing Stations stretcher cases will be evacuated direct to their Casualty Clearing Stations at AGNEZ-LES-DUISANS by the motor cars of the 4 Divisions and those of the 15th motor Ambulance Convoy — all under the direction of O.C. 15th M.A.C. Walking wounded will be directed to the Corps Collecting Station in the British School Rue BAUDIMONT and PORTE d'AMIENS, whence they will be evacuated by wheeled transport, to the rail-head at WARLUS. As the attack progresses the enemy A.D.S.'s may move forward with arrangements made by the 3 leading Divisions. 48th Field Ambulance will hold two tent Sub-Divisions ready to move forward to form an A.D.S. which it's proposed to locate near the eastern outskirts of FEUCHY. The equipment of these A.D.S.s will have to be carried by man and pack transport. The CAMBRAI road when repaired will probably be too congested for Ambulance transport evacuation, but it is hoped that evacuation by the FEUCHY CHAPELLE – FEUCHY road, and thence to ARRAS, will be possible. Bearer subdivisions attached to Brigades will maintain close touch with the medical personnel of the Battalions and O.s.C. Sub-Divisions will endeavour to keep them in reserve until the Brigades to which they are attached attack —–. O.C. will also note any suitable position for the establishment of A.D.Ss. in or near the positions	

Army Form C. 2118.

WAR DIARY
or
INTELLIGENCE SUMMARY.
(Erase heading not required.)

48 FIELD AMBULANCE

63

Place	Date	Hour	Summary of Events and Information	Remarks and references to Appendices
TERNAS	28.3.17		Indicated above and will send such information to the A.D.M.S. as early as possible. Lt. Col. D.P.WATSON. R.A.M.C. will co-ordinate the work of all the Tienes Sub-Divisions in action and will establish a report centre at a place to be selected hereafter — he will be supplied with a cycle orderly and, if possible, will be in telephonic communication with A.D.M.S. The Divisional A.D.S.s at FEUCHY and FEUCHY CHAPELLE will be reinforced as early as possible and the Divisional Field Ambulances will move up to these points as soon as circumstances permit."	DPW
"	30.3.17		Lt. A.W.HARE. R.A.M.C. reported for duty with the F.A. Lt. Col. D.P.WATSON. attended a conference at Office of A.D.M.S. Vth Corps on med arrangements for forthcoming operations.	DPW

D.P. Watson Lt. Col.
Commdg. 48th F.A.

Confidential War Diary

of

48 Field Ambulance

From 1st April To 30 April.

1917.

(Volume 21.)

B.E.F.

SUMMARY OF MEDICAL WAR DIARIES OF 48th F.A. 37th Div.

      6th Corps   3rd ARMY.
     18th Corps from April 14th.
     17th Corps from April 19th.
     18th Corps from April 30th.
      6th Corps from May 18th.

Operations on Western Front - April - May 1917.

        Officer Commanding = Lt.Col. D.P. WATSON.

SUMMARISED UNDER THE FOLLOWING HEADINGS:-

Phase "B" - Battle of Arras - April - May 1917.

1st Period - Attack on Vimy Ridge - April 1917.

2nd Period - Capture of Siegfried Line - May.

B.E.F.

48th F.A. 37th Div. 6th Corps. 3rd ARMY.   WESTERN FRONT
Officer Commanding = Lt.Col. D.P. Watson.   April 1917.

PHASE "B" - Battle of Arras - April - May 1917.
-1st Period - Attack on Vimy Ridge -   April 1917.

Headquarters at Ternas.

April 5th. Moves.   To Manin.

7th.   To Duisans.

8th. Medical Arrangements.   Following personnel under
      Moves. Detachment.
      command of Lt.Col. D.P. Watson Officer Commanding 48th
      F.A. proceeded to Louez - area of 111th Infantry
      Brigade.

              A.Br. S.D. 48th F.A. under Capt. Findlater.
              B. "   "   "   "   )
              C. "   "   "   "   ) under Capt. Evans and
                                        Sgt Pishmore.

              B. T.S.D. 48th F.A.) under Capt. Pearson with
) Capt. Mackwood,
              C. " "   "   ) and Capts Leigh and
) Grellet of 50th F.A.

              A. Br. S.D. 49th F.A. under Capt. Burgess.
              A. Br. S.D. 50th F.A. under Capt. Stafford.
              B. T.S.D.   49th F.A. under Capt. Low and 2 Off.
                                         of 50th F.A.

              41 of Divisional Band as Stretcher Bearers.

9th. Operations R.A.M.C. Zero day. 1 and B and C Br.
      S.Ds. with 100 Infantry attached went into action with
      111th Infantry Brigade.

      Medical Arrangements.) Pack transport of 3 Field Am-
      Transport.   )
      bulances of 37th Division assembled at point East of
      Arras G.23.C.2.9. (Sheet 51 B) in readiness to go
      forward with materials for establishment of A.D.S's at
      Feuchy and Feuchy Chapelle.

10th. Medical Arrangements.) Divisional Band sent to work
      Assistance.   )
      in co-operation with Br. Personnel of 15th Div. until
      morning of 12th.

      Operations. Attack of 3rd 12th and 15th Divs successful

B.E.F.

3.

48th F.A. 37th Div. 6th Corps. 3rd ARMY.   WESTERN FRONT
Officer Commanding = Lt. Col. D.P.WATSON.   April 1917.

To 18th Corps from 14th April.

PHASE "B" - Battle of Arras - April - May 1917.
 -1st Period - Attack on Vimy Ridge - April.

April 11th.   Medical Arrangements. A.D.S. Feuchy reinforced by 1 T.S.D. of 49th Field Ambulance.

A.D.S. Tilloy reinforced by 1 T.S.D. of 49th Field Ambulance and 1 of 48th Field Ambulance.

Supplementary A.D.S. established at Feuchy Chapelle by "A" T.S.D. 48th Field Ambulance.

Evacuation. As wheeled transport could now proceed along Arras-Cambrai Road cases were evacuated from Br. P. Feuchy Chapelle, to A.D.S. Tilloy by Horse Ambulances and from A.D.S. Tilloy to Arras by Motor Ambulances of 15th M.A.C.

In afternoon Divisional Motor Ambulances which had been pooled under Officer Commanding 51st M.A.C. were returned to their Divisions owing to delay in arrival of 37th Divisional M. Ambs. 200 wounded were accumulated at A.D.S. Tilloy until morning of 12th when all were cleared.

12th.   Military Situation. 37th Division relieved in afternoon and night.

Casualties R.A.M.C. 0 & 3 wounded.

14th.   Moves. To Ambrines, and to 18th Corps.
& Transfer.

B.E.F.

48th F.A. 37th Div. 18th Corps. 3rd ARMY.   WESTERN FRONT.
                                                April 1917.
Officer Commanding = Lt.Col. D.P. WATSON.

17th Corps from April 19th.

PHASE "B" - Battle of Arras - April & May 1917.
   -1st Period - Attack on Vimy Ridge - April.

April 14th. Transfer. To 18th Corps.

    15th. Medical Arrangements.) 2 Nissen Huts taken over for
           Accommodation.   ) hospital accommodation.

    19th. Moves.   To Agnez-Les-Duisans.
           Transfer.
                    To 17th Corps.

~~21st.~~

B.E.F.

<u>48th F.A.   37th Div. 17th Corps. 3rd ARMY.</u>   WESTERN FRONT
                                                    April 1917.
<u>Officer Commanding = Lt. Col. D.P. WATSON.</u>

18th Corps from 30th April.

<u>PHASE "B" - Battle of Arras - April - May 1917.</u>
   <u>1st Period - Attack on Vimy Ridge   - April.</u>

April 19th.   <u>Transfer.</u> TO 17th Corps.

    21st.   <u>Moves.</u>   ) To Haute Avesnes and took over
         <u>Medical Arrangements.</u>   )
         <u>Moves. Detachment.</u>   ) M.D.S. from 10th F.A.
         and
         1/"C" T.S.D. to Berlette and took over Combined D.R.S.

         O & 26 to 37th C.C.S. at Avesnes.

    22nd.   <u>Moves and Transport.</u> 3 Horse Ambulances and 4 Motor
         Ambulances to 49th Field Ambulance.
         <u>Moves Detachment.</u> 1 & 45 Bearers to 111th Infantry
         Brigade.

    23rd.   <u>Casualties.</u> Wounded began to arrive at 9. a.m. and
         continued steadily until 5 p.m. about 200 admitted.
         <u>Evacuation.</u> Satisfactory. Cases sent by cars of 24th
         M.A.C. from M.D.S. to C.C.S. at Aubigny.

    24th.   <u>Casualties.</u>   ) 30 and 490 wounded admitted including
         <u>Casualties Gas.</u>)
         1 & 3 gassed up to 9 a.m.

    25th.   <u>Casualties.</u>) Noon 24th to Noon 25th 10 and 140 wounded
         <u>Med. Arr.</u>   )
         passed through, including many who had
         been dressed within 1 or 2 hours. These if comfortable
         and dressings in good order sent straight to C.C.S.
         after a wash and meal.

    26th.   <u>Casualties.</u> Few.
    28th.   <u>Operations.</u> 37th Division attacked in early morning.
         <u>Casualties.</u> Began to arrive at 9 a.m. - very few - about
         60 admitted.

    30th.   <u>Moves.</u> To Lignereuil.
         <u>Transfer.</u> 37th Div. transferred to 18th Corps.

B.E.F.

48th F.A. 37th Div. 6th Corps. 3rd ARMY.   WESTERN FRONT:
                                              April 1917.
Officer Commanding = Lt.Col. D.P. Watson.

PHASE "B" - Battle of Arras - April - May 1917.

-1st Period - Attack on Vimy Ridge -   April 1917.

             Headquarters at Ternas.

April 5th.   Moves. To Manin.

    7th.   To Duisans.

    8th.   Medical Arrangements.   Following personnel under
             Moves. Detachment.
command of Lt.Col. D.P. Watson Officer Commanding 48th

F.A. proceeded to Louez - area of 111th Infantry

Brigade.

             A.Br. S.D. 48th F.A. under Capt. Findlater.
             B. "   "   "   "   )
             C. "   "   "   "   ) under Capt. Evans and
                                                 Sgt Pishmore.

             B.T.S.D. 48th F.A.) under Capt. Pearson with
) Capt. Mackwood,
             C. "   "   "   ) and Capts Leigh and
) Grellet of 50th F.A.

             A.Br. S.D. 49th F.A. under Capt. Burgess.
             A. Br. S.D. 50th F.A. under Capt. Stafford.
             B.T.S.D.   49th F.A. under Capt. Low and 2 Off.
                                          of 50th F.A.

             41 of Divisional Band as Stretcher Bearers.

    9th.   Operations R.A.M.C. Zero day. 1 and B and C Br.

S.Ds. with 100 Infantry attached went into action with

111th Infantry Brigade.

             Medical Arrangements.) Pack transport of 3 Field Am-
             Transport.   )
bulances of 37th Division assembled at point East of
Arras G.23.d C.2.9. (Sheet 51 B) in readiness to go
forward with materials for establishment of A.D.S's at
Feuchy and Feuchy Chapelle.

    10th.   Medical Arrangements.) Divisional Band sent to work
             Assistance.   )
In co-operation with Br. Personnel of 15th Div. until

morning of 12th.

             Operations. Attack of 3rd 12th and 15th Divs successful

B.E.F.

48th F.A.   37th Div.   6th Corps.   3rd ARMY.   Western Front.
Officer Commanding - Lt.Col. D.P. WATSON.   April 1917.

PHASE "B" - Battle of Arras - April - May 1917.
– 1st Period - Attack on Vimy Ridge -   April.

April 10th. contd.

Operations contd. on "Black", "Blue" and "Brown" lines.

Medical Arrangements.) B T.S.D. 49th F.A. with pack
Moves Detachment.   )
transport proceeded to Feuchy and established A.D.S.

B & C T.S.Ds 48th Field Ambulance with pack transport proceeded to point East of Tilloy H.32 C.8.4 and established A.D.S. in ruined house.

A. Br. S.D's of 49th and 50th Field Ambulances proceeded to Feuchy to reinforce Bearers with 63rd Infantry Brigade.

A Br. S.D. 48th Field Ambulance proceeded to Feuchy Chapelle to reinforce bearers of 112th Infantry Brigade.

10th.

Medical Arrangements. Br. Post at Feuchy Chapelle established

Evacuation. On Feuchy Side evacuation was entirely by hand carriage to Arras over very difficult ground. Cases brought from R.A.P's to A.D.S. Feuchy by A.,B., and C Br. S.D's of 49th Field Ambulance/and from Feuchy to Hermes Trench. H 19. C.60.95 by A Br. S.D. 50th F.A. and from this point to Arras by Bearers of 15th Div. at times assisted by bearers of 50th Field Ambulance.

In the centre Bearers of "B"&"C" S.D's 48th F.A. assisted by 100 Infantry cleared down the centre at first in conjunction with bearers of 12th Division and for some time carried to Arras. On establishment of A.D.S. East of Tilloy Wounded of 111th Brigade were evacuated through Br. Post at Feuchy Chappelle.

On night Bearers of "B" and "C" Sub Divisions of 50th Field Ambulance cleared at first in conjunction with bearers of 3rd Division and later to A.D.S. East of Tilloy.

B.E.F.

48th F.A.   37th Div.   6th Corps.   3rd ARMY.   WESTERN FRONT
                                                  April 1917.
Officer Commanding = Lt. Col. D.P. WATSON.
To 18th Corps from 14th April.

PHASE "B" - Battle of Arras - April - May 1917.
   -1st Period - Attack on Vimy Ridge - April.

April 11th.   Medical Arrangements. A.D.S. Feuchy reinforced by 1
                T.S.D. of 49th Field Ambulance.
                            A.D.S. Tilloy reinforced by 1
                T.S.D. of 49th Field Ambulance and 1 of 48th Field
                Ambulance.
                Supplementary A.D.S. established at Feuchy Chapelle
                by 1 T.S.D. 48th Field Ambulance.
                Evacuation. As wheeled transport could now proceed
                along Arras Cambrai Road cases were evacuated from Br. P.
                Feuchy Chapelle, to A.D.S. Tilloy by Horse Ambulances
                and from A.D.S. Tilloy to Arras by Motor Ambulances of
                15th M.A.C.
                            In afternoon Divisional Motor Ambulances
                which had been pooled under Officer Commanding 51st
                M.A.C. were returned to their Divisions owing to delay
                in arrival of 37th Divisional M. Ambs. 200 wounded
                were accumulated at A.D.S. Tilloy until morning of
                12th when all were cleared.
     12th.   Military Situation. 37th Division relieved in afternoon
                and night.
                Casualties R.A.M.C. O & 3 wounded.
     14th.   Moves. To Ambrines: and to 18th Corps.
                & Transfer.

B.E.F.

48th F.A.   37th Div. 17th Corps. 3rd ARMY. WESTERN FRONT
                                                April 1917.
Officer Commanding = Lt. Col. D.P. WATSON.
18th Corps from 30th April.

PHASE "B" - Battle of Arras - April - May 1917.

   1st Period - Attack on Vimy Ridge   - April.

April 19th.   Transfer. TO 17th Corps.

21st.   Moves.   ) To Haute Avesnes and took over
        Medical Arrangements.   )
        Moves. Detachment.   ) M.D.S. from 10th F.A.
        and
        1/"C" T.S.D. to Berlette and took over Combined D.R.S.

        O & 26 to 37th C.C.S. at Avesnes.

22nd.   Moves and Transport. 3 Horse Ambulances and 4 Motor
        Ambulances to 49th Field Ambulance.
        Moves Detachment. 1 & 45 Bearers to 111th Infantry
        Brigade.

23rd.   Casualties. Wounded began to arrive at 9. a.m. and
        continued steadily until 5 p.m. about 200 admitted.
        Evacuation. Satisfactory. Cases sent by cars of 24th
        M.A.C. from M.D.S. to C.C.S. at Aubigny.

24th.   Casualties.   ) 30 and 400 wounded admitted including
        Casualties Gas.   )
                             1 & 3 gassed up to 9 a.m.

25th.   Casualties.) Noon 24th to Noon 25th 10 and 140 wounded
        Med. Arr.   )
                      passed through, including many who had
        been dressed within 1 or 2 hours. These if comfortable
        and dressings in good order sent straight to C.C.S.
        after a wash and meal.

26th.   Casualties. Few.

28th.   Operations. 37th Division attacked in early morning.
        Casualties. Began to arrive at 2 a.m. - very few - about
        60 admitted.

30th.   Moves. To Lignereuil.
        Transfer. 37th Div. transferred to 18th Corps.

Army Form C. 2118.

WAR DIARY
or
INTELLIGENCE SUMMARY.
(Erase heading not required.)

48 FIELD AMBULANCE

Place	Date	Hour	Summary of Events and Information	Remarks and references to Appendices
TERNAS	1.4.17		The C.O. with Capts. MACKWOOD, PEARSON & GODFREY and Capt. BROUGH of the 47th F.A. and Sergt. ASHMORE went to ARRAS to become acquainted with the medical arrangements there.	
"	2.4.17		The C.O. with Capt. MACKWOOD selected a site for an advanced dump of medical stores in the basement of a house at G.23.a.12.12. It is unprotected and may very possibly be torn up by shell fire. Capt. O.A. RENWICK, left for England his contract having expired and he not wishing to renew it. The C.O. attended a conference on administrative matters held at HOUDAIN HOUDAIN-EVILLE. by. A.A.+ Q.M.G 37th Div. The weather is very severe. There was a heavy fall of snow this afternoon.	#P2
"	3.4.17	4 pm	After a sharp frost last night there is a thaw and thin morning. 111th Inf Bgde Instructions No 1 + 2. And addenda received with map showing positions of units at post of divinity on Z day. Instructions to accompany medical arrangements operation no 27. received from A.D.M.S. 37th Div.	#P3 #P4

Army Form C. 2118.

WAR DIARY
or
INTELLIGENCE SUMMARY.
(Erase heading not required.)

48 FIELD AMBULANCE

Place	Date	Hour	Summary of Events and Information	Remarks and references to Appendices
TERNAS	4.4.17	8 A.M.	111th Inf Brigade Order No 103 received with march table for 5th & 6th April. From TERNAS. MANIN. Starting point Line Route MAZIERES. Road junction AMBRINES. B.16. 6.05. 6.5. 10.2 A.M. Operation order by Lt Col D PATTISON Commdg 48th F.A. The Ambulance with parade at 9.40 and will march at 9.45 to MANIN by MAZIERES and AMBRINES. Sergt CARTWRIGHT with 12 other ranks with remain behind to clean up billets and then proceedings & will report to 2nd in Major TERNIK on completion and then after loading the blanket lorry with march to rejoin the Ambulance at MANIN.	4th
MANIN.	5.4.17 7 p.m		The Ambulance marched with 111th Inf Bgde to MANIN and went into billets at 12.30 p.m. Operation order for 6.4.17. The Ambulance will parade at 9 A.M and will march at 9.10 p.m. Starting point 51.C. J. 11. & 5.9 to be passed at 10.42. Sergt CARTWRIGHT and 12 O.Rs. with remain behind to clean up billets and will march after the Ambulance. Sergt CARTWRIGHT with obtain a certificate from the town Major before leaving	DP

Army Form C. 2118.

WAR DIARY
or
INTELLIGENCE SUMMARY.
(Erase heading not required.)

66 48 FIELD AMBULANCE

Place	Date	Hour	Summary of Events and Information	Remarks and references to Appendices
MANIN	5.4.17	6 p.m.	Instructions received from ADMS and from 111th Inf. Bgde that the Bgde will not move tomorrow. Orders cancelled accordingly.	JPW
"	6.4.17		Amended march table. Ambulance parts starting point at 10.2 a.m. per march order. The Ambulance will parade at 9.15 a.m. and will move off at 8.30 a.m. marching to their new area. The advanced party will remain behind to clean up billets.	JPW
DUISANS	7.4.17		The ambulance marched to DUISANS via HABARCQ & GOUVES & went into billets at 1.30 p.m. Ambulance tents were also pitched for some of the personnel. Arrangements were made for the C.O. of the I.H. to take up the Tent Subdivisions of 143rd F.A. to accompany 111th Inf Bgde together with three horse Amb-subdivisions, one from each F.A. and two tent subdivisions of 142nd F.A. with motor field amb. to the LOREZ area common to one of 49th F.A. with motor field amb. to follow in rear of the 111th Bgde two afternoon. From there they will follow in rear of the 111th Bgde two Areas on 2 day. Bombardment proceeding.	JPW
"	8.4.17		The tent & Bearer subdivisions are about to move off. The H.Q. remains at DUISANS from to under the control of Lt-Col. ROE. D.S.O. O.C. 142nd F.A. Capt. GODFREY R.A.M.C. remains in command of A tent subdivision	JPW

Army Form C. 2118.

WAR DIARY
or
INTELLIGENCE SUMMARY.
(Erase heading not required.)

48 Field Ambulance

67

Place	Date	Hour	Summary of Events and Information	Remarks and references to Appendices
DUISANS.	13.4.17.	5 P.M.	The personnel of 48th and 49th F.A. and A bearer subdivision of 50th F.A. marched from the HOPITAL ST. JEAN. ARRAS at 1 P.M. today arriving at DUISANS at 4 P.M. 48th & 49th F.A. went into huttments at DUISANS and A bearer subdivision 50th F.A. proceeded to their headquarters at BELAVESNES. On the 8th April the following personnel of the F.A.s. under the command of Lt-Col. D. WATSON Commdg 48th F.A. proceeded to LOVEZ to the area of the M⁹ 9xJ Bgde & were billeted for the night at the Sucrerie there:— A bearer subdivision 48th F.A. under Capt. FINDLATER. B " " " " " C " " " " " Capt. EVANS & Sergt ASHMORE. B Tent subdivision 48th F.A. under Capt. PEARSON with Capt. MACKWOOD and Capts C " " " " LEIGH & G. RELLET of 50th F.A. A bearer subdivision 49th F.A. under Capt. BURGESS B " " under Capt. BAIRD ? A bearer subdivision 50th F.A. under Capt. STAFFORD. B Tent subdivision of 49th F.A. under Capt. LOW. with Capt. WAY of 50th F.A. and Lt. PIGGOTT. Also 41 o.Rs. of the Divisional Band, who have been trained in stretcher bearing. 1. Hd. Clerk left for duty at the BASTION. (walking wounded collecting Station) 1. Sergt & 5 Ors. left to report for duty to O.C. 50th F.A. at MACONLEY. 2 Sergt + 1 Pte Clerks left for duty as clerks at A.D.M.S. Office at AGNEZ-LEZ-DUISANS.	ADS

WAR DIARY or INTELLIGENCE SUMMARY

Army Form C. 2118.

48 FIELD AMBULANCE

Place	Date	Hour	Summary of Events and Information	Remarks and references to Appendices
QUISANS	13.4.17	5 pm	On the 9th April, 'Zero' day, the F.A. personnel at LOUEZ proceeded with the 111th Inf. Bgde. Capt EVANS with B + C sections bearer subdivisions of 48th F.A. and 100 infantry men, each carrying one stretcher, provided by 111th Inf. Bgde. Moved in rear of the 13th Rifle Bgde. — in front of 154 F. Coy. R.E. + went into action with the 111th Inf. Bgde. B+C Section subdivns. of 46th + 50th F.As similarly joined the 63rd + 112th Bgdes. respectively + went into action with them. The remaining personnel under Lt. Col. D.T. WATSON marched in rear of the Bgdes to a point on the eastern side of ARRAS where advanced divisional dumps of medical stores had been established, Map 57.B. G.23. C.2.9. and bivouaced for the night in ruined buildings there. From this point Lt. Col. WATSON was in telephonic communication with the A.D.M.S. at battle H.Q. of the Division — 'Horse Shoe Cave', FAMPOUX Rd. The pack transport of the 3 field ambulances was also assembled at this point in readiness to go forward with material for the establishments of advanced dressing stations at FEUCHY and FEUCHY CHAPELLE. On the morning of the 10th the divisional band were sent to work in cooperation with bearer personnel of the 15th Div., carrying cases from 'McCRACKEN'S POST' G.23. d. 3.4. to the dressing station at NOUVEAU Q.041. 6.21. 6.7.6. This they did until the morning of the 12th. When they returned, and were not further employed. The attack by the 3rd, 12th and 15th Division on the 'Blue', 'Brown' lines having been successful, B tent subdivision of 49th F.A. proceeded to FEUCHY & the pack transport to station an A.D.S. there.	JW

WAR DIARY
or
INTELLIGENCE SUMMARY.

Army Form C. 2118.

48 FIELD AMBULANCE

Place	Date	Hour	Summary of Events and Information	Remarks and references to Appendices
DUISANS.	13.4.17	6 p.m.	10th April continued. B and C tent-subdivisions of 48 F.A. similarly proceeded to a ruined house on the ARRAS - CAMBRAI road east of TILLOY, at H.32.c.8.4. and established an A.D.S. there. At 2 p.m. A. bearer subdivision of 49th & 50th F.A. proceeded to FEUCHY to reinforce bearer subdivisions of 63rd Inf. Bgde & A. bearer subdivision 48th F.A. proceeded to FEUCHY CHAPELLE to reinforce bearers of 112th Inf. Bgde. Evacuation on the FEUCHY or northern side was entirely by hand carriage back to ARRAS, the carrying being over very difficult ground. Cases were brought in from the Regt Aid Posts to the A.D.S. at FEUCHY by A.B.rc. bearer subdivisions of 49 F.A. & from FEUCHY to HERMES TRENCH, H.19.c.60.90. by A. bearer subdivision 50th F.A. From there they were carried back to ARRAS by bearers of 15th Div. at time assisted by bearers of 50th F.A. In the centre the bearers of B.rc. subdivision 48 F.A. assisted by 100 infantrymen lent by the 111th Bgde cleared from the centre at first, in conjunction with the bearers of the 12th Division. For some time, however, the bearers of this Bgde had to carry right back to ARRAS. After the establishment of the A.D.S. 200 of 740 x wounded from this Brigade were evacuated through the bearer post at FEUCHY CHAPELLE. On the right the bearers of B.rc. subdivision of 50th F.A. cleared at first in conjunction with bearers of the 2nd Division. and later to the A.D.S. at the Mill east of TILLOY. Capt. PATTERSON established a bearer post at FEUCHY CHAPELLE. Capt. FINDLATER with A bearer subdivision 48 F.A.	

Army Form C. 2118.

WAR DIARY
or
INTELLIGENCE SUMMARY.
(Erase heading not required.)

48 Field Ambulance

Place	Date	Hour	Summary of Events and Information	Remarks and references to Appendices
DUISANS	13.4.17	6 p.m.	On going up cleared back to this from the Regtt aid posts. On the 11th the ADS. were reinforced by one Sub-division of 4 F.A. to FEUCHY and one of 4 F.A. & one of 48 F.A. to the 'MILL'. On this evening Capt. GODFREY with 4 Sub-division 48 F.A. went up to establish a supplementary A.D.S. at FEUCHY-CHAPELLE. Wheeled transport was only going along the ARRAS-CAMBRAI road and on the night of the 11th a limber full of water, medical comforts & dressings, and a watercart were despatched by this road to the 'MILL'. Owing to the block of traffic they failed to get through. But the limber was got through on the morning of the 12th. Capt. MACWOOD sent from the MILL to replace mo 9/c 13th R.F. Johnston. Evacuation by Cars of 15 MAC. from the 'MILL' was begun on the 11th and Six horsed ambulance wagons were put up which plied between the lower post at FEUCHY CHAPELLE and the MILL. On the afternoon of the 11th the Divisional Motor ambulances, which had been posted under the DDMS 15 MAC were called in to be redistributed to their divisions. Owing to their being delay in the return of the Cars of the 37th Div. there was a break down in the evacuation of cases from the MILL and some 200 were accumulated there on the morning of the 12th. The divisional cars however were now available and Evacuation proceeded smoothly	

Army Form C. 2118.

WAR DIARY
or
INTELLIGENCE SUMMARY.
(Erase heading not required.)

48 Field Ambulance

Place	Date	Hour	Summary of Events and Information	Remarks and references to Appendices
QUISANTS	13.4.17	6 pm	On the 12th the Division was relieved and in the course of the evening all ambulance personnel of the Division returned to HQ etc. We were all billeted at the Hopital St. Jean with the exception of Oct Bearer Sub division of 50th S.A. who were billeted by the 112th Inf Bgde. On the 11th Inf Bgde being relieved from MONCHY LE PREUX, some wounded were left in dugouts there with a supply of relevants & personnel & performed to hand them over to the relieving brigade. Now it had been impossible to evacuate. Capt EVANS evacuated sick on the morning of the 12th. The 48th F.A. marched from DUISANS at 10.30 am via HONEZ LEZ DUISANS.	JM
AMBRINES	14.4.17	6 pm	HERMAVILLE, IZEL-LEZ-HAMEAU and VILLERS-SIR-SIMON, to AMBRINES, where it went into billets at 3 pm. The only accommodation obtained for sick at present is a delapidated barn. The ambulance is brigaded with 111th Inf. Bgde, whose sick it is clearing. The undermentioned men of the F.A. were evacuated wounded, no one seriously:– No. 103188 Pte BAKER G.M.A. No. 42871 " STONE. J.P. No. 36102 " CLOUGH F.	JM
"	15.4.17		The F.A. remained in billets. The day was as far as possible observed as a day of rest. Capts. P.H. WELLS and J. CROWLEY reported for duty with the F.A. Only routine inspections being carried out.	JM

Army Form C. 2118.

WAR DIARY
or
INTELLIGENCE SUMMARY.
(Erase heading not required.)

72R 48 FIELD AMBULANCE

Instructions regarding War Diaries and Intelligence Summaries are contained in F. S. Regs., Part II. and the Staff Manual respectively. Title pages will be prepared in manuscript.

Place	Date	Hour	Summary of Events and Information	Remarks and references to Appendices
AMBRINES	15.4.17		Two Nissen huts have been taken over in addition for hospital accommodation	SPh
"	16.4.17		It was hoped to do a practice formation of an A.D.S. today, but the bad weather has cancelled/postponed	SPh
"	17.4.17		Capt. J.C. MACWOOD transferred to Medical Charge of 13th Dr. Fusiliers & is struck off.	SPh
"			The Strength of the Field Ambulance	SPh
"	18.4.17		The weather has continued too bad for the practice formation of A.D.S. to be carried out.	SPh
AGNES-LEZ-DUISANS	19.4.17		The Ambulance marched with 111th Bgde. by VILLERS-SIR-SIMON - IZEL-LEZ-HAMEAU and HERMAVILLE to AGNEZ-LEZ-DUISANS and went into billets at 1.30 pm. There is one Nissen hut for hospital accommodation.	SPh
"	20.4.17	9.A.M.	Preliminary movement orders from a.d.m.s received at 1 A.M. 48th F.A. will relieve 10th Field Ambulance at HAUTE AVESNES and will form a main dressing station there (1 Tent sub-division and 20 bearers). One tent subdivision to join Combined Divisional Rest Station at BERLETTE. Date and time to be notified later. The Ambulance is standing by ready to move.	SPh
HAUTE AVESNES	21.4.17		At 5.30 pm. yesterday the DADMS arrived to say that 10th F.A. had evacuated their site here, except for a taking over party. An advanced party under Capt. PEARSON with Capt. GODFREY was at once sent on by Ambulance cars to take over the remainder of B. tent subdivision marching up at the same time. At 7.45 am this morning Capt. FINDLATER with an advanced party of 1 Lieut & 18 men left to report to O.C. Combined Divisional Rest Station at BERLETTE.	SPh

Army Form C. 2118.

WAR DIARY
or
INTELLIGENCE SUMMARY.
(Erase heading not required.)

73 48 Field Ambulance

Place	Date	Hour	Summary of Events and Information	Remarks and references to Appendices
HAUTE AVESNES	2.4.17	8 AM	The Field Ambulance marched to HAUTE AVESNES and took over two French huts, one Nissen hut and 26 Marquees. Field Ambulance site vacated by 104 F.A.	
			At the same time the remainder of C tent subdivision under Capt CROWLEY marched to the Combined Divisional Rest Station at HAUTE AVESNES BERLETTE.	SPW
			3 NCOs and 23 other ranks were sent for duty to No. 37 C.C.S. at AVESNES, relieving a similar party from 50th F.A. Who are being returned to their unit at ST. NICHOLAS.	
		4 pm	Operation order No. 30 received from A.D.M.S. 37th Div. States:- 3. Advanced Report Centre will be at H.14.a.0.9. Office of A.D.M.S. will be moved with one clerk at ETRUN, with rear echelon of Divisional Headquarters. On the Advanced Report Centre on evening of 22nd inst.	
			4. Two bearer sub-divisions will form from each of the Brigades on the evening of Y day. Thereafter rationed under Brigade arrangements. Rationed for Champotier on "Z" day.	
			5. ---------- The reserve bearer sub-divisions of all three Field Ambulances will also report to O.C. 50th Field Ambulance on Y day.	
			8. The present advanced dressing station is established on the ST LAURENT - ATHIES road at a railway crossing on the south side of the road. (H.13.b.9.2)	SPW

WAR DIARY
or
INTELLIGENCE SUMMARY.

Army Form C. 2118.

48 FIELD AMBULANCE

Place	Date	Hour	Summary of Events and Information	Remarks and references to Appendices
HAUTE AVESNES	21.4.17	4/am	9. The Divisional Collecting Station will be at the Oil Factory Part of ST NICHOLAS (G.17.C. Central) O.C. 49th F.A. will be in command.	
			11. The Divisional main dressing station will be HAUTE AVESNES, O.C. 48th F.A. in command; also of the Divisional Rest Station at BERLETTE to which such cases urgently needing evacuation will be sent.	
			12. Returns and Reports will be made out Divisionally in the normal manner.	
			13. ---- Evacuations from the Divisional Collecting Station and Main dressing Station will be carried out by 24 Motor Ambulance Convoy to Casualty Clearing Stations at AUBIGNY. Abdominal Cases will be sent direct to C.C.S. at AGNEZ and Self Inflicted Wounds to 37th C.C.S. at AVESNES. Infectious Cases to No 12 Stationary Hospital ST POL to No 33 Advanced Depot of medical stores is at St VY.	SD/
"		6.30p	I at once went to see ADMS to point out to him the distribution of my personnel and that I have only 46 bearers available. The ADMS knows out but the D.A.D.M.S. took down my figures. I am allowing 67 O.R. for the manning of the Main Dressing Station which is the absolute minimum. I also asked permission to recall Capt CROWLEY from Divisional Rest Station	SD/

WAR DIARY
or
INTELLIGENCE SUMMARY.
(Erase heading not required.)

Army Form C. 2118.

75 — 48 FIELD AMBULANCE

Place	Date	Hour	Summary of Events and Information	Remarks and references to Appendices
HAUTE AVESNES	22.4.17	2pm	Instructions received from ADMS at 10 am. to despatch 3 horsed ambulance wagons and 5 large motor ambulance cars to report to O.C. 49th F.A. The 3 horsed wagons and 4 cars were despatched forthwith, the 5th being to go to the workshop. I am now without any motor ambulance of my own. The A.D.M.S himself arrived about 11 AM. He informed me that today is "Y" day, and that the bearers must form 111th Bgde today. I asked that I might recall Capt CROWLEY, and the ADMS said he would arrange for another medical officer to be sent to the main dressing station. Capt GODFREY with 45 bearers left at 1.30 pm by G.S. wagons to join the 111th Bgde. I am now left with only two officers at the main Dressing Station.	SPL.
"	"	6.30 pm	Rode over to see the tent-subdivision running Divisional Rest Station at BERLETTE. The C.O. informed me he could spare one of my officers there. I arranged to send Pte BROWN there as clerk in place of Pte WOOLLEY on return. Rang up the ADMS office & asked DADMS to phone DDMS for permission to withdraw Capt CROWLEY to the main dressing Station. I also asked DADMS to phone to ADMS at advanced report centre to ask if he had arranged for Capt POYSER RAMC of 37 Div from to be attached to main dressing station, as informed this morning.	SPL.

WAR DIARY or INTELLIGENCE SUMMARY

Army Form C. 2118.

48 FIELD AMBULANCE

Place	Date	Hour	Summary of Events and Information	Remarks and references to Appendices
HAUTE AVESNES	22.4.17	7 pm	Rang up D.A.D.M.S. again to their about he had me more officer. Learned that D.D.M.S. refused withdrawal of Capt CROWLEY. D.M.M.S. rang up later. D.A.D.M.S. stated he was ringing up A.D.M.S. to know what arrangements he had made - Also stated that A.D.M.S. 34th Div had stated his inability to find personnel.	Appx.
		9.30.	Got having heard from A.D.M.S. office rang up D.D.M.S. Request permission to recall Capt CROWLEY. Was answered by D.D.M.S. Clerk + left message with him to the effect that I had only 2 officers at Main Dressing Station and additional were absolutely necessary.	Appx.
		10 pm.	D.A.D.M.S. rang up to say that Capt POYSER, No. 142 3⁷⁶ and Capt. CROWLEY has been instructed by D.D.M.S. to return from Corps Rest Station. The Rev - HARDY reported for duty with the ambulance.	Appx.
"	23.4.17	5 am.	Capt CROWLEY returned from BERLETTE this morning and Capt POYSER, No. 142 3⁷⁶ Div. Train & reported for duty. Wounded began to arrive about 9 am and have continued in a fairly steady flow. About 200 have up to now been admitted. The majority of the wounds are severe, shell wounds largely predominating. Evacuation has proceeded without a hitch. 2.4. M.T.C. have 10 cars constantly circulating between the combined Main Dressing Station (now being stations of 5th, 37th, 34th F.As.) and C.C.S. at AUBIGNY	

Army Form C. 2118.

WAR DIARY
or
INTELLIGENCE SUMMARY.
(Erase heading not required.)

77 **48 FIELD AMBULANCE**

Place	Date	Hour	Summary of Events and Information	Remarks and references to Appendices
HAUTES AVESNES	23.4.17	5 pm	O.C. 103rd Fd Ambly lent the services of an officer for part of the day, which was a Church Parade. DDMS XVII Corps paid a short visit in the morning & discussed the question of personnel &c.	SPR
"	24.4.17	9 am	30 Officers & 400 ORs admitted up to this morning. Seven cases of penetrating wound of the lung were detained at the main dressing station, and 1 Offic. and 3 other ranks suffering from the effects of gas. These latter are treated in a Marquee having the wall down on one side. Oxygen is administered hourly for 5 minutes. A relief of H.S. Horses for Ambulance wagons and 1 NCO ATC were sent up to O.C. 49th F.A. last night.	
"	25.4.17		10 Officers and 140 other ranks of the Division passed thro' from rest bivouac. Many cases come down who have been detained within one or two hours at the ADS. There is comfortable a bivouac in good order are passed straight to CCS after a wash and meal. Lt. RODOLPH RAMS of the 104th Fd Fd. was posted for duty to this unit last night to take over duties at the Entraining Station. DDMS XVII Corps visited the main dressing station in the morning.	SPR
"	26.4.17		Few casualties came thro' today.	SPR
"	27.4.17		A quiet O.C. O.C. visited ADS at Railway Embankment in morning, and Colonel Gen Rest Sta in afternoon. The Division is expected attack early tomorrow morning.	SPR

Army Form C. 2118.

WAR DIARY
or
INTELLIGENCE SUMMARY.
(Erase heading not required.)

48 Field Ambulance

Place	Date	Hour	Summary of Events and Information	Remarks and references to Appendices
HAUTE AVESNES	28.4.17		Wounded began to arrive about 9 A.M. D.D.M.S. XVIII Corps visited the F.A. at 9.30 A.M.	59/6
"	"	6 p.m.	Wounded have come in very sparingly — only about 60 during the day	
"	29.4.17	8 A.M.	37th Div. Operation Order No. 87. Received 1. The 9th Div. is relieving the 37th Div. on the nights 28/29th and 29/30th April. 5. The 37th Div. will be transferred to XVIIIth Corps from 12 noon on April 30th. 6. Divisional Headquarters will ...... spend LIGNEREUIL at 10 A.M. on 30th April Table of Reliefs and Movements attached. 48th F.A. from HAUTE AVESNES to LIGNEREUIL. Capt T. CROWLEY detailed to relieve Capt. FINDLATER, sick, at Combined Divisional Rest Station. BERLETTE.	ARH
"	30.4.17	6 A.M.	The Ambulance moves this afternoon to LIGNEREUIL by HERMAVILLE. The party from BERLETTE to move independently. The bearers under Capt. GODFREY have not yet returned, but it is expected they will arrive this morning in the cart & horsed wagons of the F.A. from the oil factory	59/21

D. Murdoch ?
Commdg 48th F.A.

Medical

Confidential
War Diary
of
48 Field Ambulance

From 1st May To 31st May.

1917.

(Volume XXII.)

COMMITTEE FOR THE
MEDICAL HISTORY OF THE WAR
Date 10 JUL 1917

B.E.F.

SUMMARY OF MEDICAL WAR DIARIES OF 48th F.A. 37th Div.

6th Corps 3rd ARMY.
18th Corps from April 14th.
17th Corps from April 19th.
18th Corps from April 30th.
6th Corps from May 18th.

Operations on Western Front - April - May 1917.

Officer Commanding = Lt.Col. D.P. WATSON.

SUMMARISED UNDER THE FOLLOWING HEADINGS:-
Phase "B" - Battle of Arras - April - May 1917.
1st Period - Attack on Vimy Ridge - April 1917.
2nd Period - Capture of Siegfried Line - May.

B.E.F.

<u>48th F.A. 37th Div. 18th Corps. 3rd ARMY. WESTERN FRONT.</u>
May 1917.
<u>Officer Commanding = Lt. Col. D.P.WATSON.</u>

PHASE "B" - <u>Battle of Arras - April - May 1917.</u>
    2nd Period - <u>Capture of Siegfried Line - May.</u>

May 2nd.	<u>Moves</u>. Detachment. 1 & 22 to 19th C.C.S. - Returned to Headquarters on 6th inst.
3rd-18th.	Operations R.A.M.C. Routine.
18th.	<u>Transfer</u>. 37th Division transferred to 6th Corps.

B.E.F.

48th F.A. 37th Div. 6th Corps. 3rd ARMY. WESTERN FRONT.
May 1917.
Officer Commanding = Lt. Col. D.P.WATSON.

PHASE "B" - Battle of Arras - April - May 1917.
2nd Period - Capture of Siegfried Line - May.

May 18th.   Transfer. 37th Div. transferred to 6th Corps.
            Moves. To Berneville.

19th.   Moves.   ) To Tilloy-Les-Hafflaines and took
            Med. Arrangements.   )
            Accommodation.   ) over A.D.S. from 2nd/3rd London
            Field Ambulance. A.D.S. situated among debris of houses
            and shell-pitted gardens - One fairly protected
            dressing room, and tents.
            Br. Posts at Marlière N. 17. d. 3.4. and Gun Pits
            N. 11.a.7.7 taken over in conjunction with 50th F.A.

20th.   Operations. 56th Division carried out small attack - Heavy
            artillery fire.
            Casualties. 24 wounded sent to M.D.S.

22nd.   Moves. Detachment. 1 & 24 rejoined Headquarters from
            37th C.C.S.

24th.   Operations Enemy. Vicinity of A.D.S. shelled.

25th.   Decorations. Cpl. Brooker C.E.   )
                         a/Cpl. Dent G.   ) awarded M.M.
                         Pte. Clough F.   )
                         "   Stone J.F.   )

26th.   Operations Enemy.
            Shell from German H.V. gun burst close
            to A.D.S.
            Casualties.
                    O & 1 killed.
                    O & 2 wounded.
            Casualties R.A.M.C. O & 2 wounded.

28th.   Military Situation. 111th Brigade relieved 112th Brigade
            in the line from Coteuil River to Trench Junction
            0.8.d.1.9.
            Medical Arrangements. 1 & bearers took over Br. P. at

2.

B.E.F.

<u>48th F.A. 37th Div. 6th Corps. 3rd ARMY.</u>   WESTERN FRONT.
                                                May 1917.
<u>Officer Commanding - Lt.Col. D.P. WATSON.</u>

<u>PHASE "B" - Battle of Arras - April - May 1917.</u>
   <u>2nd Period - Capture of Siegfried Line - May.</u>

May 28th (contd) <u>Medical Arrangements</u> contd. at Gun Pits.

                   1 & Bearers took over Br. Post at Marliere.

30th-31st. <u>Operations</u>. 111th Infantry Brigade carried out minor operations in conjunction with 86th Infantry Brigade on night 30th - 31st.

<u>Casualties</u>. Up to 8.30 a.m. 31st 39 wounded passed through A.D.S.

B.E.F.

48th F.A. 37th Div. 6th Corps. 3rd ARMY. WESTERN FRONT.
May 1917.
Officer Commanding = Lt. Col. D.P.WATSON.

PHASE "B" - Battle of Arras - April - May 1917.

2nd Period - Capture of Siegfried Line - May.

May 18th. Transfer. 37th Div. transferred to 6th Corps.
Moves. To Berneville.

19th. Moves.   ) To Tilloy-Les-Hafflaines and took
Med. Arrangements.)
Accommodation.   ) over A.D.S. from 2nd/3rd London
Field Ambulance. A.D.S. situated among debris of houses
and shell pitted gardens - One fairly protected
dressing room, and tents.
Br. Posts at Marliere N. 17. d. 3.4. and Gun Pits
N. 11.a.7.7 taken over in conjunction with 50th F.A.

20th. Operations. 56th Division carried out small attack - Heavy
artillery fire.
Casualties. 24 wounded sent to M.D.S.

22nd. Moves. Detachment. 1 & 24 rejoined Headquarters from
37th C.C.S.

24th. Operations Enemy. Vicinity of A.D.S. shelled.

25th. Decorations. Cpl. Brooker C.E.   )
              a/Cpl. Dent G.   ) awarded M.M.
              Pte. Clough F.   )
              "   Stone J.F.   )

26th. Operations Enemy.
Shell from German H.V. gun burst close
to A.D.S.
Casualties.
    O & 1 killed.
    O & 2 wounded.
Casualties R.A.M.C. O & 2 wounded.

28th. Military Situation. 111th Brigade relieved 112th Brigade
in the line from Coteul River to Trench Junction
O.8.d.1.9.
Medical Arrangements. 1 & bearers took over Br. P. at

48th F.A. 37th Div. 6th Corps. 3rd ARMY. WESTERN FRONT.
May 1917.
Officer Commanding - Lt.Col. D.P. WATSON.

PHASE "B" - Battle of Arras - April - May 1917.
2nd Period - Capture of Siegfried Line - May.

May 28th.contd). Medical Arrangements contd. at Gun Pits.
1 & Bearers took over Br. Post at Marliere.

30th-31st. Operations. 111th Infantry Brigade carried out minor operations in conjunction with 86th Infantry Brigade on night 30th - 31st.

Casualties. Up to 8.30 a.m. 31st 79 wounded passed through A.D.S.

Army Form C. 2118.

WAR DIARY
or
INTELLIGENCE SUMMARY.
(Erase heading not required.)

Vol 22 / 79 / 48 FIELD AMBULANCE

Place	Date	Hour	Summary of Events and Information	Remarks and references to Appendices
LIGNEREUIL	1.5.17		The Ambulance marched yesterday at 11 a.m from HAUTE AVESNES to LIGNEREUIL arriving at 4.30 p.m. The party from BERLETTE under Capt CROWLEY marched independently arriving at 6 p.m. Capt. GODFREY with the bearers came by motor bus with 111th Bgde. A French hut has been taken over as hospital. The personnel are billeted in barns, accommodation not very good. Lt. Qr. HAYNES was evacuated last night to 37. C.C.S. sick.	87th
"	2.5.17		Lt. DEAKIN R.A.M.C. appointed actually Field Ambulance for duty last summary. Lt RODOLPH with 92 O.Rs proceeded to No 19. C.C.S. for temporary duty. Capt. H.M.GODFREY. Left for duty with XIX Corps Cavalry Mx and 3rd R.R M.R. acting thereupon.	28/11 3/20
"	3.5.17		Capt. MERRIN R.A.M.C. was attached for duty to the F.A. on 28th April. Capt. S. SCOTT R.A.M.C. posted for duty to the F.A. vice GODFREY.	
"	5.5.17		Two tent subdivisions formed a practice A.D.S. on the Church at E of the LIGNEREUIL — AMBRINES Road ½ mile from AMBRINES. Casualties, evacuated were supplied by 58 F.A. The tent subdivisions were under the Command of Capt CROWLEY. Capt MERRIN proceeded to take temporary medical charge of the 9th Bn Sch at DENIER vice DEAKIN. The transport was inspected in the morning by Lt Col Syte Adv Adm, who reported him as well satisfied with the mount.	

WAR DIARY or INTELLIGENCE SUMMARY.

48 FIELD AMBULANCE

Army Form C. 2118.

Place	Date	Hour	Summary of Events and Information	Remarks and references to Appendices
DANNEBROEK	6.5.17		Notification received that Capt H.W. EVANS has been sent sick to ENGLAND. He is struck off the strength accordingly. Strength of the F.A. at present: Officers 9, Other ranks 157. N.C.O.s 41.	A.Phs
"	11.5.17		Pte RODOLPH No 22 was returned from duty at No 19 C.C.S. Re-inoculation of the unit with T.A.B. commenced. Capt A.MERRIN and Lt H.V. DEAKIN returned to duty with the 2nd 13th K.R.R.C. Capt A.MERRIN	A.Phs
"	12.5.17		Capt J. CROWLEY is posted for duty with 10th Ry. Fusiliers. Capt P.H. WELLS, who evacuated to No 6 Sty Hosp. suffering from P.U.O. is posted for duty with 13th K.R.R.C.	A.Phs
"	15.5.17		A considerable number of men of the unit have been reporting sick with severe slight diarrhoea. The majority belong to B. Section. Their billets clean and inspection does not suggest any special unhygienic condition. The billet has been sprayed with Cresol.	A.Phs
"	17.5.17 12.45pm		Rec'd 57th Div Order No 31 re-issue + The 37th Div Gen Artillery with reliever the 50th Div is taking the line from the 117th Div extract O.M.6.3.0 to GRAPH TRENCH exclusive to 0.8 a 8.8 by the morning of 18/19 May 1917. 2nd Bgde will relieve	A.Phs

Army Form C. 2118.

WAR DIARY
or
INTELLIGENCE SUMMARY.
(Erase heading not required.)

48 Field Ambulance

81

Place	Date	Hour	Summary of Events and Information	Remarks and references to Appendices
LIGNEREUIL	17.5.17	12.15	H.Q. 2nd Army, under orders to be moved later.	APP.
"	"	6.5pm	Order no 112 of III E Bgde received with march table. The Ambulance will march to BERNEVILLE via WANQUETIN & WARLUS, passing Starting Point at 1.36 a.g.1. at 12.40 p.m.	APP.
BERNEVILLE	18.5.17 1.9pm		The Ambulance marched by above route, arriving at BERNEVILLE at 5.pm. The march was 8 hrs, as the Tuck [lorry] Bike was moving by the same roads and there were few rests. On arrival the C.O. went with Capt. Scott and an advanced party by motor Ambulances to TILLOY, on the ARRAS-CAMBRAI road, to take Fd positn in PRINZ RUPPRECHT STRASSE occupied by the 2/3 London F.A. and returned leaving the party there to commence taking over. Sets from R.A.M.C 37th Division Order no 32. 18th May. 1917. (2) "48th Field Ambulance will move to TILLOY-LES-MOFFLAINES that S.B. H.31. d. on 19th May, and will take over the advanced Dressing Station from the 2/3 London Field Ambulance. The relief to be completed by 6 pm on the 19th." An advance party 5th proceed in the afternoon of the 18th. Details of the relief to be arranged between Os. C Field Ambulances concerned.	APP.

WAR DIARY
or
INTELLIGENCE SUMMARY. 48 Field Ambulance

Army Form C. 2118.

Place	Date	Hour	Summary of Events and Information	Remarks and references to Appendices
BERNEVILLE	18.5.17	9/ra.	(3) 49th Field Ambulance will move to ARRAS and take over the main dressing station at HOPITAL ST JEAN - - - - .	
			(5) Two bearer subdivisions of 50th Field Ambulance will be attached to the 1/12th Bgde. and will take over the bearer posts N.11. a.77 (gun pits) and MARLIERE N.117. d. 3.4 on the evening of the 19th E. Relief to be completed by 10. A.M on the 20th. These bearer subdivisions will come under the Command of the O.C 48th Field Ambulance, who will be responsible for the clearing of the forward area. They will be relieved by the O.C. 48th Field Ambulance.	
			(6) The clearing of the wounded from the left Bearer post N.11. a.79 will be by hand carriage to the ARRAS- CAMBRAI Road, and thence by motor Ambulance Car to the Advanced dressing Station TILLOY. The clearing of the wounded from the Right bearer post MARLIERE N.17.d.34 will be by hand carriage to the WANCOURT - TILLOY Road, and thence by Motor Ambulance Car to Advanced dressing Station TILLOY	
			(7) The Evacuation from the advanced dressing station TILLOY to the Main dressing Station HOPITAL ST JEAN will be carried out by Divisional Cars along the CAMBRAI - ARRAS Road. "	

Army Form C. 2118.

WAR DIARY
or
INTELLIGENCE SUMMARY. 48 FIELD AMBULANCE
(Erase heading not required.)

Instructions regarding War Diaries and Intelligence Summaries are contained in F. S. Regs., Part II. and the Staff Manual respectively. Title pages will be prepared in manuscript.

Place	Date	Hour	Summary of Events and Information	Remarks and references to Appendices
TILLOY-LES-MAFFLAINES	19.5.17	7.p.m.	The remainder of the Ambulance marched with the 111th Inf. Bgde. this morning to ARRAS, and thence on to TILLOY, where it arrived at 3.30 p.m. and took over from the 2/3 London F.A. The site occupied is among the debris of houses and shell pitted grounds. There is one fairly protected dressing room. The rest of the treatment of the wounded is carried out in tents. Very much requires to be done in the way of cleaning up the ground etc. Some of the Ambulance personnel are accommodated in dugouts – the remainder in tents. The remainder O.C. in the open half a mile away. Capt. C.H. LLOYD R.A.M.C. and Capt. H. McINTYRE R.A.M.C. from the 3rd Gunner Reported tonight for temporary duty.	(JH)
"	20.5.17	9 a.m.	The 58th Div. tent "night carried out a trench attack". Heavy artillery fire thro' the night. 4 lying and 20 sitting cases of wounded only were sent to the Main Dressing Station during the night.	JH
"	21.5.17		The C.O. visited bearer posts at MARLIERE and the Comforts at N.11.b.38 m.p. 57.B. At MARLIERE the bearer party are in extensive underground caves, where the R.A.P. of The two Battalions in the line are also situated. The bearers camp by hand near to the TAULDAY but about ½ mile distant on the TILLOY-WANCOURT Road.	

WAR DIARY or INTELLIGENCE SUMMARY

Army Form C. 2118.

48 Field Ambulance

Place	Date	Hour	Summary of Events and Information	Remarks and references to Appendices
TILLOY-LES-MAFFLAINES	22.5.17		Two cars were kept here by the outgoing F.A. one at the loading post, another about 300 yards in front of this, as this part is frequently shelled on account of our numerous gun positions in the neighbourhood. The car at the loading post is being withdrawn. When casualties are brought down a runner is sent ahead to fetch the other car into the loading post. The other loading post is in an old German gun position about 150 yards from the ARRAS–CAMBRAI road. Some of the protection to road, but it requires to be improved in parts, as this spot is at times heavily shelled. Two cars were kept on the main road about ½ mile from N.W. of the dressing post. One of these is to be withdrawn.	S.P.W.
"	23.5.17		Lt. A.W. HARE and 24 O.R.s returned from duty at No. 37 C.C.S. ADMS has requested CRE to improve protection at gun pits. Lt. G.H. RODOLPH placed in close arrest.	S.P.W.
"	24.5.17		All personnel of A.D.S. took to the dugouts last night on account of shelling. No shell has fallen in or burst actually over the A.D.S. but several have been very close, & casualties have been carried amongst the neighbouring troops. The C.O. visited D.M.S. at Army H.Q. in conference with an order received this morning. Eight O.R. R.E. there proceeded	

WAR DIARY
or
INTELLIGENCE SUMMARY.
(Erase heading not required.)

Army Form C. 2118.

48 FIELD AMBULANCE

Place	Date	Hour	Summary of Events and Information	Remarks and references to Appendices
TILLOY-LES-MAFFLAINES	24.5.17		to the bearer post at the Jum position to improve the protection there. They will remain there and be relieved by this F.A.	JHh
"	25.5.17		The C.O. attended a conference of A.D.s. M.S. C.Os. F.As. + Sanitary Officers at office of D.D.M.S. VIth Corps. The following O.Rs. of the F.A. have been awarded the military medal by VIth Corps Commander for acts of gallantry in the field. No. 38024 Cpl. C.E. BROOKER. No. 38225 Cpl. (A/Cpl.) G. DENT. " 38162 " F. CLOUGH. " 42871 " J.F. STONE. Half the personnel from A.D.S. at Crumpits returned to A.D.S. under Lt. DEAKIN & were relieved by personnel of 46th F.A. under Lt. HARE.	
"	26.5.17		A shell from a German H.V. gun burst close to the A.D.S. killing one & wounding two of the sick parade & wounding Pte's CROMER and FODEN of the 48th F.A.	JHh
"	27.5.17		C.O. visited bearer posts at MARLIERES and the Crumpits. Lt. HARE with Bearers from 46th F.A. relieves Lt. DEAKIN & half bearer personnel of 50th F.A. at the Crumpits. Cpl. BROOKER & bearers from 48th F.A. relieves half bearer personnel of 50th F.A. at MARLIERES. R.A.M.C. 37th Division Order No. 33. received – (1) The 111th Inf. Bgde. – will relieve the 112th Inf. Bgde +-- in the line from the COJEUL RIVER	

WAR DIARY
or
INTELLIGENCE SUMMARY

Army Form C. 2118.

86 **48 FIELD AMBULANCE**

Place	Date	Hour	Summary of Events and Information	Remarks and references to Appendices
TILLOY-LES-MAFFLAINES	27/5/17		to the French Junction O.8.d.1.9. on the night May. 28/29th. The relief to be completed by 6.0. am. May 29th.	
			2(a) The 112th Bde Bde ---- will move in relief to ATRAS - and ACHICOURT.	
			4. The 63rd Inf Bde ---- will relieve the 111th Inf Bde in support on the night 28th-29th May	
			5. Two bearer sub-divisions of 48th Field Ambulance will relieve the two bearer sub-divisions of 50th Field Ambulance at Cropits at N.11.a.77. and MARLIERE N.17.d.34. Relief to commence on 27th inst & to be completed by 28th inst. Time to be arranged by O.C. 48th F.A.	
			6. The two bearer sub-divisions of 50th Field Ambulance will return to the Headquarters of 50th F.A. at HOPITAL - ST. JEAN.	SPO.
"	28.5.17.	8 p.m.	Capt CHILD and bearers of 48th F.A. relieved remainder of 50th F.A. Personnel at Cropits & MARLIERE.	
			Capt PEARSON " " " " " "	
			R.A.M.C. 37th Division Order No. 34. received :-	
			1. The 29th Division has been ordered to capture HOOK Trench with a view to the eventual occupation of Infantry Hill.	
			2. For this operation the 8th East Lancs. Regt. 112th Inf. Bde, and one coy of the 9th N. Staff. Regt. will be placed under the orders of the 88th Inf. Bde from 6. am 29th May. 88th Inf. Bde from 6. am 29th May.	
			7. Medical arrangement will be under the administration of the ADMS. 29th Division.	

WAR DIARY
or
INTELLIGENCE SUMMARY.

87 / 48 FIELD AMBULANCE

Army Form C. 2118.

Place	Date	Hour	Summary of Events and Information	Remarks and references to Appendices
TILLOY-LES-MAFFLAINES.	28.5.17		8. O.C. 49th Field Ambulance will detail one bearer subdivision to reinforce the bearer subdivision at N.11.a.7.7. (gun pits). Party to arrive at 2 p.m. 29th inst.	
			9. O.C. Bearer Subdivisions on arrival, will report to O.C. 87th Field Ambulance at N.5 Central (gun pits) and act under instructions from him.	N.P.L.
"	29.5.17	8 am	CO. visited Bearer post at GUNPITS and invited Capt. CHILD to get into close touch with Regtl MOs & gather all possible information about tonight's operations. An extra car has been sent up to each bearer post.	
			Rame 37th Div. Order no 35 received	
			1. The 37th Div -- will be relieved by the 61st Div --	
			7(a) 48th Field Ambulance will hand over the advanced dressing station at TILLOY and the Bearer posts N.11.a.77 and MARLIERE Cave N.17.d.3.4. to the 2/1st Field Ambulance 61st Div. Relief to be completed by 6 pm on the 31st June. Details of relief to be arranged by O.C. Field Ambulances concerned.	
			(b) 48th Field Ambulance will march from TILLOY to ARRAS on the evening of 1st and will send a representative to report to the A.D.M.S. Commandant's Office, BOULEVARD CARNOT, ARRAS to arrange for billets, at least 24 hours beforehand.	

WAR DIARY
INTELLIGENCE SUMMARY. 48 Field Ambulance

Army Form C. 2118.

Place	Date	Hour	Summary of Events and Information	Remarks and references to Appendices
THOY-LES-MAFFLAINES	29.5.17	8 pm	7. (c) Dismounted portion of 48th Field Ambulance will move by bus under orders of G.O.C. 111th Brigade on June 2nd to AMBRINES - LIENCOURT area. (d) Transport of 48th Field Ambulance will move under orders of G.O.C. 111th Brigade on June 2nd to AMBRINES - LIENCOURT area. 8. O/c Field Ambulances will arrange to clear the sick of their brigades.	SP2
"	30.5.17	11 am	Telegraphic instructions received last night for C.O. to report to D.M.S. 3rd Army for temporary duty. C.O. handed over temporarily to Capt Scott Ritchie (T) S Ritchie Lt-Col.	
		6 pm	Capt Hirst R.A.M.C. of the 2/1 South Midland Field Ambulance reported at 3 pm in the afternoon with 11 other ranks, Capt Hirst & 5 other ranks proceeded to the Bearer Post at the Quarries, 1 N.C.O. & 5 other ranks to the Bearer Post at Blanchire for instruction & duty. Lieut Ashmore R.A.M.C. 49th Field Ambulance reported at 4 pm for temporary duty with this ambulance until midday June 13th. Lieut Hart R.A.M.C. upon being relieved by Capt Hirst R.A.M.C. returned to A.D.S.	

Army Form C. 2118.

WAR DIARY
or
INTELLIGENCE SUMMARY.   48 FIELD AMBULANCE
(Erase heading not required.)

Place	Date	Hour	Summary of Events and Information	Remarks and references to Appendices
TILLOY-LES-MOFFLAINES	30.5.17		Operation Orders No 36 received from A.D.M.S. 3rd Division (1) The 111th Inf Bde will carry out a minor operation in conjunction with the 86th Inf Bde on night 30/31st (2) The cross roads at O.8.d.1.2 will be captured & consolidated	S.S.
	31.5.17	8.30 am	A Bearer Sub-Division was held in readiness to reinforce Bearer Sub-Division at the Bearer Post N.11.a.4.3. (Sun Rly), but it was not called upon. Evacuation of wounded was carried out by a Arras-Cambrai Road & to Wancourt Trolley Road. Two stretcher & thirty seven walking cases passed through the A.D.S. during the night & early morning up to 8.30 am. Strength of Field Ambulance R.A.M.C. 155 A.S.C. 49 Total 204 Ten reinforcements posted on the 26th inst., the Ambulance is 27 under strength S. Scott Capt RAMC T. for O.C. 48th Field Amb.	S.S.

Confidential

War Diary

of

48 Field Ambulance.

From 1st June to 30th June.

1917

(Volume XXIII)

Army Form C. 2118.

WAR DIARY
or
INTELLIGENCE SUMMARY.
(Erase heading not required.)

48 Field Ambulance

VOL 23
90

Place	Date	Hour	Summary of Events and Information	Remarks and references to Appendices
TILLOY-LES- MOFFLAINES	31/5/17	10 pm	Orders received from A.D.M.S. 34th Division to clear the sick of "B" Echelon Div Amm Column on June 2nd & following days. They will leave Achicourt 10 am on 2/6 for Boys-en-Artois, attached to Sains-les-Bains on the 3rd June. Capt C.N. Lloyd RAMC & Capt H. R. INTYRE RAMC left & rejoin their units. Very few wounded or sick came through to-day. In the evening the bearer-posts situated at RARLIÈRE the GUN PITS were relieved by 1 officer & 12 O.R.s of the 2/1 South Midland Field Ambulance, 61st Division. Capt GHILD RAMC & Capt PEARSON RAMC returning to TILLOY.	S.S.
	1/6/17	10 pm	Operation order No 122 by the 111th Inf Brigade received in the morning, march tables & disclination of Units shown. During the morning Lieut DEAKIN RAMC proceeded to ARRAS & reported to the Town Commandant to arrange for billets for the night of June 1/2nd. Capt GHILD RAMC rejoined the 60th Field Ambulance. An advance party of the 2/1 South Midland F.A. reported in the morning followed by the main body commanded by Col Thompson in the afternoon. We were relieved by the 2/1 South Midland Field Ambulance at 6.65 pm. Marched to the billets at ARRAS, officers at 32 Rue d'Amiens, men at 16 Rue Henri de Gête.	S.S.
ARRAS.	2/6/17	8.30 am	Transport of the Ambulance under command of Lieut ASHMORE RAMC left the lines at 4.45 am to proceed to ARSIRINES via DAINVILLE, WARLUS,	

Army Form C. 2118.

WAR DIARY
or
INTELLIGENCE SUMMARY.
(Erase heading not required.)

48 Field Ambulance

Place	Date	Hour	Summary of Events and Information	Remarks and references to Appendices
ARRAS	2/6/17		WANQUETIN, HAUTEVILLE, AVESNES reaching their destination without incident. Lieut RODOLPH RAMC Transferred before a Field General Court Martial held at 10 am in the SCHRAMM barracks ARRAS. Capt PEARSON RAMC acted as escort. Lieut DEAKIN RAMC gave evidence; the accused was acquitted. ARRAS was shelled during the morning, no casualties in unit. Morning & afternoon spent in usual inspections. Dismounted portion of Field Ambulance entrained in the RUE de LILLE at 4.50 pm leaving at 6.30 pm, travelling to CAMBRINES by St POL ARRAS road — HABARCQ—AVESNES arriving at AMBRINES at 9 pm in the evening.	S.S.
AMBRINES	3/6/17	6.30	Orders from A.D.M.S. 33rd Division received at 1.30 am ordering us to proceed to LIENCOURT early in the morning. Lieut ASHMORE RAMC reported to the 49th Field Ambulance marched from AMBRINES arriving at LIENCOURT 12 mid day. Capt HARMAN RAMC joined this unit for duty.	S.S.
LIENCOURT	4/6/17	8.0	In view of an early move from this area no effort was made to establish a large hospital at LIENCOURT, only the Brigade sick being collected & evacuated in the usual way to No 6 Stationary Hospital FRÉVENT. Route march for men not otherwise employed in the morning, kit & clothing inspection in the afternoon. We were visited by the A.D.M.S in the afternoon.	S.S.

Army Form C. 2118.

WAR DIARY
or
INTELLIGENCE SUMMARY.
(Erase heading not required.)

92 48 Field Ambulance

Place	Date	Hour	Summary of Events and Information	Remarks and references to Appendices
LIENCOURT	5/6/17	9.0	111 Brigade sick collected & evacuated during the day. Physical Drill & Squad Drill in morning, G.O's inspection in afternoon; at night a very successful Whist Drive was held for the men, there being about 80 players.	S.S.
LIENCOURT	6/6/17	9.15	111th Inf Brigade Orders No 123 received in the early morning, extracts as follows "The 37th Division less Artillery ... will be transported from the 3rd Army Area to the 1st Army Area & will be in G.H.Q. reserve." Billeting Party under Capt PEARSON RAMC sent on in advance to FIEFS & arrange billets for ambulance. Transport under Capt DEAKIN with LIEUT NARE in charge of horsed ambulances moved off at 6.30 a.m. to join the 111th Brigade Transport Column at the Cross Roads 250 yds S. of S. en MAZIERS at 7 a.m. following the route AVER-DOINGT — MARQUAY — BRYAS — VAL HUON, making FIEFS without incident at about 2 p.m. Dismounted portion of Field Ambulance left LIENCOURT at 9 a.m, entrained at AMBRINES, followed route via ARRAS - ST. POL road — TINQUES — MONCHY-BRETON — PERNES — SACHIN, debussed at SAINS lez PERNES & from there marched to FIEFS reaching there about 1 p.m. Rest of day spent in resting. 111th Inf Brigade Orders No 124 received in the early morning, extracts as follows	S.S.
FIEFS.	7/6/17	4.30	"111th Inf Brigade group will move to the ROMY area on 4th June 1917." Billeting Party under Capt PEARSON. RAMC. sent on in advance to ERNY-ST-JULIEN. 48th Field Ambulance marched in column of route reaching the starti point cross roads 1000 yds S. of MONTGORNET, at 11.46 a.m & following route by FLECHIN to	

WAR DIARY or INTELLIGENCE SUMMARY

Army Form C. 2118.

48th Field Ambulance

Page 93

Place	Date	Hour	Summary of Events and Information	Remarks and references to Appendices
ERNY-ST-JULIEN			which was reached by 2.30 p.m.; LIEUT DEAKIN was in charge of Transport of Ambulances; three motor ambulances & followed half of brigade, who marched by LAIRES — BEAUMETZ road, three horsed ambulances & one motor ambulance followed remainder of Brigade who marched by FLECHIN — EUHEM road, these conveyances picked up 29 casualties on the road & conveyed them to their respective units destinations; men marched in light marching order; the packs being left behind at FIEFS under a guard to be brought on later under Brigade arrangements. Lieut HARE was left behind to dispose of such & to follow later in ambulance cars. Very good accommodation for officers & men, but poor hospital accommodation, there being only room for about 20 lying cases in the only barn set apart as a hospital. Orders received from A.D.M.S. 37th Division for Lieut G.N. RODOLPH R.A.M.C to proceed forthwith & report for duty with the 14th Division, Lieut RODOLPH left about 2 hours after arrival in village. Capt G. CLARKE R.A.M.C. arrived in the early evening & takes over the command of the 48th Field Ambulance, command should over to him accordingly	S.S

Army Form C. 2118.

WAR DIARY
or
INTELLIGENCE SUMMARY.

(Erase heading not required.)

94 **48 FIELD AMBULANCE**

Place	Date	Hour	Summary of Events and Information	Remarks and references to Appendices
ERNY ST JULIEN	June 7	7.30pm	Capt C. Clark RAMC arrived from duty as O.C. 16 Motor Ambulance Convoy and took over command of No 48. Field Ambulance from Capt Scott R.A.M.C	C
do	8th		Major D.P. Watson appointed D.A.D.M.S Sanitation Third Army and struck off the strength of 48 Field Ambulance.	C
do	9th		Capt E.A Pearson left for "leave of absence in Scotland" today. (The personnel of 1 to 8 field ambulances have been employed during 7th–9th in cleaning Billets, preparing latrines ablution places etc and arranging for accommodation of patients. A large barn capable of holding 30 stretcher cases has been prepared as a temporary Hospital Ward and any of an injurious field has been prepared as a convalescent camp for such discharged from Hospital. Four bell tents and an operating tent and as a treatment tent being utilised.	C
do	10th		Sgt. Major D. Stewart arrives to take over duties of Sgt Major to the unit. Field Training commenced. Section A under Capt Marannan and Section B under Capt Scott checked all equipment during the morning and reported all deficiencies to Adj Officer for replacement.	C
do	11th			C

WAR DIARY
or
INTELLIGENCE SUMMARY.

(Erase heading not required.)

Army Form C. 2118.

95 **48 Field Ambulance**

Place	Date	Hour	Summary of Events and Information	Remarks and references to Appendices
ERNY-St Julien	11	2 pm	Capt Scott marched out to a point on the ERNY – ENGUINEGATTE road half a mile south of ENGUINEGATTE and putting an advanced dressing station. Detachment marched back to ERNY-St Julien in the evening leaving 1 N.C.O. and 4 men in charge of tents, wagons and equipment (B section).	C
do	12	9 A.M.	A section with transport under Capt Marmor marched out to a point on the PETIGNY – COYECQUE road midway between these towns and pitched an advanced dressing station. B section completed formation of advanced dressing station and were executed in advanced dressing station work. C section formed a Main Dressing Station at ERNY and received cases sent in from advanced Dressing Station. Sgt Major L. J. Brown proceeded for duty to No 6 General Hospital was S.M. Steward. Lieut J. P. Howe U.S. Medical Corps arrived for duty and was taken on the strength of the unit.	C

Army Form C. 2118.

WAR DIARY
or
INTELLIGENCE SUMMARY.
(Erase heading not required.)

Instructions regarding War Diaries and Intelligence Summaries are contained in F. S. Regs., Part II. and the Staff Manual respectively. Title pages will be prepared in manuscript.

96 48 FIELD AMBULANCE

Place	Date	Hour	Summary of Events and Information	Remarks and references to Appendices
ERNY-St- JULIEN.	June 13.		Capt. J. G. T. Thomas RAMC arrived for duty and was taken on the strength of the unit today. Sections A & B. entrenched in advanced dressing station work. Section C engaged in main dressing station work.	ce
do	14	9 am	Authority received from 37 Division H.Q. for Capt. C. Clark to act as Badges of rank of Lieut Colonel while in command of No 48 field Ambulance. Training continued. A & B Sections advanced dressing station work. C Section main dressing station work.	ce
do	15th		Training continued. C Section providing staff for main dressing station Hospital.	ce
do	17th		A section relieve C section and takes over Main Dressing Station. C section with transport entrained in formation of advanced dressing station at a point in the PETIGNY L'OYE C g de mal. B Section Company keyed drill with field exercises.	a

A 5834 Wt.W4973/M687 750,000 8/16 D. D. & L. Ltd Forms/C.2118/13.

WAR DIARY
or
INTELLIGENCE SUMMARY. 2/8 Field Ambulance

Army Form C. 2118.

Place	Date	Hour	Summary of Events and Information	Remarks and references to Appendices
ERNY St JULIEN.	18th		A section engaged in main dressing station work. B " " " " Field Brant work. C " " " " Advanced dressing station work. Sanitary School for training men in sanitation and water duties formed today. Men posted for training from units of 111th Brigade.	C
	19		Training School for training men in sanitation and water duties.	C
	20th		Training School for 111th Brigade continued. Regimental orderlies opening today.	
	21st		Sections examined and cleaned all equipment. C.O. inspecting 2 p.m. full parade of Field Ambulance. Plans etc. Orders received from A.D.M.S. 37th Division on 20.6.17 N° 4 2/8 Field Ambulance to move from BOMY and to St HILAIRE Cc men under orders from 111th Brigade. Sanitary and water school for Brigade (111) closed today.	CC
	22nd		Orders received from H.Q. 111th Brigade on 21st June. 2/8th Field Ambulance to march on 23rd June from ERNY St JULIEN to GUARBECQUE. Starting point road junction north of ESTRÉE BLANCHE at 9.22 A.M. June 23. 1917.	C

Army Form C. 2118.

WAR DIARY
or
INTELLIGENCE SUMMARY.
(Erase heading not required.)

98 48 FIELD AMBULANCE

Place	Date	Hour	Summary of Events and Information	Remarks and references to Appendices
ERNY. St JULIEN.	23 June	8 am	No 48 Field Ambulance paraded at ERNY St Julien at 7.45 am. under the command of Lieut Col P. Clarke RAMC and proceeded by column of route to starting point at ESTREE BLANCHE arriving	
		9.20	there at 9.20 am. Field Ambulance marched past saluting point of the III Brigadier General. At road junction north east of Lt M in Mazingham (HAZEBROUCK map 5A) 100,000 Major General Williams Commanding The 48th Field Ambulance marched past. March was continued through LAMBRES 37th Division.	HAZEBROUCK 5.A
		2 pm.	MOLINGHEM to GUARBECQUE when the field ambulance arrived at 2 pm and was billeted in barns.	
GUARBECQUE	24 June	3.45 am	Field Ambulance paraded at 3.45 AM and proceeded by column of route through the following towns. GUARBECQUE. St VENANT. MARBECQUE. HAZEBROUCK to KREULE where the unit was billeted in Barn arriving N KREULE at 2 pm. Field Ambulance passed the G.O.C 37th Division on the road north of MARBECQUE.	Map referring W

Army Form C. 2118.

WAR DIARY
or
INTELLIGENCE SUMMARY.
(Erase heading not required.)

48 Field Ambulance

Place	Date	Hour	Summary of Events and Information	Remarks and references to Appendices
KREULE	25 June	6.30 am	48th Field Ambulance paraded at 6.15 am and marched by column of route at 6.30 am through the following towns KREULE. METEREN. ROUGE CROIX. BAILLEUL. LA BREARDE LOCREHOF FARM. where the unit was billeted in huts arriving there at 1 pm. At METEREN the 48th Field Ambulance marched passed the G.O.C. 2nd Army and G.O.C. 37th Division.	Map reference HAZEBROUCK 5A
LOCRHE	26th	8 am	20489 Field Ambulance cleared sick from 111th Brigade and evacuated men seriously sick to Casualty Clearing Stations in BAILLEUL. Lieut HARE R.A.M.C. relieved Lieut HOWE. Ambulance lorry who was temporarily attached 37. Div. R.E. Lieut DEAKIN R.A.M.C. adm. to Casualty Clearing Station suffering from P.U.O.	
LOCHRE	27th	8 am	2/48th Field Ambulance cleared sick from 111th Brigade. Report received that Lieut DEAKIN. R.A.M.C. had been evacuated to Base. B section 48th F.A. under Capt Scott moved to Rest Station KEERSEBROM.	

Army Form C. 2118.

WAR DIARY
or
INTELLIGENCE SUMMARY
(Erase heading not required.)

48 Field Ambulance

Place	Date	Hour	Summary of Events and Information	Remarks and references to Appendices
Lochre	June 28	9 am	Sick cleared from 111th & 112th Brigades. A section and C section 2/4 B.F.A. transferred from Lochrehof farm to KEERSEBROM. Small rearguard party left at Lochrehof farm. (12 men & a Corporal) to clear up grounds and huts.	
KEERSEBROM 29.		9 am	Under instructions received from A.D.M.S. 37 Division two horsed ambulance wagons and two motor ambulance wagons were transferred to O.C. 2/9th field ambulance for duty at LOCHRE. Equipment, stores, tents etc. taken out from 109th Field Ambulance History forming Dressing station and Rear station at KEERSEBROM.	HAZEBROUCK 5/7 troops refused chow Completed [?]
KEERSEBROM 30		9 am	No 109th Field Ambulance relieved Lieut Col M Gill D.S.O. marched out from KEERSEBROM today at 6 am — took over Rest Camp Capt Scott with B section personnel } 48 FA with A section & C section personnel } — took over Dressing station	

Army Form C. 2118.

WAR DIARY
or
INTELLIGENCE SUMMARY.
(Erase heading not required.)

48 FIELD AMBULANCE

101

Place	Date	Hour	Summary of Events and Information	Remarks and references to Appendices
KEERSEBROM.	June 30.	6.10 pm	Col. Morphew, DSO AMS, ADMS 37 Division inspected Ambulance and Rest Camp at KEERSEBROM at 6.10 p.m. on 29th June 1917 which the camps were being handed over from 109th FA to 48th FA. The following points were noted during his tour of inspection. MAIN DRESSING Station. Bath house in the course of erection. ABLUTION room, urinals and latrins dirty. Soapy water not properly trapped but flowing over court of drainage pit and soaking adjacent ground. A grease trap close to ablution room was very dirty and contained trains + food refuse exposed to flies. A bell tent close to a ward tent was in use as a combined bath house and latrine for the ward patients. REST. CAMP. Surface of rest camp ground untidy, empty fives, match ends, bits of paper etc about. Many FIRE Buckets half empty, water in many were very dirty and contained in general sundry scraps. SAND buckets showing to rain	

Army Form C. 2118.

WAR DIARY
or
INTELLIGENCE SUMMARY.
(Erase heading not required.)

102 **48 FIELD AMBULANCE**

Inspecting A. HAZEBROUCK 1/100,000

Place	Date	Hour	Summary of Events and Information	Remarks and references to Appendices
KEERSEBROM.	30 June		contained a caked mass of sandy earth.	
			LATRINES. Seats not automatically closing; some latrines had openings at the back and were not fly proof.	
			INCINERATOR. The ground around the incinerator was very untidy and contained a fair quantity of strewn refuse which was not burnt.	
			KITCHENS. The preparation room of the kitchen was very untidy, tins, match ends, paper, unlying about on the floor. The cutting up table improperly taken and in splinters, tenders being covered with grease. The grease trap near kitchen contained a large quantity of the bones and was in a dirty irregular state. The A.D.M.S. 37 Division was informed that the above points were to be attended to on the camp being taken over from the 109th Field Ambulance.	
			O Clarke Lt Col R.A.M.C. O.C. 48th Field Ambulance. 30/6/17	

Confidential
War Diary
OF

48th Field Ambulance

From :- 1st July To :- 31st July

1917.

(Volume XXIV)

COMMITTEE FOR THE MEDICAL HISTORY OF THE WAR
Date 10 SEP. 1917

Army Form C. 2118.

VOL.2A.
103

WAR DIARY
or
INTELLIGENCE SUMMARY.
(Erase heading not required.)

48 FIELD AMBULANCE

Instructions regarding War Diaries and Intelligence Summaries are contained in F.S. Regs., Part II. and the Staff Manual respectively. Title pages will be prepared in manuscript.

Place	Date	Hour	Summary of Events and Information	Remarks and references to Appendices
KEERSEBROM	July 1st		A Section of Field Ambulance employed as carpenters, painters, gardeners, handling spade etc. for the Camp. B Section personnel supply Fatigues of Rest Camp. C Section " " for main Dressing Station	Map reference HAZEBROUCK 1/100,000. German F.A. 13 5/4
do.	2.		Capt. Morrison posted for temporary duty with 315 Army F.A. 13 5/4. 2 cars (motorised) returned for duty and use posted to Astation. Dr. Hardie reported today for duty and was posted to Astation. Strength of unit R.A.M.C. 182 / O.R. 49 / = 231	do. 5.A
do.	3rd		Intimation received through A.D.M.S. 37 Div. that Capt. Pearson R.A.M.C. had been granted extension of leave to 1st July	do.
do.	6th		Capt. Thomas R.A.M.C. returned from leave today	do.
do.	7th		Capt. Pearson has not returned from leave up to date. Advice reporting to A.D.M.S. 37th Division	North East Europe

A 5834. Wt: W4973/M687 750,000 8/16 D.D. & L. Ltd. Forms/C.2118/13.

Army Form C. 2118.

WAR DIARY
or
INTELLIGENCE SUMMARY.

(Erase heading not required.)

104 / 48 Field Ambulance

Place	Date	Hour	Summary of Events and Information	Remarks and references to Appendices
KEERSEBROM	8 July		Average number of patients in Rest Camp during first week in July was 230. The majority of the patients were convalescent P.U.O. cases or septic infection of skin cases.	a
do	9 July		Constructional work carried out by unit. A large outdoor workshop for carpenters & painters has been made by using a tarpaulin for roof and canvas screening for sides. The huts occupied by patients in the Rest Camp being without tables or forms, on table and two forms on being made for each hut; hay for huts has now been equipped as above. A large hot spray bath (3 compartments) has been erected in a marquee. Patients never lost clothes/rack company personnel over a week. A corrugated iron roof has been fitted to the showerbath of Rest Camp which was without a roof	a

A 5834 Wt. W4973/M687 750,000 8/16 I.D.D.&L.Ltd. Forms/C.2118/13.

Army Form C. 2118.

WAR DIARY
or
~~INTELLIGENCE SUMMARY~~
(Erase heading not required.)

48 FIELD AMBULANCE

Place	Date	Hour	Summary of Events and Information	Remarks and references to Appendices
KEERSEBROM	10th July		Lieut Stow returned for duty with 48th Field Ambulance	a
do	12 July		Capt Marmion rejoined the unit for duty (sick)	a
do	13 July		Lieut Martin transferred for duty as M.O. 27 Labour Group R.E. Lieut Howze do— for duty (living) as M.O. 13th Royal Fusiliers	a
do	14th July	10 A.M.	Conference of O.C.'s commanding Field Ambulances in 37th Division held at Jeffers J. A.D.M.S. intentions with reference to future operations received from Col Morphew D.S.O. Capt Thomas left unit for temporary duty as M.O. 8th Lincolns	c
		5.30 P.M.	A.D.M.S. held medical Board at 48th Field Ambulance on 9 men of 13th K.R.R. recommended to an unfit for M.O. Regt.	a

Army Form C. 2118.

WAR DIARY
or
INTELLIGENCE SUMMARY.
(Erase heading not required.)

106. 48 FIELD AMBULANCE.

Instructions regarding War Diaries and Intelligence Summaries are contained in F. S. Regs., Part II. and the Staff Manual respectively. Title pages will be prepared in manuscript.

Place	Date	Hour	Summary of Events and Information	Remarks and references to Appendices
MEERSEBROM	July 14th	2.30 pm	D.D.M.S IX Corps inspected 48th Field Ambulance, and issued the following instructions.	
			1) MAIN DRESSING STATION a) Personnel of unit to be billetted in adjacent Barns (Bc 13th K.A.R.) now in occupation of Barns to be reported to vacate them. Huts to be used for Hospital purposes only.	
			b) Chicken wire to be fixed around supports of Hospital huts to keep ground clean underneath.	
			2) REST CAMP a) All patients to sleep on stretchers and not as at present on straw mattresses. Stretchers to be drawn from Corps dump at DRANOUTRE.	C
			b) All windows to be provided with new oiled silk.	
			c) All patients permitted to use Dining Room.	
			d) Cement floors to be repaired where necessary.	

Army Form C. 2118.

WAR DIARY
or
INTELLIGENCE SUMMARY.
(Erase heading not required.)

48 Field Ambulance

107

Place	Date	Hour	Summary of Events and Information	Remarks and references to Appendices
KEERSEBROM.	15 July		In compliance with instructions received from D.D.M.S. IX Corps, Area Commandant was written to and Farm Billets now occupied by B.C. 13th K.R.R. applied for. O/C Corps Stretcher Dump in reply to request for 300 stretchers stated that he only had 150 stretchers in his possession.	C
do.	16 July	10 AM	150 stretchers received from IX Corps Stretcher Dump.	
		10 pm	Telephone message from A.D.M.S. 37th Div. regarding a report to be sent tomorrow stating number of stretchers on charge with 48th F.A. Barn Yards etc adjacent to Rest Camp & MAIN Dressing Station to be searched for spare stretchers.	E
do	17th	10 AM	A.D.M.S. notified that a total of 236 stretchers were held on charge at present. No stretchers found in Barns or Huts. Capt MARMION left today to take medical charge of 17th H.A.G.	

Army Form C. 2118.

WAR DIARY
or
INTELLIGENCE SUMMARY
(Erase heading not required.)

108 — **48 Field Ambulance**

Place	Date	Hour	Summary of Events and Information	Remarks and references to Appendices
KEERSEBROM.	July 17th		Capt THOMAS struck off strength and posted as MO of 8th Bn Lincolns. Capt Pearson struck off strength of unit from 4. July 1917.	CC
	July 18th		Capt Wishart reported for duty from 17th H.A.G. Personnel of Ambulance accommodated in Barns instead of tents & tents. Accommodation arranged for patients. Rest Camp 400. could be increased to 510 if required. Main Dressing Station 200.	CC
	July 19th		Secret report with reference to a new type of gas shell in use at Ypres received. reported action on Eyes and skin noted.	CC
	July 21st		Operation order No 48 received from ADMS 37 Division and following orders issued for future action. 3 Horsed Ambulance wagons to be ready to proceed to 48 & 49th Field Ambulance 4 Motor Ambulance wagons " " " " " " " 50th " " " One Bearer subdivision and one tent sub-division to be held in readiness	CC
	July 23rd		21. Cases of Gas Shell poisoning admitted to Rest Camp from 50th F.A. majority of cases Exhibited severe conjunctivitis and inflammatory redness of face neck hands. in some cases actual vesication produced	CC

Army Form C. 2118.

WAR DIARY
or
INTELLIGENCE SUMMARY.
(Erase heading not required.)

109   48 FIELD AMBULANCE

Place	Date	Hour	Summary of Events and Information	Remarks and references to Appendices
KEERSEBROM	July 23rd		The gassed cases reported that they were gassed while in dugouts near WYTSCHAETE night July 22nd by gas shells. Gas appeared to have very slight odour, difficult to detect. Severe conjunctivitis burning of skin and respiratory irritation without bronchitis later. Treatment: Eyes washed out with Boracic lotion and then treated with Castor oil drops. Skin washed with Bicarbonate of soda & Boric ac solution and then smeared with Boric ointment. Cases were seen and examined by 37 Stn gas officer Lt Isaacs. 15 cases required Oxygen + Brandy (enough nys & Bri strychnine + digitalis also as Stretcher cases, admitted 12.3 July were evacuated to C.C.S. cases 11.30 am	TRENCH MAP FRANCE Sheet 28 S.W. Ed 5A
	July 24th		58 cases of gas shell poisoning admitted. AM 4 pm from 50th F.A. Cases similar to those admitted 23 July but much milder in character. Conjunctivitis & skin inflammation of face and hands much more marked. Cases were gassed by shell gas. Night July 22nd	

A 5834 Wt. W 4973/M687 750,000 8/16 D. D. & L. Ltd. Forms/C.2118/13.

Army Form C. 2118.

WAR DIARY
or
INTELLIGENCE SUMMARY.

48 Field Ambulance

(Erase heading not required.)

Place	Date	Hour	Summary of Events and Information	Remarks and references to Appendices
KEERSEBROM	July 25		Mild cases of gas poisoning still recurring. Conjunctivitis the chief symptom, a few cases exhibit dermatitis especially about groin & axillary spaces but of only slight degree	
	July 26		Lieut Howz U.S Army rejoined the unit today from 13. Royal Fus.	
	27"		Charge Sheet received from A.P.M. 37th Div. against Pte McCarthy No 50217, B. Sec same together with evidence (documentary) of three Frenchmen who stated that they had seen Pte McCarthy with a boy in a French Farmer's field of peas. Evidence taken down in writing. Pte McCarthy willed evidence to prove an alibi. Summary of evidence referred to higher authority.	
	28"		Patches to act as Divisional Badges received to be sewn on back sleeves of all ranks immediately below the regimental title	

Army Form C. 2118.

WAR DIARY or INTELLIGENCE SUMMARY

(Erase heading not required.)

48 FIELD AMBULANCE

Place	Date	Hour	Summary of Events and Information	Remarks and references to Appendices
KEERSEBROM	July 29	12.15 pm	Divisional Rest Station and 48th Field Ambulance visited and inspected by Lt.Col. Browne A.A.+Q.M.G. 37 Division	Trench Map FRANCE Sheet 28 SW ed 5A
	30	12.30 pm	Secret order received from A.D.M.S. 37 Division stating that 30/7/17 was Y day. In compliance with previous arrangements 3 horsed ambulance wagons were sent at 3 pm to O.C. 49th Field Ambulance at PARRAIN FARM and at 4.30 pm 4 motor ambulance cars were sent to O.C. 50th F.A. at DRANOUTRE. Two clerks were sent to O.C. 59th Field Ambulance at 3 pm. Two clerks for all 37 Div cars passing through to act as Walking wounded station KEMMEL BREWERY.	
		4.30	12 stretcher bearers sent to O.C. 50th F.A. from Asylum	
		7 pm	Secret order received from A.D.M.S. containing instructions for new covertion in B.A.B. TRENCH order notice received that 3.50 AM 31/7/17 was Zero hour for operations &c	Clerk W.O.W. Rouse

Army Form C. 2118.

WAR DIARY
or
INTELLIGENCE SUMMARY.
(Erase heading not required.)

112 **48 FIELD AMBULANCE**

Place	Date	Hour	Summary of Events and Information	Remarks and references to Appendices
KEERSEBROM	July 31	11:30 A.M.	Main Dressing Station and Rest Camp organized for the reception of 600 patients. Bay No 9 Bartus Buildings shelters also the temporary accommodation could be increased to 800 patients. Sent Subdivision and Bearer Subdivision (100×12 hours) @ A station held in readiness to move if required under Capt Wishart, RAMC. Clarke Major O C 48 F A	∈

Medical

Confidential
War Diary.
of
48 Field Ambulance

From 1st August To 31st August
1917.
(Volume XXV)

COMMITTEE FOR THE MEDICAL HISTORY OF THE WAR
Date -1 OCT 1917

Army Form C. 2118

Vol 25
Instructions regarding War Diaries and Intelligence Summaries are contained in F.S. Regs, Part II. and the Staff Manual respectively. Title pages will be prepared in manuscript.

113

WAR DIARY
or
INTELLIGENCE SUMMARY.
(Erase heading not required.)

48 FIELD AMBULANCE

Place	Date	Hour	Summary of Events and Information	Remarks and references to Appendices
KEERSEBROM	August 1st		No cases have been received in the Rest Station of wounded from IX Corps front. Extra Beds & accommodation prepared have not been required.	Map Reyrnia HAZEBROUCK 1/100,000
		2nd	Instructions received from DDMS IX Corps 41/150 stretchers to be carried in futurity field ambulance	5.A.
	do	3rd 1pm	DDMS IX Corps Col Wilson AMS visited 48th Field Ambulance and issued instructions for the unit to be prepared for an early move and to be communicated. All Red Cross Stores held by the unit to be handed over to another unit when 48th Field Ambulance received present staff. Detailed instructions to be issued later by DDMS after receipt of Auf. 9 Red Cross Stores.	
	do	4th	Instructions received to hand out 6 riding horses from the unit to OC W2C Divisional Train (37) on 6. August. Subsequently to be handed in to DADOS 6/8/17 pursuant reduction of horses held by field ambulance 37 Div	C

Army Form C. 2118.

WAR DIARY
or
INTELLIGENCE SUMMARY
(Erase heading not required.)

1/4 48 Field Ambulance

TRENCH MAP SHEET 28. S.W. 5A

Place	Date	Hour	Summary of Events and Information	Remarks and references to Appendices
KEERSEBROM	August 4th	—	Application for trial of No 50217 Pte McCarthy 48th FA by Field General Court Martial transmitted to A.D.M.S. 37th Divn.	
	5th	12:30pm	Lieut Fletcher R.A.M.C. posted for duty with 48th F.A. arrived today	
	6th	12pm	Lt. W. McClure R.A.M.C. " " " 48th FA	
		midnight	Orders received from A.D.M.S. 37th Division order No. 52. 6/8/17. 48th Field Ambulance to hand over Rest Camp KEERSEBROM to 13th Australian F.A. and to take over KEMMEL Brewery from 59th FA. 48th Field Ambulance to take over Advanced Dressing Stations from 59th F.A. & 57th F.A. and to be responsible for the clearing of the whole line to the Main Dressing Station. (49th F.A. Hospice LOCHRE). 48th FA over by 48th FA (Johnny posts N.1h. Kakun) PALMA POST (N.18. a. 6.9) DAMSTRASSE (O.19 c.3.8) KLEIN VIERSTRAAT (N.10 a. 9.9) NORTH HOUSE (O.19.b.9.9)	

WAR DIARY
or
INTELLIGENCE SUMMARY.
(Erase heading not required.)

Army Form C. 2118.

48 Field Ambulance

Place	Date	Hour	Summary of Events and Information	Remarks and references to Appendices
KEERSEBROM	6/Aug.		Advance changes to Hr. completed by 10 a.m. 8/8/16.	
	7.	Any	Advance parties sent in the morning to take over posts in the line from 57th & 59th Field Ambulances.	cc
			Rest Camp KEERSEBROM handed over to 13th F.A. (Australian)	TRENCH MAP Sheet 28 S.W. A
KEMMEL	8	10 a.m.	All posts mentioned above in 37/ADMS/order 52 taken over from 57th & 59th Field Ambulances at 10 a.m. 8/8/17 being Portion of 48th Field Ambulance on Holland.	
			Mount Kemmel Brewery. KEMMEL.	
			No 1. Advanced Dressing Station (Right half) KLEIN VIERSTRAAT. (N10 a 9.9)	
			(Left half) DAMSTRASSE (O19 c 3.5)	
			No 2. Advanced Dressing " (Right half) Regimental Aid Post in DENY'S WOOD.)	
			wounded evacuated by trolleys from (Left half Regimental Aid Post in DENY'S WOOD.)	
			in OUSTERVERNE WOOD.) and (IN DER STERCKS CABARET (O.15 a 3.2)	
			to trolley line Head west (IN DER STERCKS CABARET (O.15 a 3.2) ce	
			wounded carried by Trolley line to PALMA POST. (N.18 a 6.9) and thence	
			by Ambulance cart to Advanced Dressing station at KLEIN VIERSTRAAT.	

Army Form C. 2118.

WAR DIARY
or
INTELLIGENCE SUMMARY.
(Erase heading not required.)

1/6 48 FIELD AMBULANCE

Place	Date	Hour	Summary of Events and Information	Remarks and references to Appendices
KEMMEL	Aug 8th		From the Advanced Dressing Station N. KLEIN VIERSTRAAT the wounded are carried to the Main Dressing Station No 49 F.A. in LOCHRE HOSPICE. No 3. A.D.S. formed by the first subdivision of other section in KEMMEL Brewery for local sick and wounded, which are evacuated to LOCHRE Hospice.	
	8th	4 pm	Main Dressing Station (49 F.A.) by Ambulance Car. Pts/AHERN.D./FOLEY.T/ANNAL.J/THOMPSON.G/FAY.J/CLARKE.E admitted to Hospital suffering from gas poisoning the advance shelling military gas / mustard and protecting equipment you. 48 F.A. 6 Aug 18	
KEMMEL ADS			Lieut P.R Witlington. U.S.A. reported for duty and protecting C section	
KEMMEL	Aug 10th		Capt Poyser R.A.M.C. posted for duty with 48th F.A. reported his arrival today. Capt Poyser placed in charge of A.S.C. attached and Horse Transport.	

Army Form C. 2118.

WAR DIARY
or
INTELLIGENCE SUMMARY
(Erase heading not required.)

48 FIELD AMBULANCE

Place	Date	Hour	Summary of Events and Information	Remarks and references to Appendices
KEMMEL	Aug 11th		Court Martial assembled 10th Aug to try charge against McCarthy Rfmr 48th FA under Sec 6 AA stealing 7 pkts from a French Woman — re arrested today found guilty — previous 7 convict not guilty	C.
do	Aug 12		Pte Thompson J. of 48th Field Ambulance guard which on transit duty in Outtersteen Jn. reported to have died from effects of gas poisoning on 11/8/17 at No 1 Australian C.C.S.	
do	13 Aug		A.D.M.S. 37 Div inspected the A.D.S. Klein Vierstraat and notified me that 48th F.A. might be required to clear the line from the Railway O.10.c.4.4. to the junction of present line with the Ypres–Comines Canal O.4.a. With this extra work in view an application was transmitted today to the A.D.M.S. for a branch trolley line to run from main trolley line at O.14.a.8.2. to Bain Strasse O.9.c.3.7.	
do	14 Aug		Work commenced at formation of a new Advanced Dressing Station at PALMA POST N.7.c.3.1. using iron cupolas & sandbags provided by R.E. at PALMA POST	

Army Form C. 2118.

WAR DIARY
or
INTELLIGENCE SUMMARY.
(Erase heading not required.)

118 **48 FIELD AMBULANCE**

Place	Date	Hour	Summary of Events and Information	Remarks and references to Appendices
KEMMEL	Aug 14.		Transport Coins of 2/48" F.A. reported today to Major General H.B. Williams. C.B. D.S.O. Commanding 37. Division.	C.C. Trench MAP Sheet 28. S.W. 1/20,000
do	Aug 15"		In compliance with instructions received from A.D.M.S. 37 Div 100 stretchers were sent today to 50" F.A. Haegedoorne. Instructions were also received to supply Bailleul. M.O.P. 8/Somersets with 5 stretchers today, when sent-off. Secret order received today stating that the 112" Inf Brigade at present in the line was to be relieved tonight by 63rd Inf Brigade	ce
do	Aug 16"		Capt Royset R.A.M.C. evacuated sick to 2nd/9" Field Ambulance today.	
do	Aug 17"		In Compliance with secret instructions received from A.D.M.S. the wounded from line O.11.b.60 to O.12.b.4.4. N. perrow shared by 132 Field Ambulance were transferred with a view to 2/48 Field Ambulance taking over this clearing of this portion of the line in addition to its present work.	
do	Aug 18"		Above instructions with reference to relieving 132 Field Ambulance cancelled by A.D.M.S. until further orders.	

WAR DIARY
or
INTELLIGENCE SUMMARY.

Army Form C. 2118.

48 Field Ambulance

Place	Date	Hour	Summary of Events and Information	Remarks and references to Appendices
KEMMEL	Aug 18th		The trenches of A section at present occupied by the right half of the 63rd	TRENCH MAP SHEET 28 S.W. S.A
		9 AM	Brigade front will be relieved by the trenches of 1/3 section	
		5 pm	Above change completed	
			Lieut. McClusk RAMC. took over charge of the advanced dressing station at Donn Monen DAMM STRASSE today in relief of Lieut. Hours U.S.A.	
do	Aug 19th		A German aeroplane was shot down by anti-aircraft battery today near DAMM STRASSE. The occupants, a Lieutenant and Warrant Officer, were found through the A.D.S. The Lieutenant with fractured right thigh and other bullet wounds. The Warrant Officer with bullet wounds right leg, both evacuated to 49 F.A.	a
do	Aug 21st		The Dump Station at the foot of the French Battery on the VIERSTRAAT-WYTSCHAETE road was shelled today with about six rounds of 5.9 H.E. shells. Our men was killed and three wounded. Other parts of the A.D.S. were not injured. The it hits at present	c
do	Aug 23rd		Shelling has intensified scoring M.E. & gas shell, shelling Cmcurlt Down Monen & Damm Strasser. Sick + wounded evacuated daily average about 48 in number	e

119

Army Form C. 2118.

WAR DIARY or INTELLIGENCE SUMMARY
(Erase heading not required.)

120 2/3 FIELD AMBULANCE

Place	Date	Hour	Summary of Events and Information	Remarks and references to Appendices
KEMMEL	Aug 25		Shelling of the DAMM STRASSE is in the vicinity usually takes place about 7–9 a.m. daily. H.E. 5.9 shells. Information received today that the 11th Warwick Regt. wanted our wagon line in front of OOSTAVERNE O.21.b. in squares 57 & 58 from 8.18.3 tomorrow. 2/3 Field Ambulance reported to take over wounded from regimental stretcher bearers at point O.16.c.5.1. after 2 A.M. 26/8/17	TRENCH MAP Sheets 28 S.W.5A
do	Aug 26		Stand for Brewery relays arranged today. 8 bearers which to wheeled stretcher carriage to evacuate wounded from O.16.c.5.1. to Rgt Aid post at O.15.a 5.10. from these point wounded to be evacuated by 2/3rd Field Amb. to PALMA Dump N.12.c.51	do
do	Aug 27th		Raid arranged above carried out after 2 a.m. this morning. 5 wounded evacuated (1 Officer 4 O.R.) from the 49. FA. suffering from pyrexia. Lieut. WITHINGTON evacuated sick to 49 FA suffering from Pyrexia and diarrhoea today.	do
do	Aug 28		Orders received from A.D.M.S. 37 Division today stating that 63rd Inf Brigade, was relieving 117 Inf Brigade on 29/8/17. Line to be taken	do

Army Form C. 2118.

WAR DIARY
or
INTELLIGENCE SUMMARY.
(Erase heading not required.)

121 / 48 FIELD AMBULANCE

Place	Date	Hour	Summary of Events and Information	Remarks and references to Appendices
	Aug 28.		out hospital from FORRET FARM O.11.c. 2.1. to YPRES - COMINES Canal at O.6.a.9.1. 2nd & 5th Field Ambulance to clear wounded from the line relieving us 132 Field Ambulance. 29/8/17.	SHEET 28/5A Trench Map
	Aug 29th		48th Field Ambulance relieved 132 Field Ambulance today. 68 Stretcher bearers having been sent yesterday 28/8/17 from 4/9th Field Ambulance for this purpose and placed under O.C. 48 F.A. Posts taken over Reg. Aid Posts 0.5.a.2.1 // Bearer Posts 0.4.a.6.z. do - do - 0.4.a.8.2.1 // do 0.3.d.3.6.	" "
	Aug 30th		Wounded evacuated by hand carriage and tram trolley to 0.3.c.4.1 and from this place by ford car to VOORMEZEELE. where a large motor car is stationed. From VOORMEZEELE wounded are carried by amb. car to A.D.S. KLEIN VIERSTRAATE. N10.a.9.9. Line quiet except for occasional shelling.	"

A5834 Wt. W4973/M687 759,000 8/16 D. D. & L. Ltd. Forms/C.2118/13.

Army Form C. 2118.

WAR DIARY
or
INTELLIGENCE SUMMARY.
(Erase heading not required.)

48 FIELD AMBULANCE

122

Place	Date	Hour	Summary of Events and Information	Remarks and references to Appendices
C	May 31st		Notice received that 10 R.F. would raid German trenches early Sept 1st. Evacuation of wounded &c. to be conducted in the same way as for raid on night of 26/8/16.	C
			Strength of unit 31/8/17	
			RAMC 173	
			att ASC 49	
			222	

C. Clarke Major RAMC
O.C. 48 F.A.

Army Form C. 2118.

Vol. 26.

123 48 FIELD AMBULANCE

WAR DIARY
or
INTELLIGENCE SUMMARY.
(Erase heading not required.)

Place	Date	Hour	Summary of Events and Information	Remarks and references to Appendices
KEMMEL	Sept 1st		(0.21.6.6.7) Recce conducted on German Trenches in front of OOSTTAVERNE. Casualties one officer wounded by machine gun from pavend Chemy. A.D.S. and men evacuated to 49 F.A.	SHEET 28/57 Trench MAP
	Sept 2nd		In compliance with instructions received from A.D.M.S. Order 55. 112th Brigade relieving 116th Brigade in front. autd 2/9/17 J.31.a.75.75. YPRES - COMINE'S - CANAL. up to No 48 Field Ambulance to relieve 134 Field Ambulance and evacuate all sick and wounded to main Dressing Station LOCRE. Change to be completed by 10 pm today. Combined R.A.P. at 1.36.a.2.7. A.D.S. at NORFOLK. Lodge on north bank of Canal N. Lock 6 1.33.d.2.6. Beau Poot SPOIL BANK 1.33.a.2.2.	SHEET 28. ENL 3
KEMMEL			O.C. 48.F.A. to hand over to a Field Ambulance of 30th Div (97 FA) dan following posts. DOME HOUSE 0.9.c.3.8 NORTH HOUSE 0.19.6.9.9. OOSTAVERNE WOOD 0.15.c.2.8 GARRAIN FARM N.25 6.6.9 (about huts) ONRAET WOOD 0.14.c.5.8 Above relief completed 10 pm 2/9/17	C.C

Army Form C. 2118.

WAR DIARY
or
INTELLIGENCE SUMMARY.
(Erase heading not required.)

124 — 48 FIELD AMBULANCE

Place	Date	Hour	Summary of Events and Information	Remarks and references to Appendices
KEMMEL	Sept 3rd		37th Divisional front now extends from FORRET FARM O.11.b.6.0. to J.31.a.75.75 astride the YPRES. COMINES. canal. No. 8 Bearer ? A & m ?A clear the front South ? the canal " " " ? A " " " North ? the canal Both group ? Bearer camp wounded from R.A.P.s to A.D.S. at NORFOLK LODGE Lock 6. I.33. d.2.6. wounded are conveyed from the A.D.S. and from? wheeled stretchers to SHELLY FARM. O2.6. 9.1. and from there to LOCRE. Main Dressing Station by Ambulance Car. Evacuation { wounded. sitting cases sick. 4 lying and 13 sitting	SHEET 28 EAST 2 Ce
				Ce
				Ce
do	Sept 4th		Evacuation { wounded 3 lying sick 16 sitting	Ce
do	Sept 5th		Evacuation { wounded 8 lying and 3 sitting sick 1 lying and 13 sitting	Ce

Army Form C. 2118.

WAR DIARY
or
INTELLIGENCE SUMMARY.
(Erase heading not required.)

Instructions regarding War Diaries and Intelligence Summaries are contained in F.S. Regs., Part II. and the Staff Manual respectively. Title pages will be prepared in manuscript.

/25

Place	Date	Hour	Summary of Events and Information	Remarks and references to Appendices
Kemmel.	Sept 6th		111th Infantry Brigade relieved 63rd Infantry Brigade in the trench front — JOTTET FARM — YPRES COMINES CANAL. Evacuation { wounded 13 lying 1 sitting; sick 9 sitting }	C
KEMMEL	Sept 7th		8th East Lancs relieved 11th Warwicks; 10th Loyal N. Lancs " 6th Bedfords. Lieut G.P. Hoar posted to the 10th R.F. vice M.O.? Batchelor and struck off strength unit. Evacuation { wounded 6 lying; sick 1 lying and 7 sitting }	C
do.	Sept. 8th		Lieut J. ROTE } U.S.M.R.C. arrived today posted for duty with 18th F.A. Lieut W.F. SCOTT } Two officers and 100 men arrived today from 58 & 59th Field Ambulances 19th Div. in order to prepare anywhere sites for wounded in the three Officers and 50 men places at KLEIN VIERSTRAAT 25mm at LATERIE YORK RD. & 25mm at PALMA DUMP. Evacuation { wounded 5 lying 2 sitting; 8 sitting }	C

Army Form C. 2118.

WAR DIARY
or
INTELLIGENCE SUMMARY.
(Erase heading not required.)

Place	Date	Hour	Summary of Events and Information	Remarks and references to Appendices
KEMMEL	Sept 9th	10 am	Sick and Wounded evacuated from Line during last 24 hrs	C.E.
			Wounded. 8 # a dying	
			Sick (5 cav ? Demham) 37 P.U.O + 1 Dental abscess.) + 4 otherwise.	
KEMMEL	Sept 10th		Orders received today from ADMS 37th Division works 58. 9/9/17	e
			as follows.	
			"Horse lines at M.12.d.2.8	
			O.C. 48th Field 2 KEMMEL BRASSERIE . . . to 58th Field Ambulance.	
			Ambulance Posts [1.35 central, 1.34 d 8.8.	
			to hand over { R57 Field Ambulance	
			O.4 ~ d.7.7.	
			O.3 ~ d.2.6.	
			N.10. ~ 9.7.	
			N.15. a. 6.9.	
			N.16. d.1.3	
			O.C. 49th Field TYRONE FARM M.36. a.9.4. from 57th Field Ambulance	
			Ambulance to taken over	
KEMMEL	Sept 11th		Advanced parties for all the changes mentioned in detail above (ADMS. order 58/57) 37th Dn posted today	C.E.

Army Form C. 2118.

WAR DIARY
or
INTELLIGENCE SUMMARY.
(Erase heading not required.)

Place	Date	Hour	Summary of Events and Information	Remarks and references to Appendices
TYRONE FARM DRANOUTRE M.36.a.9.4	Sept 12		Transfers ordered by A.D.M.S 37 Div taken place by 12 noon. 4/8th Field ambulance established today at TYRONE FARM M.36 a.9.4 and clearing sick of 111th Brigade commencing tomorrow Sept 13th.	c
do	Sept 13.		Sick cleared by ambulance cars from units of 111th Brigade to 50th Field ambulance's Barrieul. Lt Col C. Clarke name O.C 4.8 F.A proceeded on 10 days leave (14th - 24th Sept) today to England. address whilst on leave C/o HSBCo 3 Whitehall Place. Capt Scott R.A.M.C took an O.R. F.A. in absence of C.O. Lieut 9. Fletcher proceeded to take temporary duty with 4th Middlesex Regt as Their Regimental Medical Officer	c

Army Form C. 2118.

WAR DIARY
or
INTELLIGENCE SUMMARY.
(Erase heading not required.)

128.

Place	Date	Hour	Summary of Events and Information	Remarks and references to Appendices
			Lieut T. St G. McClure proceeded to take temporary medical charge of 8th E. Lancs in the absence of Lieut Ashworth	S.S
Dranoutre	Sept 14th		Morning spent in usual camp fatigues, clothing & kit inspection in afternoon. During the day orders were received from A.D.M.S 37th Division to send 1 large car with drivers & orderly to D.G. 54th Ft Amb.	S.S
Dranoutre	Sept 15th		at the HOSPICE, LOCRE. This was complied with. 111th Inf Brigade went into the line during the evening. Usual camp fatigues in morning, smoke helmet respirator & P.H. helmet inspection & drill in afternoon	S.S
Dranoutre	Sept 16th		5D stretcher were handed over to O.C 5th Field Ambulance in accordance with orders received from A.D.M.S 37th Div	S.S
Dranoutre	Sept 17th		As G. sections paraded in light marching order & were taken a route march via NEUVE EGLISE DE KENNEBAT CABINET & DRANOUTRE in the morning. B section did camp fatigues. During the afternoon there was a pay parade.	

WAR DIARY
or
INTELLIGENCE SUMMARY.
(Erase heading not required.)

Army Form C. 2118.

Place	Date	Hour	Summary of Events and Information	Remarks and references to Appendices
DRANOUTRE	Sept 17th		In the evening orders were received from A.D.M.S. 34th Division to furnish a working party of 100 men to report to O.C. 8 Army Tramways Coy at VESUVIUS at 9 am to-morrow.	S.S
DRANOUTRE	Sept 18th		100 N.C.O.s & men under Capt SCOTT RAMC proceeded to VESUVIUS to report to O.C. 8 Army Tramway Coy. They were conveyed by Motor Ambulances & Horsed Ambulance Wagons. There being no O.C. 8 A TT Coy (light railway order), they were handed over to the construction gang worked all day until about 4 pm on the construction of a trench Tramway. Quiet day, very little hostile shelling.	S.S.
DRANOUTRE	Sept 19th		Previous days fatigue party supplied again, this time they were taken to their destination in Motor Lorries under arrangements of S.R.T.O IX Corps; party covered track at DRANOUTRE at about 6 pm	
			Orders received from A.D.M.S. 37th Division that the Ambulance must hold itself in readiness to move at short notice consequently all ranks confined to billets until further notice. 111th Inf. Bgde came into billets in neighbourhood of Dranoutre, sick collected by motor ambulances & transferred to 50th Fd Amb.	S.S

WAR DIARY or INTELLIGENCE SUMMARY

Army Form C. 2118.

Place	Date	Hour	Summary of Events and Information	Remarks and references to Appendices
DRANOUTRE	Sept	20th	Morning & afternoon spent in camp fatigues. Capt WISHART R.A.M.C. & Lt ROTE U.S.A.N.O.R.C. proceeded for temporary duty to No 2 C.C.S. at OUTERSTEEN. Orders received from A.D.M.S. 39th Div to provide 2 working parties of 50 other ranks to work under N.E. officers in neighbourhood of LOCRE in section of bulments, to report to-morrow at 8.45 until rations for day. In the evening hostile shelling commenced at about 9.45 pm. The projectiles were long range, high velocity shells bursting on percussion, they came from the direction of NAUBOURDIN (South Easterly direction), they were about 20 or 30 in number & some fell in neighbourhood of Camp.	S.S
DRANOUTRE	Sept	21	The shelling continued during the night & stopped at about 4 a.m. Extent of damage done was 2 N.Q. horses killed, 1 H.Q. horse wounded & 1 rider wounded (necessitating evacuation) 2 G.S. wheels damaged; 3 tents damaged, 1 limber & 1 G.S. wagon damaged — no casualties amongst personnel. Two working parties of 50 each reported at 8.45 to R.E. officer & worked until 4 p.m. in afternoon.	S.S
DRANOUTRE	Sept	22	Previous night was quiet. Working parties of previous day resumed. Orders received from A.D.M.S. to field Ambulance in readiness to proceed at 2 hours notice note given. Sick bearer to go into DRANOUTRE between the hours	S.S

WAR DIARY or INTELLIGENCE SUMMARY

Army Form C. 2118.

Place	Date	Hour	Summary of Events and Information	Remarks and references to Appendices
DRANOUTRE	Sept 22		Orders received from A.D.M.S. to despatch to O.C. 49th Fd. Amb. Bearers at the BRASSERIE 2 large Motor Ambulances for the will) showing & car orderlies to take 2 days rations. R.A.M.C. Order No 68 received informing no that (1) 112 Inf Bgde no relieving 118 Inf. Bgde (39th Div.) in the line on the 22/23 Sept. (2) O.C. 49 Field Ambulance will detail 1 officer & 30 other ranks & where bearers of the 134 Field Amb in the line, they will be responsible for the evacuation of the line. After to the A.D.S at ZWARTELEN.	S.S. S.S.
DRANOUTRE	Sept 23		Working parts of 100 men detailed to work with R.E.s at the same working party of 100 men proceeded to work with R.E.s at same place than on previous days.	
DRANOUTRE	Sept 24		R.A.M.C. Order No 59 received (1) O.C. 49th Fd Amb will move on Sept 26th & relieve 95th Field Amb at KEERS BROM & MAGILLIGAN camps (2) He will form a dressing station at MAGILLIGAN camp. (3) Advance parties to be sent on 25th Sept (4) O.C. 48th Fd Amb will continue to collect the sick 111 Inf Bgde & will treat them so far as possible in MAGILLIGAN CAMP. Lieut ROTE U.S.A.O.R.C reported back for duty from No 2 C.C.S under orders of D.M.S. 2nd Army. Lieut WOODSEND RAMC reported for duty taken on strength of field ambulance.	S.S.

Army Form C. 2118.

WAR DIARY
or
INTELLIGENCE SUMMARY.
(Erase heading not required.)

Place	Date	Hour	Summary of Events and Information	Remarks and references to Appendices
DRANOUTRE	25		Lieut FLETCHER R.A.M.C. posted to permanent medical charge of 4th Middlesex Regt. Lt Col Clark returned from 10 days leave of absence in England.	
do	26		48th Field Ambulance marched today from TYRONE FARM (M36 a 9.4) to MAGILLIGAN CAMP (Sq. d.8.1.) at 10 a.m. arriving at 11 a.m. Camp at KEERSEBROM was also taken over. S10.D.6.6. TYRONE FARM was left unoccupied. MAGILLIGAN & KEERSEBROM camps were taken over from 98th F.A. 56 slightly sick and convalescent patients were taken over at both these camps.	
KEERSEBROM	27		Lieut McClure R.A.M.C. returned to duty with 48th F.A. today from 8th E.Lancs in compliance with orders received from A.D.M.S. 37 Division. 74 Pearsants were sent up at 6.30 p.m. today by three motor lorries to report for duty with 49th F.A. at V. ORMERZEELE Capt Scott & Lieut Scott U.S.A. also proceeded to 49th F.A. for temporary duty	

WAR DIARY
or
INTELLIGENCE SUMMARY.

(Erase heading not required.)

Army Form C. 2118.

Place	Date	Hour	Summary of Events and Information	Remarks and references to Appendices
KEERSEBROM	28th		37th A.D.M.S. order No. 60 received 27/9/17. Orders received from A.D.M.S. 37th division to send a third team subdivision (1 person) to report for duty with 49th Field Ambulance	C.C.
do	29th		24 hours schedule making total of 1 9.8. teams supplied to 49th F.A. under instructions received from A.D.M.S. 37th Div. above party to proceed & carry tomorrow	Sheet 28 Ed 3
			Lieut Rote U.S.A. proceeded to day at 8am with the 24 hours for duty with O.C 49 F.A	ce
do	30th		Capt Wishart R.A.M.C returned for duty with 48th F.A today from No 2 C.C.S.	ca

C Clarke Lt Col RAMC
O.C. 1st 8th Field Ambulance
30/9/17-

Confidential

War Diary
of
48th Field Ambulance.

Vol. 27

From 1st Oct: 1917 to 31st Oct: 1917.

VOLUME 22
124.

Army Form C. 2118.

WAR DIARY
or
INTELLIGENCE SUMMARY.
(Erase heading not required.)

48th FIELD AMBULANCE

Place	Date	Hour	Summary of Events and Information	Remarks and references to Appendices
REIGERSBURG	Oct 1st		111th Brigade Order No 161 App 14 received stating that an offensive attack would take place early morning of 2/3 oct a day	a
	Oct 2nd		A.D.M.S. order 37th Div RAMC No 62 copy 1 received stating that 111th & 63rd Brigades would attack on a two Brigade front on a path to be notified D.R.	
			A.D.M.S. 37th Division instructed O.C. 48th F.A. to form an Advanced Dressing Station for walking wounded at Voormezeele. O.C. 48th Field Ambulance to be responsible for the evacuation of walking wounded. Track to be clearly marked by pointing hand flags as follows —	a
			Regimental aid posts — CANADA STREET — TROLLEY LINE to KNOLL ROAD — WOODEN ROAD — a point about 1.28.c.8.9. — along TROLLEY LINE via LOCK 8 to Walking Wounded Collecting Station at VOORMEZEELE.	

Army Form C. 2118.

WAR DIARY
or
INTELLIGENCE SUMMARY.
(*Erase heading not required.*)

Place	Date	Hour	Summary of Events and Information	Remarks and references to Appendices
KEERSEBROM	Oct 3rd		Tent Subdivisions of B & C sections transferred from KEERSEBROM by Horse Ambulance Wagons to VOORMEZEELE. 1.31.c.3.9. to form advanced dressing station for walking wounded. Walking wounded to be evacuated to 58th Field Ambulance KEMMEL BREWERY. Tomorrow by motor lorries.	
VOORMEZEELE	Oct 4		37th Div. (111th & 63rd Brigades attached) commenced operations SHREWSBURY FOREST at 6 a.m. today J.25. JSheet 28. Edition 3. 48th Field Ambulance stationed at VOORMEZEELE 1.31. to receive walking wounded about mid-day. Large numbers of the wounded walking down by track. Regimental Aid Posts – CANADA STREET – Wooden Road – Jolley Lunn, put lock 8 to VOORMEZEELE reported that they had been held up by heavy barrage fire. All wounded men were given hot coffee & bread, wounds were re-dressed and anti tetanus serum loss units given.	

Army Form C. 2118.

WAR DIARY
or
INTELLIGENCE SUMMARY.
(Erase heading not required.)

Place	Date	Hour	Summary of Events and Information	Remarks and references to Appendices
VOORMEZEELE	Oct 4th		Cases were then evacuated to KEMMEL Brewery by motor lorries supplied by Corps	a
do	Oct 5th		Walking wounded from the Battle of BROODSENDE continued to arrive at No 48 F.A. A.D.S. throughout the day and night. The great majority of the cases were mild due to H.E. Shell fragments.	a
do	Oct 6th		Wounded from the battle have practically ceased to arrive and an order was received from A.D.M.S. 37 Div to close A.D.S. at VOORMEZEELE at 12 mid-day today. Total walking wounded evacuated at 48th F.A. (A.D.S.) Oct 4th - 6th = 347. Above order from A.D.M.S. cancelled. A.D.S. at VOORMEZEELE to remain open. Staff to consist of two subdivisions.	a

Army Form C. 2118.

WAR DIARY
or
INTELLIGENCE SUMMARY.
(Erase heading not required.)

Instructions regarding War Diaries and Intelligence Summaries are contained in F.S. Regs., Part II. and the Staff Manual respectively. Title pages will be prepared in manuscript.

137

Place	Date	Hour	Summary of Events and Information	Remarks and references to Appendices
GON 6W VOORMEZEELE	6/10	OM	Batt of BROODSENDE. ON 1/10 personnel to the 1048th F.A. under instructions received from A.D.M.S 137 Div. had reported to O.C. 49 F.A. 3 Brant Advanomos = 98 m.m. and 3 officers. Other Brant Advanomos and officers worked under orders of O.C. 49 F.A. who was responsible for clearing the line of wounded. Lim { Adv sector J.20.d.5.8. { Angle sector J.25.6.2.8. 1048 { Two medical officers stationed at CANADA STREET (A to G) F.A. { on medical " " " LARCH WOOD (A to G) Gallant Conduct 1 Pte. Cart. B section. 46 F.A. whom a number of bearers squad 4 m.m. pushing trolley from CANADA STREET to LARCH WOOD was struck in thigh by shell fragment but continued to push trolley to LARCH WOOD when he collapsed. Str. 18 wounded near FOSSE WOOD. reported by Cpt Scott Barnes	

Army Form C. 2118.

WAR DIARY
or
INTELLIGENCE SUMMARY.
(Erase heading not required.)

Place	Date	Hour	Summary of Events and Information	Remarks and references to Appendices
VOORMEZEELE	Oct 6		Gallant Conduct. Oct 3rd at BODMIN COPSE between 2.30 & 3 A.M. A soldier was buried by shell fire. German shells were bursting within a few yards every 5 seconds. Pte Milne 48 F.A. R.A.M.C. showed a fine example of courage, he rallied his party and rescued the buried man after 10 minutes work, to extricate the wounded man. Pte Milne encouraged the men who helped him throughout the time. Recommended by Capt. J.E. Mackenzie M.O. i/c 13th R.F.	a
	Oct 8		A.D.M.S. ordt. 2064 Copy W.I. recurring O.C. 48th F.A. to be responsible for the clearing of the line from Regimental Aid Posts to LARCH WOOD. He will have at his disposal: 9. 48 F.A. 2 Bearers. 2 Bearers 49 F.A. 6.0 Bearers 50. F.A.	a

WAR DIARY
or
INTELLIGENCE SUMMARY.

Army Form C. 2118.

Place	Date	Hour	Summary of Events and Information	Remarks and references to Appendices
LARCH WOOD. HILL. 60	Oct 8		In compliance with A.D.M.S. order No 64 - 8/10/17. today went to (LARCH WOOD) TUNNELS. HILL 60 and made his Headquarters there at 9 p.m. (I.29.c.2.7)	O.C. 48 Fd
I.29.c.2.7			At 10 p.m. O.C. 48th Field Ambulance in company with Capt. Wishart R.A.M.C. O/c 112th Brigade at Headquarters visited O.C. CANADA STREET (A.D.S.) & HEDGE STREET TUNNELS. It was reported (by Pigeon Post) that some wounded were at the Central R.A.P. East of DUMBARTON LAKES. 7 stretcher bearers were asked for to clear this post. Guide arranged for by 112th Brigade H.Q. to call at CANADA STREET A.D.S. at 8 a.m. 9/10/17 to guide 3 squads to the post. N trying impossible to reach the post across the Dumbarton Lake district by night.	
do.	Oct 9th		Three squads (12 Bearers & 1 NCO) and Brigade guide left CANADA STREET A.D.S. at 8 a.m. this morning. The 3 squads were heavily shelled before they	

A 5834 Wt. W4973/M687 750,000 8/16 D. D. & L. Ltd Forms/C.2118/13.

Army Form C. 2118.

WAR DIARY
or
INTELLIGENCE SUMMARY.
(Erase heading not required.)

Instructions regarding War Diaries and Intelligence Summaries are contained in F. S. Regs., Part II. and the Staff Manual respectively. Title pages will be prepared in manuscript.

Place	Date	Hour	Summary of Events and Information	Remarks and references to Appendices
LARCH WOOD	Oct. 9th		had advanced more than 2 or 3 hundred yards towards the Front line, when a shell burst near them, killing the guide from the Brigade H.Q. and one stretcher bearer. 5 other stretcher bearers were wounded. The remainder returned to CANADA STREET A.D.S. Officers of CANADA STREET. A.D.S. reports that night of Oct 8th-9th was quiet. Only 2 stretcher cases & 2 walking wounded passing through.	a
Do.	Oct 10th	9 a.m.	Officer i/c CANADA STREET A.D.S. reports that during last 24 hours 2 stretcher cases and 79 walking cases have been passed through the A.D.S. to LARCH WOOD. The Jolly run from CANADA STREET to LARCH WOOD is shelled daily by "shell fire", this line is in my opinion for evacuation of wounded. Yesterday 14 casualties occurred amongst the personnel of the Bearer Company. 4 killed or died of wounds (Pte BARNES, LOVEKIN, Pte BEDFORD, SIMS.) 10 wounded.	a

Army Form C. 2118.

WAR DIARY
or
INTELLIGENCE SUMMARY.
(Erase heading not required.)

Place	Date	Hour	Summary of Events and Information	Remarks and references to Appendices
LARCH WOOD HILL 60	Oct 10		The Central R.A.P. mentioned on 9th Oct. was closed & wounded by Sgt Carthy 49th F.A. with 5 squads of bearers. Disposition of bearer squads. 112th Brigade holding the line. 3 Battalions in the front line south of YPRES Rd to MENIN was TOWER HAMLETS. 1 Battalion in support at BODMIN COPSE. Right RAP = 4 squads + 1 N.C.O. Centre RAP = 3 " " " Left RAP = 2 " " " Support RAP = 4 " " " at CANADA STREET A.D.S. 2 Medical Officers + 8 squads in advanced reserve. at LARCH WOOD in Reserve 15 squads. Each Bearer squad which collected a case at an R.A.P. carried the case back to LARCH WOOD (A.D.S) when the squad rejoined the Reserve and took its place at bottom of Roster. The squads worked on the ration chain principle	c

Army Form C. 2118.

WAR DIARY
or
INTELLIGENCE SUMMARY.
(Erase heading not required.)

Place	Date	Hour	Summary of Events and Information	Remarks and references to Appendices
LARCH WOOD	Oct 11th		Capt Wishart RAMC O/c A.D.S. CANADA STREET reports that 112 cases passed through the A.D.S on their way to LARCH WOOD during the last 24 hours. Most of the cases were wounded at CANADA STREET by shell fire amgst. Ration parties and reinforcements being caught by enemy shell fire on their way up to front line. No casualties reported amongst the personnel.	a
do	Oct 12.		O/c CANADA STREET A.D.S. LARCH WOOD reports that 70 cases were evacuated to A.D.S. LARCH WOOD during last 24 hours forward posts clear, no casualties amongst personnel.	a
	Oct 13.		O/c CANADA STREET ADS reports 73 cases evacuated through his A.D.S during last 24 hours. No casualties amongst personnel. O.C. 48th F.A. handed over command of forward Bearer to O.C. 49. F.A. today under instructions received from A.D.M.S. 2nd Division	a

A5834 Wt.W4973/M687 750,000 8/16 D. D. & L. Ltd. Forms/C.2118/13.

Army Form C. 2118.

WAR DIARY
or
INTELLIGENCE SUMMARY.
(Erase heading not required.)

Place	Date	Hour	Summary of Events and Information	Remarks and references to Appendices
McGILLIGAN CAMP.	Oct 14.		Sent Subaltern with equipment of No 1 & 8th F.A. posted at Voormezeele. To deal with walking wounded in connection with 49 F.A.	
BAILLEUL			No 14 & 48 F.A. under instructions received from A.D.M.S. 37 Division withdrawn today to Capt. MARSHALL posted to Heavy Artillery Group	
	Oct 15		LIEUT WOODSEND returned today to 48 F.A. from duty in the line with 49th F.A.	
	Oct 16		Bearer squads returned from duty in the line with 49th F.A. today being transported from VOORMEZEELE by MOTOR BUSSES to BAILLEUL	
			Capt WISHART returned to duty today from 49th F.A.	
	Oct 17		From today sick of 111th Brigade situated in LOCRE. DRAVOUTRE area to be dealt daily by 49th F.A. McGILLIGAN CAMP to be run as a DRESSING STATION 37 Division being most withdrawn from the line.	

WAR DIARY or **INTELLIGENCE SUMMARY**
Army Form C. 2118.

Place	Date	Hour	Summary of Events and Information	Remarks and references to Appendices
6 NOV 17. McGILLIGAN CAMP. BAILLEUL.			List of Casualties incurred by 1/48th Field Ambulance in fighting about TOWER HAMLETS - SHREWSBURY FOREST. from Sept 28th to October 11th 1917. **Killed in action** 9/10/17 37409. Pte. BEDFORD. T. H. 2/10/17 38012. Pte. BROADBENT. O. B. **Died of wounds** 3/10/17 38827 Pte. BAIN. J. 9/10/17 39324 Pte. BARNES. M. 9/10/17 50213 Pte. LOVERIN. W. 6/10/17 36188 Pte. FLEMING. J attached A.S.C. .. H.T (17th H.L.I.)	

Army Form C. 2118.

WAR DIARY
or
INTELLIGENCE SUMMARY.
(Erase heading not required.)

Place	Date	Hour	Summary of Events and Information	Remarks and references to Appendices
McGILLIGAN CAMP BAILLEUL	Oct '17		Wounded	
			1/10/17 (40508) Sgt Ashmore T slight in arm. returned to duty.	
			2/10/17 38024 " Brookes. C.E. gassed.	
			3/10/17 89246 " Jait. A.Y. gassed.	
			2/10/17 38134 Corp. Fray. R. gassed.	
			2/10/17 38106 L/Corp. Chapman. J.H. gassed.	
			2/10/17 42679 2/Corp. Park. D. gassed.	
			5/10/17 92971 Pte. Baillie. W.	
			9/10/17 40422 pte Barker. B.	
			30/9/17 38333 pte Botterill. W.J. gassed	
			3/10/17 37413 pte Bradshaw. A.	
			5/10/17 93879 pte Butro J.M. gassed	
			3/10/17 58575 pte Catt. E.	
			4/10/17 40465 pte Cartlidge J.G.	
			1/10/17 78637 pte Cottingham A.	
			9/10/17 93861 pte Graham D. gassed	
			1/10/17 69210 pte Herron W gassed	
			5/10/17 42467 pte Lewis A gassed	
			3/10/17 50217 pte McCarthy. J.	
			28/9/17 47312 pte O'Connell. O	
			29/9/17 7182 pte Onejet	
			6/10/17 74156 pte O'Rhum gassed	
			9/10/17 88227 pte Pye. A.E.	
			3/10/17 42698 pte Williams A.G. gassed	
			9/10/17 78215 pte Woolley. W.	C

WAR DIARY
or
INTELLIGENCE SUMMARY.
(Erase heading not required.)

Army Form C. 2118.

Place	Date	Hour	Summary of Events and Information	Remarks and references to Appendices
M^cGILLIGAN CAMP	Oct 10		In compliance with instructions received from A.D.M.S. 37 Division O.C. 1 & 8th Field Ambulance took over KEERSEBROM CAMP BAILLEUL from O.C. 134 Field Ambulance today. 57 patients in the Camp were also taken over from O.C. 134 F.A.	u
do	Oct 14		23323 Pte MILES & 38545 Pte CARR both 1 & 8th Field Ambulance were awarded the Military Medal today for gallant conduct in the field. Pte MILES on Oct 3rd for "BODMIN COPSE" Pte Carr Oct 12th near LARCH WOOD	a
do	Oct 20		The Camp at M^c GILLIGAN CAMP is now used as a Dressing Station which the KEERSEBROM Camp is used as a Rest Station. The patients in each camp numbering about 80. Trench feet & Catarrh account for most of the patients. The patients are admitted from 111th Brigade	u

WAR DIARY
or
INTELLIGENCE SUMMARY.

Army Form C. 2118.

Place	Date	Hour	Summary of Events and Information	Remarks and references to Appendices
McGILLIGAN CAMP	Oct 22nd		Lt. W. St Clair McClure RAMC posted to 37th Div. R.E. as presumed medical Officer in Charge.	
	25th		1st Lt J. C. Rote U.S.M.C. took over temporary medical charge 10th Royal Fusiliers.	
	26th		Owing to the shelling of Bailleul by a high velocity german gun 150 patients were transferred today to KEERSEBROK Camp for a few hours. 2 p.m. – 6.30 p.m. as the shell was falling near 50th Field Ambulance in BAILLEUL.	a
	do		Inspection of 48th Field Ambulance by Col. Wilson DDMS IX Corps. Verbal intimation received from DDMS 6 marquees were indented for from IX Corps for KEERSEBROM CAMP.	c
	30th		BAILLEUL shelled by german long range gun again today. 9 am to 5 pm. Shell being fired as they hourly intervals 1/50 patients transferred from 50th F.A. to 48th F.A. for period 10am – 7 pm.	a

WAR DIARY
or
INTELLIGENCE SUMMARY.
(Erase heading not required.)

Army Form C. 2118.

Place	Date	Hour	Summary of Events and Information	Remarks and references to Appendices
McGILLIGAN CAMP.	Oct 30th		1st Lieut J. M. Bloomfield U.S.M.C. posted to 48th F.A. for duty.	
do	Oct 31st		1st Lt. S. R. Marcum U.S.M.C. posted to 48th F.A. for duty. Sgt Brockert R.A.M.C. awarded a bar to his M.M. and 2 Cpl field a M.M. for gallantry in the field. Under instructions received from A.D.M.S. 37th Div. today, the 50 stretchers supplied by 48 F.A. to the HAGEDOORNE CAMP, Bailleul (Dysentery Hospital) are to be replaced by 63 stretchers from McGILLIGAN CAMP. MEDICAL EQUIPMENT. The 50 stretchers on loan to the Dysentery Hospital to be part of the McGILLIGAN MEDICAL EQUIPMENT on temporary loan.	

Clark Lt Col A.M.C.
O.C. 48th F.A.
Ambulance

VOLUME 28
PAGE 149

WAR DIARY
INTELLIGENCE SUMMARY

Army Form C. 2118.

Place	Date	Hour	Summary of Events and Information	Remarks and references to Appendices
McGILLIGAN CAMP BAILLEUL	Mar 1st		Telephone message received from A.D.M.S. 37th Div. Capt WISHART R.A.M.C. to report for duty with O.C. 50 F.A. in "Nor 2" at HAEGEDOORNE CAMP. BAILLEUL.	a short Ed. 3.
do	2nd		Capt Wishart proceeded for duty with 50 F.A. in compliance with above order	"
do	5th		Instructions received 9 the award of D.C.M. to Sgt Ashurn 9/48th F.A.	" Ed. 3.
do	6th		Lt Woodward proceeded for temporary duty with 6th Bradford Regt.	"
do	10th		Transport Completion 37 Divisnry & 8th F.A. now 1st pony ford, transport 9 a field ambulance.	"
do	11th		Lieut Scott U.S.M.S. posted to permanent change as medical officer 9 10th York & Lancashire Regt.	"

WAR DIARY
or
INTELLIGENCE SUMMARY.
(Erase heading not required.)

Army Form C. 2118.

Place	Date	Hour	Summary of Events and Information	Remarks and references to Appendices
McGILIGAN CAMP	Jan 7th		Capt Martin R.A.M.C. proceed for duty today with 48th F.A. In compliance with A.D.M.S. order 69 an advance party was sent under Cpl Scott to KEMMEL BRASSERIE to take over. Clearing of line from O.C. 58th F.A. 19th Div.	
	Jan 8.		The Bearer Sp. of 8th Field ambulance relieving the Bearer Sp 58th field ambulance today. 19 spuds four teams each hung with in the Compound. The line being cleared extended from the YPRES COMINES CANAL Spout HOLLEBEKE thence in front 7 H.4.60 to a point east of MOUNT SORREL when the front of the Division in the line joins the front hill by that of the Division. 19th Division in the line & cleared by 8th F.A. 37 Division	

Army Form C. 2118.

WAR DIARY
or
INTELLIGENCE SUMMARY.
(Erase heading not required.)

Instructions regarding War Diaries and Intelligence Summaries are contained in F. S. Regs., Part II. and the Staff Manual respectively. Title pages will be prepared in manuscript.

Place	Date	Hour	Summary of Events and Information	Remarks and references to Appendices
KEMMEL	Nov 8		The following posts are then nor. A.D.S at LARCH. WOOD & at SPOIL BANK RELAY Post at VESUVIUS and S.T ELOI crossroads. Headquarters of 48th Field Ambulance are situated from MCGILLIGAN. CAMP. BAILLEUL. to BRAISERIE	
do.	9.		KEMMEL. Capt MARTIN 48 F.A. remained at McGILLIGAN CAMP. in charge of the Dressing Station there 102 patients (exclusive of the Hospital cases) 58th Field Ambulance marched from KEMMEL today to BAILLEUL when they are accommodated in the KEERSEBROM CAMP.	

Place	Date	Hour	Summary of Events and Information	Remarks and references to Appendices
KEMMEL	Aug 10		The 63rd Infantry Brigade marched today from the LOCRE area to BOIS AREA (O.i.e.) (N.6.d) (N.12.a) Brigade closed in the march by 48th F.A.	
KEMMEL	Aug 11		Lieut MAXEIMER U.S.M.S. on detail today to proceed to VOORMEZEELE with an advanced party and look over the A.D.S. there. Ambulance cars moved from LATERIE YORK R? KEMMEL to VOORMEZEELE. Instructions received from A.D.M.S. 37 Div about 70. 48 field ambulance was detailed to take over posts from 96 fld ambulance at IRON BRIDGE (O.4.6.3.3) and at the MOUND near ST. ELOI. can Roads. taking over completed today	

Army Form C. 2118.

WAR DIARY
or
INTELLIGENCE SUMMARY.
(Erase heading not required.)

Place	Date	Hour	Summary of Events and Information	Remarks and references to Appendices
KEMMEL and VOORMEZEELE	Nov. 12th		A.D.M.S. orders W.71. received today. 2 & 3rd Field Ambulance to hand over KEMMEL BRASSERIE to 49th F.A. and proceed to VOORMEZEELE.	Sheet 28. Ed. 3
do	13.		Had quarters D.1 & 8th Field Ambulance. Transferred to VOORMEZEELE. A.D.S. Train.	
			Lieut ROTE U.S.M.S. posted for temporary medical charge to 10th Loyal North Lancs.	u
			28 sick and 11 wounded evacuated to 49th Field Ambulance. Kemmel.	u
VOORMEZEELE	14th		54 sick and 11 wounded evacuated to 49th F.A. today.	
VOORMEZEELE	15th		A.D.M.S. order W.72 dated 15.11.17. received. 42 sick and 5 wounded evacuated to 49th F.A.	u
			6 sick and 4 wounded evacuated to C.C.S. BAILLEUL x.e. 12 tunnels in divisional area.	u

Army Form C. 2118.

WAR DIARY
or
INTELLIGENCE SUMMARY.
(Erase heading not required.)

Place	Date	Hour	Summary of Events and Information	Remarks and references to Appendices
VOORMEZEELE	16th		30 sick evacuated to 4th 9th F.A. at KEMMEL. 16 sick and 5 wounded evacuated to C.C.S. BAILLEUL	a
do	17th		In compliance with A.D.M.S. order 72. dated 15-11-17. McGILLIGAN CAMP and KEERSEBROM CAMP. BAILLEUL were handed over to O.C. 50th F.A. today. Capt MARKIN and personnel of 4th 8th F.A. joining Headquarters of 48th F.A. at VOORMEZEELE today. 30 sick and 15 wounded evacuated to 4th 9th F.A. 1 sick and 6 wounded evacuated to C.C.S. BAILLEUL	
do	18th		Plans submitted to A.D.M.S. 37 div. for construction of A.D.S. at VOORMEZEELE. 9 & 3 Elephant iron shelters each 27 ft long. with shell proof covering 9 concrete. Plans also submitted for Field Ambulance Horse lines at Brasserie Vierstraat	

WAR DIARY
or
INTELLIGENCE SUMMARY.

Army Form C. 2118.

Place	Date	Hour	Summary of Events and Information	Remarks and references to Appendices
VOORMEZEELE	18th		31 sick and 1 wounded evacuated to 49th F.A.	c
do.	19th		7 sick and 8 wounded evacuated to C.C.S. BAILLEUL	c
			34 sick evacuated to 49th F.A	
			3 sick and 7 wounded evacuated to C.C.S. BAILLEUL	c
do	20th		4 sick and 3 wounded evacuated to 49th F.A.	c
			2 sick and 3 wounded " " C.C.S BAILLEUL	
do	21st		Work commenced today on the construction of the new A.D.S. Shelters at VOORMEZEELE. under direction from R.E. 37 Div. – 29 sick + 4 wounded evacuated to 49th F.A – 4 wounded to C.C.S. The Bearers from 48th, 49th + 50th Field Ambulances work in three separate parties. Each party of 60 N.C.O. + men doin 3 days duty in the Bearer Posts and 6 days resting in VOORMEZEELE or BRASSERIE VIERSTRAAT.	c

WAR DIARY or INTELLIGENCE SUMMARY

Army Form C. 2118.

Place	Date	Hour	Summary of Events and Information	Remarks and references to Appendices
VOORMEZEELE	22		22 sick and 1 wounded evacuated to 49th F.A.	
do	23		3 wounded evacuated to C.C.S. Lieut Woodward RAMC posted for duty as M.O. 6. 6th Beds.	c
do	24		Capt. MARTIN. RAMC detailed for duty as M.O. to Middlesex. 22 sick and 10 wounded evacuated to 49th F.A. 1 wounded evacuated to C.C.S.	
do	25		27 sick and 1 wounded evacuated to 49th F.A. The dead body of Dr McGINLEY was brought to the ADS VOORMEZEELE from 146 Co. ATRE death was due to bullet wound left thigh, reports I sent on were AIM 39 on white[?]	c
do	26		16 sick and 1 wounded evacuated to 49th F.A.	c
do	27		31 sick and 2 wounded evacuated to 49th F.A. 23 sick and 1 wounded " " 49th F.A	c

WAR DIARY
or
INTELLIGENCE SUMMARY.
(Erase heading not required.)

Army Form C. 2118.

Place	Date	Hour	Summary of Events and Information	Remarks and references to Appendices
VOORMEZEELE	28th		23 sick and 15 wounded evacuated to 1/49th F.A.	
			Lieut. ROTE (U.S.) (R.C.) att. Troop duty, on M.O. to 10th Loyal North Lancs front and sustained injury admitted to Hospital. (sick)	
do	29		Lieut WATKINS U.S.M.O.R.C reported for temporary duty from 50th F.A.	
			31 sick and 11 wounded evacuated to 1/49th F.A.	
do	30th		Lieut TOULSON. U.S.M.O.R.C returned to 1/49th F.A for duty from 1/8th F.A.	
			21 sick and 20 wounded evacuated to 1/49th F.A.	

C Clarke Lt Col R.A.M.C.
O.C 48th Field Ambulance

CONFIDENTIAL

War Diary
of 48th Field Ambulance
from 1st Decr 1917 to 31st Decr 1917.

Volume 29.

COMMITTEE FOR THE MEDICAL HISTORY OF THE WAR
Date -1 FEB. 1918

VOLUME 29

WAR DIARY
or
INTELLIGENCE SUMMARY.

Army Form C. 2118.

Place	Date	Hour	Summary of Events and Information	Remarks and references to Appendices
VOORMEZEELE	Dec 1st		General Situation. H.Q. 5th Field Ambulance Headquarters at Voormezeele Brasserie. Advanced Dressing Station and Ambulance Car Stand with Chief Advanced Dressing Station at LARCH WOOD — Lypsalis (down to Voormezeele). " " " " SPOIL BANK — Crate " " " " VESUVIUS (S² 3.107³) — Ryper Statin Railway Post Erection of new horse lines at Brasserie VIERSTRAAT commenced today.	YPRES BRASSERIE 28 N W4 Ed 3 3
do	1st		Evacuation of Casualties: 6 "49" F.A. sick 14. wounded 4	4
do	2.		Evacuation of Casualties: 6 "49" F.A. s 25. " 4	3
do	3.		Evacuation of Casualties: 6 "49" F.A. s 14. " 2	2

WAR DIARY
or
INTELLIGENCE SUMMARY.
(Erase heading not required.)

Army Form C. 2118.

Place	Date	Hour	Summary of Events and Information	Remarks and references to Appendices
VOORMEZEELE	Dec 4th		Lt. WATKINS R.A.M.C. returned to duty with 50th F.A. from 48th F.A.	a
	5th		Evacuation of Casualties to 49th F.A. 23 sick and 1 wounded	a
	6th		do do 22 sick and 10 wounded	a
			do do 17 sick and 1 wounded	
	Dec 7th		Capt. Scott R.A.M.C. evacuated sick to 49th Field Ambulance.	a
			Evacuation of Casualties to 49th F.A. 16 sick and 4 wounded.	a
			" " " " 6 sick and 2 wounded	
	Dec 8th		" " " " 18 sick and 7 wounded	a
	Dec 9th		" " " "	a
	Dec 10th		" " " " 15 sick and 10 wounded	a
			Considerable progress has been made with constructional work by the	

Army Form C. 2118.

WAR DIARY
or
INTELLIGENCE SUMMARY.
(Erase heading not required.)

Place	Date	Hour	Summary of Events and Information	Remarks and references to Appendices
VOORMEZEELE	Dec 16	null	84 NCOs and men are signed constantly in the line to staff the Lyts. Central and Right Beam Posts. The Beams are relieved every third day, each party spend working for 3 days in the line and 6 days out of the line. During the time out of the line the parties are distributed as follows: 20 men at KEMMEL on working party constructing HQ 11th FA Home line. 20 men at Brasserie. VIERSTRAAT " " 48 F.A. 25 men at VOORMEZEELE constructing concrete dugouts for A.D.S. stationed at VOORMEZEELE. The cupola iron & concrete dugouts at VOORMEZEELE are constructed to hold 36 stretcher cases and about 60 walking cases. Three iron cupolas each 27 feet long are being built side by side with a concrete passage way connecting the three cupolas. One cupola is being fitted up as an operating room, 2 cupolas in waiting rooms for cases which have been dressed	

Army Form C. 2118.

WAR DIARY
or
INTELLIGENCE SUMMARY.
(Erase heading not required.)

Place	Date	Hour	Summary of Events and Information	Remarks and references to Appendices
VOORMEZEELE	Dec 10		The cupolas open in to the road, when the ambulance cars are stationed and the lack of running water to the VOORMEZEELE Station is the lack of the A.D.S. M. McClure reported for temporary duty today. Evacuation of Casualties to 49th F.A. Sick 19, wounded 3. Capt Southam returned today.	ce
do	Dec 11		" " " " Sick 16, wounded 7.	ce
do	Dec 12		" " " " Sick 20, wounded 2.	ce
do	Dec 13		" " " " Sick 33, wounded 4.	ce
do	Dec 14		" " " " Sick 11, wounded 4.	ce
do	Dec 15		" " " " Sick 22, wounded 5.	ce
do	Dec 16		A.D.S. VOORMEZEELE inspected today by D.D.M.S. IX Corps and A.D.M.S. 37 Div.	ce
do	Dec 17		Evacuation of casualties to 49th F.A. Sick 24, wounded 9	ce
do	Dec 18		" " " 49th F.A. " 35 " 10	ce

WAR DIARY
or
INTELLIGENCE SUMMARY.
(Erase heading not required.)

Army Form C. 2118.

Place	Date	Hour	Summary of Events and Information	Remarks and references to Appendices
VOORMEZEELE.	Dec 19th		Capt S. Rutherford RAMC and Lieut M.B. GUNN RAMC arrived today for duty with 48th Field Ambulance.	
do			Lieut W. St. C. McClure rejoined his unit 37th D'v R.E. today. Evacuations to 49th Field Ambulance sick 16 wounded 8	
do	Dec 20th		Lieut Gunn detailed for temporary medical charge 8" Somerset L.I. Evacuations to 49th Field Ambulance sick 19. wounded 13.	
do	Dec 21st		Lieut Marcus U.S. MO.R.C. detailed to take medical charge of 8" Somerset L.I. vice Lt Gunn. Evacuations to 49th Field Ambulance sick 14: wounded 3.	
do	Dec 22nd		Lieut Bloomfield U.S. M.O.R.C detailed to medical charge 13 K.R.R.C. vice Capt Martin RAMC Evacuations sick 16. wounded 15.	
do	Dec 23rd		Capt Martin RAMC reported for duty today with 48th Field Ambulance Evacuations sick 8 - wounded 19.	

WAR DIARY or INTELLIGENCE SUMMARY

Army Form C. 2118.

Place	Date	Hour	Summary of Events and Information	Remarks and references to Appendices
VOORMEZEELE	Dec 24		Evacuations Sick 13. and wounded 7. A considerable number of gas cases occur, they are slight in character, chief symptoms are slight vomiting, conjunctivitis, pharyngitis. German gas shells are fired nightly on ridges of Mt60 and BATTLE WOOD	
			Evacuation Sick 11 wounded nil.	
do.	Dec 25		Evacuation Sick 13 wounded 7. Some of the milder gas cases were observed in LARCH WOOD tunnels.	
	Dec 26		Trench feet. The troops occupying the hard hits are on changed every 24 hours. The men's feet are thoroughly washed and then powdered with Camphor and Boracic Ac. powder. Dry socks are supplied and frequently changed. The ground is frozen hard, and weather conditions are established. A few cases of Trench feet evacuated through the A.D.S. are few in number and mild in character. The prevailing type being painful and oedematous in character.	

WAR DIARY or INTELLIGENCE SUMMARY

Army Form C. 2118.

Place	Date	Hour	Summary of Events and Information	Remarks and references to Appendices
VOORMEZEELE	Dec 26.		During the present month the average number of cases evacuated per day has been 2.	
do	Dec 27.		Evacuations Sick 36 wounded 6.	
do	28		Evacuations Sick 46 wounded 7.	
do	Dec 29th		Lieut Grimm R.A.M.C. evacuated to Hospital sick with Bronchial Catarrh on the night train of 29th Dec (eng). Evacuations sick 13 wounded 2.	
do	Dec 30th		Capt. Milton R.A.M.C. evacuated sick to Hospital train 102° P.O.O. D.S.R. MAJ EINER U.S.M.O.R.C. posted to permanent to Medical Charge of 8th Surreal R.J.	
do	Dec 31st		Evacuations Sick 30. wounded 3. Cumulative Sick 13 wounded 4. Including 31 Dec. 59 cases of sickness has been evacuated during the month. Strength of the unit Officers 6. R.A.M.C. personnel 180. A.S.C. personnel { Horse transport 25, R.B. men 6, M.T. 11. Wanting to complete strength Officers 3. — O.R. R.A.M.C. 2 — O.R. A.S.C. 2 — O.R. M.B. 4.	

C. Clark Lt.Col. R.A.M.C.
O.C. 4th Field Ambulance

Confidential.

WAR DIARY

48th Field Ambulance
from
1st January 1918 to 31st January 1918.

Volume 30.

Volume 30
Page 165

Army Form C. 2118.

WAR DIARY
or
INTELLIGENCE SUMMARY.
(Erase heading not required.)

Instructions regarding War Diaries and Intelligence Summaries are contained in F.S. Regs., Part II. and the Staff Manual respectively. Title pages will be prepared in manuscript.

Place	Date	Hour	Summary of Events and Information	Remarks and references to Appendices
VOORMEZEELE	Jan 1st		General Situation. J.48th Field Ambulance clearing the line. Forward fever posts situated at the 4 Regimental Aid Posts	YPRES 28. NW ed. 3
			Right R.A.P. at Iron Bridge on YPRES COMINES CANAL. O.4.a.6.2.	
			Right Centre R.A.P. at BATTLE WOOD — I.36.c.3.0	
			Left Centre R.A.P. " " — I.36.c.2.6.	
			Left R.A.P. — — — — — J.25.c.9.3	
			One medical officer at A.D.S. LARCH WOOD.	
			One medical officer at A.D.S. SPOIL BANK	
			Headquarters and A.D.S. at VOORMEZEELE.	
			83 Bearers on ground to staff the bearer posts.	
			Line of Evacuation. From Left R.A.P. by three relays to LARCH WOOD A.D.S. thence IMAGE TRENCH and via ZWARTELEN. from LARCH WOOD by BUCKSHOT TRACK to VERBRANDEN ROAD and thence by Ambulance Car to VOORMEZEELE	

Army Form C. 2118.

WAR DIARY
or
INTELLIGENCE SUMMARY.
(Erase heading not required.)

Instructions regarding War Diaries and Intelligence Summaries are contained in F. S. Regs., Part II. and the Staff Manual respectively. Title pages will be prepared in manuscript.

166

Place	Date	Hour	Summary of Events and Information	Remarks and references to Appendices
VOORMEZEELE	Jan 1st		Evacuation. From the two centre R.A.P.s by O.A.F. TRENCH to IRON BRIDGE along CANAL BANK to NORFOLK LODGE and then to SPOIL BANK A.D.S. From the Right R.A.P. at IRON BRIDGE along the CANAL to NORFOLK LODGE and then to SPOIL BANK A.D.S. From SPOIL BANK A.D.S. by ambulance car to VOORMEZEELE. From the A.D.S. at VOORMEZEELE the cases are carried by ambulance cars to KEMMEL. (49th F.A.) HORSE LINES, 9/48th F.A. are stationed at BRASSERIE VIERSTRAAT.	a
	Jan 2nd		Lieut GUNN R.A.M.C. returns from Hospital today. Evacuations to 49th Field Ambulance. Sick 22. wounded 2.	a
	Jan 3rd		Capt MERRIN R.A.M.C. returns from Hospital today. Evacuations. Sick 20. wounded 3	a
			A/Sgt M/27701 Bowler. A.E. A.S.C. M.T. reported for duty today in charge of mechanical transport vice Sgt Jeffery R/C Evacuations sick 16 wounded 1.	a

Army Form C. 2118.

WAR DIARY
or
INTELLIGENCE SUMMARY.
(Erase heading not required.)

Place	Date	Hour	Summary of Events and Information	Remarks and references to Appendices
VOORMEZEELE	Jan 5th		Continued but found progress of work on sky blue then cupolas at VOORMEZEELE. as no cement can be placed over the top of the cupolas.	
do	6"		The interior work for each cupola is largely finished two cupolas having proven to hold 36 British Cavs. (8" in cap) The cupolas are painted white inside, fitted with electric light and closed by doors at each end.	
			Evacuations wounded 2. sick 14.	
	7"		" " 4. " 15.	To A.A. 9th F.A.
	8		" " 1. " 14.	
			" " 8 " 9	
			" " 1 " 7	
do	Jan 9		In compliance with instructions received from HQRS. 1 syk (shelterum) and 8 horses with orderlies were attached to 13th K.R.R.C. this afternoon a raiding party of 5 bombers this evening, in attacking the german line, left Battle W'Good. and the extra squad on to perform the rescue.	
			Evacuations wounded 5. sick 10.	

Army Form C. 2118.

WAR DIARY
or
INTELLIGENCE SUMMARY.
(Erase heading not required.)

Instructions regarding War Diaries and Intelligence Summaries are contained in F.S. Regs., Part II. and the Staff Manual respectively. Title pages will be prepared in manuscript.

Place	Date	Hour	Summary of Events and Information	Remarks and references to Appendices
VOORMEZEELE	Jan 9		Advance party party of Major Brown and Hon Sgt 12th Aust Field Amb. arrived today at H.Q. Field Ambulance Hqrs to arrange relay of 48th F.A. from the line.	C.a.
	10th		Personnel of 12th Aust F.A. arrived today and were accommodated in billets at VOORMEZEELE. 12th A.C. F.A. transport were stationed at Siege Farm near KEMMEL for the night of the 10th having arrived in this area. Transport of 48th F.A. moved by road to STRAZEELE Jan 11th	C.C.
	11th		On 11th the Bearers of 48th Field Ambulance in the line were relieved by the bearers of 12th Aust. Field Ambulance. A.D.S. at 2 ARCH WOOD — SPOIL BANK — and VOORMEZEELE were also handed over. Personnel of 48th F.A. and transport 12 Qu MTPA withdrew to Brasserie VIERSTRAAT for night of Jan 11th-12th.	C.a.
	12th		At 8:30 am Jan 12th Personnel of 48th F.A. under command Capt Withers marched from VIERSTRAAT to DICKEBUSCH RAILWAY STATION, under instructions received from 111th Brigade and entrained at 11 am for EBBLINGHAM where unit detrained at 2.0 pm. Unit marched from EBBLINGHAM by road to billets at BANDRINGHAM. Bearers VIERSTRAAT handed over to 12th Aust F.A. on 12/1/18	C.a.

Army Form C. 2118.

WAR DIARY
or
INTELLIGENCE SUMMARY.
(Erase heading not required.)

Place	Date	Hour	Summary of Events and Information	Remarks and references to Appendices
BANDAGHEM	Jan 13		118th Field Ambulance established in Billets at Bandaghem a small empty hamlet near map reference 4.B.c.1.3. converted into a Dressing Station for Sick of 111th Brigade in WAR.ORECQUES accommodating 12 patients on stretchers and capable of accommodating 20 wounded Rest Station. 50 F.A. situated at 20 on mattresses. BAILLEUL. Corps Rest Station. 11.C.C.S. at GODEWAERSVELDE Serious cases and those requiring Hospital treatment, evacuated to 15 C.C.S. EBBLINGHAM. Sitting cases to 11. C.C.S.	SHEET 36A N.W. Ed 4 1/20000
do	Jany 14		The Billets at Bandeghem are on fairly comfortable barns with clean straw; The horse lines on the common in front of the village are too exposed the horses and mules have been broken up into small parties of 6 or 7 and accommodated in the various available farm and outhouses. Weather very cold and a considerable quantity of snow has fallen, ground frozen.	

Army Form C. 2118.

WAR DIARY
or
INTELLIGENCE SUMMARY.
(Erase heading not required.)

Instructions regarding War Diaries and Intelligence Summaries are contained in F.S. Regs., Part II. and the Staff Manual respectively. Title pages will be prepared in manuscript.

170

Place	Date	Hour	Summary of Events and Information	Remarks and references to Appendices
BANDRINGHAM	Jan 15.		Personnel of No 8th Field Ambulance were marched to the Divisional Baths at BLARINGHEM today every man being given a hot shower bath and a clean change of underclothing. Each section & the Stretcher ambulances examined and received boxing on crumbs & vermin.	SHEET 36A NW Ed.4 1/20000
do	Jan 16.		The weather continues to be very bad rain at intervals every day and owing to the absence of a drying room no attempt can be made to underclothing Personnel on billets duty on billets on ungrad duties sanitary duties etc.	"
do	Jan 17.		Capt Maclagan RAMC and Lieut Hall RAMC reported for duty today. Capt Marvin RAMC posted to temporary charge of 6th Bedfords. Training of unit continued by route marches drill and lectures.	"
do	Jan 18.		Lieut Gunn RAMC proceeded today for a weeks training at IX Corps Gas School. Admission to No 48 F.A. from 111th Brigade for week ending 20/1/18 & 46. Evacuated to C.C.S. 8. — Lt. Col C. Clarke RAMC proceeded to England today on 14 days leave Capt Scott acting as O.C. 48 F.A.	"
do	Jan 28th		training advance of Lt. Col C. Clarke in England. Capt Wishart RAMC proceeded on 14 days leave & returned today	"

A 5834 Wt. W4973/M687 750,000 8/16 D. D. & L. Ltd. Forms/C.2118/13.

Army Form C. 2118.

WAR DIARY
or
INTELLIGENCE SUMMARY.
(Erase heading not required.)

191

Place	Date	Hour	Summary of Events and Information	Remarks and references to Appendices
BANDRIGHAM	Jan 21		All sections engaged in physical drill, squad & stretcher drill in the morning. Weather conditions do not yet permit of much recreational training.	S.S.
	Jan 22		In the morning "A" & "B" sections marched to BLARINGHEM & were billeted, remainder were employed in cleaning wagons, billets etc. The battn. parade for "C" section & transport in the afternoon was cancelled by order from O.C. Divisional Baths. Capt. MERRIN R.A.M.C. reported back to the unit in the evening for duty.	S.S.
	Jan 23		C.O.'s inspection parade in full marching order was held in the morning followed by squad & stretcher drill. In the afternoon a Rugby match was played against the 10th Royal Fusiliers at WARDRECQUES in which the ambulance was beaten.	S.S.
	Jan 24		Morning spent in physical, squad & stretcher drill, afternoon in recreational training, weather has improved considerably.	S.S.
	Jan 25		A detachment of 10 other ranks under the command of Capt. Renwick were sent to ARQUES to represent the R.A.M.C. of the 37th Division at the presentation of medal ribands by the Army Commander Gen. Sir N.S. Rawlinson Bart. G.C.V.O., K.C.B., K.C.M.G. commanding 4th Army, the recipients from the 48th Field Ambulance were Serg Ashmore the D.C.M., L/Corpl Field, Pte Riles & Garr the M.M.	

A 5834 Wt. W 4973/M687 750,000 8/16 D.D. & L. Ltd. Forms/C.2118/13.

WAR DIARY
or
INTELLIGENCE SUMMARY.
(Erase heading not required.)

Army Form C. 2118.

Place	Date	Hour	Summary of Events and Information	Remarks and references to Appendices
BAVINGHEM	Jan 25 (cont)		Remainder of unit exercised in fire Drill & collection of wounded during gas attack	S.S.
	Jan 26th		In the afternoon an interaction (A v B V C) football match was played. Army horsey a demonstration with smoke puffs & R.S.F bombs was held by the 7th Divisional Gas Officer. Stretcher squads exercised in rapid adjustment of small box Respirator during real smoke clouds.	
			Capt Roda an R.A.M.C. left to take temporary medical charge of Fd 123 Field Amb. reported back this day from the Corps Gas School at STRAZEELE. R.F.A. at STRAZEELE.	S.S.
			55146 Cpl Shaw to detailed for permanent duty with No 3R 123rd Bde R.F.A.	
	Jan 27th		The unit in full marching order together with transport was inspected by B.O.C. 34th Division. Major General B Williams C.M.G. It was drawn up in line & General saluted. Given. He expressed himself as being very pleased with the turn out of the men that were not so pleased with the transport.	S.S.
			Church parade held in afternoon	
	Jan 28th		Morning occupied by route march & squad drill A stretcher drill competition was held in the afternoon, marks were given for (1) Turn Out (2) Stretcher Drill (3) Carry of wounded over rough ground (4) Viva Voce in first aid competition was won by G section	S.S.
	Jan 29th		Day occupied by loading & loading parade for all sections at BAVINGHEM.	S.S.

Army Form C. 2118.

WAR DIARY
or
INTELLIGENCE SUMMARY.
(Erase heading not required.)

1/3

Place	Date	Hour	Summary of Events and Information	Remarks and references to Appendices
BANDRINGHEM	Jan 30th		Weather still continues very fine. The 152 Field Coy, R.E. have left the loft end of the village so that we are able to provide more shelter stabling accommodation for our horses. In the morning training was devoted to the treatment & collection of wounded in the field.	S.S.
	Jan 31st		Route march in full marching order for ranks. Parade was taken by Capt. PERRIN RDFC.T. In the afternoon an association football match was played against the 4th Stationary Hospital at ARQUES. Strength of the Unit on Jan 31/13 Officers — 8 RAMC personnel — 198 A.S.C. (H.T.) — 34 D.S.C (M.T.) — 11	S.S.

Confidential.

Duplicate

WAR DIARY.

48th Field Ambulance.

from

1st February 1918 to 28th February 1918.

VOLUME 31.

COMMITTEE FOR THE MEDICAL HISTORY OF THE WAR
Date -8 APR 1918

Vol 31
174

Army Form C. 2118.

WAR DIARY
or
INTELLIGENCE SUMMARY.
(Erase heading not required.)

Instructions regarding War Diaries and Intelligence
Summaries are contained in F.S. Regs., Part II.
and the Staff Manual respectively. Title pages
will be prepared in manuscript.

Place	Date	Hour	Summary of Events and Information	Remarks and references to Appendices
BANDRINGHEM	Feb 1st		Morning occupied in physical, squad & stretcher drill for all sable sections of the field Ambulance mentioned heretofore in afternoon.	S.S.
	Feb 2nd	6.00	Inspection of Ambulance in full marching order followed by short route march & lectures by Section Officers. In the afternoon the 111th Inf Bdge held their Brigade sports. 41 sick were admitted from the 111th Inf Brigade during the last week of which 14 were evacuated to C.C.S. remainder to D.R.S. or to duty. Permission was received for 2 N.C.O.s & a Pte to wear the 1914 star.	S.S.
	Feb 3rd		Divine Services were held during the day. The Ambulance played the 13th R.B. at football in the afternoon. Capt S. RUTHERFORD RAMC. proceeded to do temp duty as R.D to the 13th Rifle Brigade.	S.9
	Feb 4th		Morning occupied with Physical, Squad & Stretcher Drill. Notification of the award of the BELGIAN CROIX DE GUERRE to No 31731 Sgt Major D. STEWART RAMC 45th Fd Ambulance was received.	S.S.
	Feb 5th		Bathing parades at BLARINGHEM & Billets fatigues during day. Lieut M.B. GUNN RAMC proceeded to take permanent medical charge of the 13th K.R.R. Corps. Lieut Col C. CLARKE RAMC returned to the Ambulance from short leave to England. 111th Inf Bdge relieved the 112 Inf Bsde in the forward area. The latter taking over the rest billets occupied by the 111th Inf Bsde.	S.S.

Army Form C. 2118.

Instructions regarding War Diaries and Intelligence Summaries are contained in F. S. Regs., Part II. and the Staff Manual respectively. Title pages will be prepared in manuscript.

175

(*Erase heading not required.*)

Place	Date	Hour	Summary of Events and Information	Remarks and references to Appendices
BANDRINGHEM	Feb 6th		Training of the unit continued daily route marches & squad drill and stretcher drill. Lt Phillpot of temporary Medical charge with Lt Waggins. Lt Bloomfield U.S. M.R.C. rejoined the unit today.	FRANCE SHEET 36 A.
do	8th		The weather has become cold and wet sections not staying with the outdoor training of the unit, the men being billeted at Barns and there being no drying room for clothes on wet days. Each Section officer holds lectures and demonstrations in the billets on "Sanitation" "First Aid." Contents and uses of equipment in the Surgical and Medical Panniers.	
do	10th		The three sections were exercised today on preparing improvised dressing stations at Barns.	
do	12th		Under instructions received from A.D.M.S 37th Division Capt Thorne with an advance party of 16 N.C.O's & men proceeded today to WINNITH CAMP near ~~Dickebuseh~~ POPERINGHE to take over the camp then from 60th Field Ambulance	

A5834 Wt. W4973/M687 750,000 8/16 D. D. & L. Ltd. Forms/C.2118/13.

WAR DIARY or INTELLIGENCE SUMMARY

Army Form C. 2118.

Place	Date	Hour	Summary of Events and Information	Remarks and references to Appendices
BANDRINGHEM	12		Roads through to Caëstre via STRAZEELE & BANDRINGHEM to STRAZEELE.	FRANCE SHEET 36 A
do	13		Men transport, Cooker & magasin brought to STRAZEELE by rail. WARATAH CAMP near DICKEBUSCH right bank canal to C. 9/6	
			Lieut W. F. SELF U.S.M.R.S. reported for duty. Today in C.E.F. Pay. 10th York & Lancs. Lieut HOLDANE reported sick today from trench nephritis.	
	14		The Adv. Group (A. & B. Echelons) under Capt. L. under the command of Capt. HOUT from BANDRINGHEM to STRAZEELE	
	15		The Personnel of the 18th Field Ambulance marched from BUS. Corner at 8 a.m. to EBBLINGHEM STATION under the command of Capt. WYLIE with 112th Bengals and E. Fraud for DICKEBUSCH. Unit detrained at DICKEBUSCH and marched to WARATAH CAMP.	

WAR DIARY
or
INTELLIGENCE SUMMARY.
(Erase heading not required.)

Army Form C. 2118.

Place	Date	Hour	Summary of Events and Information	Remarks and references to Appendices
WARATAH CAMP G15.C.2.9	2/5/15		Headquarters of 48th Field Ambulance removed this form Brandhoek to WARATAH CAMP where the H.Q. & No 2 & No 3 Sections from 66th Field Ambulance as 57 Divisional Rest Station.	BRANDHOEK Belgium & FRANCE sheets 25 & 13
WARATAH CAMP	16/6		WARATAH CAMP. On 16/6 10 workers put to work as Hospital Wards and 2 tents Hospital Marquees [illegible] as recommended. At 200 patients. 78 [illegible] complete accommodation for patients with mattresses sheets &c. at the moment sleep on stretchers supplied in trestles. It was intended on taking the camp over that several L.of C. beds were inspected next line. Arrangements were made however for the complete disinfection of all blankets &c by the steam disinfector as the survivors [illegible] give a hot spray bath and every patient on admission receives a hot spray bath and a complete change of underclothing.	

Army Form C. 2118.

WAR DIARY
or
INTELLIGENCE SUMMARY.
(Erase heading not required.)

Instructions regarding War Diaries and Intelligence Summaries are contained in F. S. Regs., Part II. and the Staff Manual respectively. Title pages will be prepared in manuscript.

178

Place	Date	Hour	Summary of Events and Information	Remarks and references to Appendices
WARATAH	Aug 16 17		37th Division at Rest Camp	
CAMP	17		R.A.M.C. Evac to C.C.S. 7 " discharged to duty 22 " admitted to camp 10. Arrangements are being made to supply B Ech. Personal with ammunition not in fixed Lewis gun posts. Shells available a fresh [illegible] in vicinity of [illegible]	
G.15.c.2.9	18		Patients Evacuated to C.C.S. 5 " discharged to duty 5 " admitted to Camp 16	Generally work is being out in the lines where we are in occupation of when not only on account of the lines being rifle pits and that was open in northern side.
	19		Patients Evacuated to C.C.S. 1 " discharged to duty 2 " admitted to L Camp 35	Sim at Blend Posh from the [illegible] Labour Company are sent to WARATAH Camp each day for evacuation to 8th CHINESE HOSPITAL at ARQUES.

Army Form C. 2118.

WAR DIARY
or
INTELLIGENCE SUMMARY.
(Erase heading not required.)

Place	Date	Hour	Summary of Events and Information	Remarks and references to Appendices
WARMYNH	Sep 20		Pat & to Convalescent to C.C.S. 11	
			discharged to Dut — 14	
			Admitted to Camp — 30	
CAMP				
G.I.S.C. 29				
do	21		Pat. b to Convalescent to C.C.S. 6	
			discharged to Dut — 6	
			admitted to Camp — 11	
do	22		Pat. b to Convalescent to C.C.S. 6	
			discharged to Dut — 11	
			admitted to Camp — 11	
do	23		Pat. to Convalescent to C.C.S. 3	
			discharged to Dut — 13	
			admitted to Camp — 25	

Army Form C. 2118.

WAR DIARY
or
INTELLIGENCE SUMMARY.
(Erase heading not required.)

Place	Date	Hour	Summary of Events and Information	Remarks and references to Appendices
WARATAH CAMP G15c2q	24		[illegible handwritten entries]	
	25		[illegible handwritten entries]	
	26		[illegible handwritten entries]	
	27		[illegible handwritten entries]	

Army Form C. 2118.

WAR DIARY
or
INTELLIGENCE SUMMARY.
(Erase heading not required.)

Place	Date	Hour	Summary of Events and Information	Remarks and references to Appendices

------- CONFIDENTIAL. -------

WAR DIARY OF

48th. FIELD AMBULANCE.

From   1st. MARCH 1918.
To.   31st, MARCH, 1918.

VOLUME.33.

Army Form C. 2118.

WAR DIARY
or
INTELLIGENCE SUMMARY.
(Erase heading not required.)

Instructions regarding War Diaries and Intelligence Summaries are contained in F.S. Regs., Part II. and the Staff Manual respectively. Title pages will be prepared in manuscript.

VOLUME 32

Place	Date	Hour	Summary of Events and Information	Remarks and references to Appendices
WARATAH CAMP G.15.c.2.9	March 1st		Patients admitted to Rcstr. Station (37 day) 17 " evacuated to C.C.S. 2 " discharged to duty 9	Hurst 28. S4/12 1/40,000
	2nd		Patients admitted 19 " evacuated to C.C.S. 15 " discharged to duty 11	
	3rd		Patients admitted 24 " evacuated to C.C.S. 3 " discharged to duty 6	Considerable progress has been made in preparing the manoeuvre area of ground within the Camp boundary for the raising of vegetables. Over 9,000 square yards have been set aside for this purpose and a labour party is employed daily in digging up the ground. Manure is being obtained from the field ambulance horse lines and a large quantity is also being collected from agjacent abandoned horse lines.

Army Form C. 2118.

WAR DIARY
or
INTELLIGENCE SUMMARY.
(Erase heading not required.)

Instructions regarding War Diaries and Intelligence Summaries are contained in F. S. Regs., Part II and the Staff Manual respectively. Title pages will be prepared in manuscript.

Place	Date	Hour	Summary of Events and Information	Remarks and references to Appendices
WARATAH CAMP	March 4th		Lieut Hall RAMC posted today as M.O/c 37th Machine Gun Battalion and struck off the strength of the unit	c
			Patients admitted to Rhos Camp 27	
			" wounded to C.C.S. 16	
			" discharged to duty 16.	
			Capt WISHART RAMC posted as command to C section from Ascherson	
			Capt MERRIN RAMC posted to A section from C section.	
do	5th		Patients admitted 21	c
			" discharged to C.C.S. 3	
			" discharged to duty 14	
do	6th		Capt. Maclagan RAMC proceeded today to take medical charge of 6th Bedford.	c
			Patient admitted 25.	
			" discharged to C.C.S. 1	
			" discharged to duty 6	
			Every effort is being made to economise in the meat/bread. The rations of personnel and patients are undertaken daily and spare bread loaves are used for the collection of bread pudding, the cheese is melted down and served to all meltings bread cheese etc. The bread is added to the stews & made up as a welsh rarebit, with the patients tea.	

A.5834 Wt. W.4973/M687 750,000 8/16 D.D. & L. Ltd. Forms/C.2118/13.

Place	Date	Hour	Summary of Events and Information	Remarks and references to Appendices
WARATAH CAMP.	March 7		Patient admitted to Bro'n Camp...34. " transferred to C.C.S...3...10. " + Capp R.S. 3. " discharged to duty......6. Capt MERRIN. R.A.M.C. appointed as Company officer and Adjutant vice Capt Scott R.A.M.C. Telegram received today at 10.30 pm from A.D.M.S. 37 Div to take Precautionary action. 38 N.C.O.s + men with 1 Horsed ambulance wagon, and 2 motor ambulance cars sent to 49th F.A. on the MENIN ROAD. 38 N.C.Os + men with 2 Horsed ambulance wagons and 2 motor ambulance cars sent to 50th F.A. at WOODCOTE HOUSE.	a
do	8th		Patients admitted 24. " to C.C.S + C.R.S. 7. " to Duty 15. In compliance with instructions received from A.D.M.S 37 Div 18 additional teams were sent to 50th F.A. today as reinforcements	a

Army Form C. 2118.

WAR DIARY
or
INTELLIGENCE SUMMARY.
(Erase heading not required.)

Instructions regarding War Diaries and Intelligence Summaries are contained in F. S. Regs., Part II. and the Staff Manual respectively. Title pages will be prepared in manuscript.

185

Place	Date	Hour	Summary of Events and Information	Remarks and references to Appendices
WARATAH CAMP	March 9th		Patients admitted to Rest Camp 39	CC
			" Evacuated to CCS 3	
			" discharged to duty 10	
	10th		Patients admitted to Rest Camp 11	CC
			" evacuated to C.C.S & C.R.S 13	
			" discharged to duty 10	
	11th		Patients admitted to Rest Camp. Sick 27 Wounded 2	CC
			" Evacuated to C.C.S & C.R.S " 11 " 0	
			" discharged to duty " 9 " 0	
	12th		Patients admitted to Rest Camp. Sick 31. — " 0	CC
			" Evacuated to C.C.S & C.R.S " 11 " 0	
			" discharged to duty " 4 " 2	

A5834 Wt. W4973/M687 750,000 8/16 D. D. & L. Ltd. Forms/C.2118/13.

WAR DIARY
or
INTELLIGENCE SUMMARY.

(Erase heading not required.)

Army Form C. 2118.

Place	Date	Hour	Summary of Events and Information	Remarks and references to Appendices
WARATAH Camp	March 13th		The 18 trains sent to 57th Field Ambulance on 8th on special reinforcement rejoined the unit today	G.
			Patients admitted to the Rest Camp Sick 35	G.
			" evacuated to CCS & CRS " 7	
			" discharged to duty 13	
do	14th		Patients admitted to the Rest Camp Sick 22	
			" evacuated to CCS & CRS " 19	G.
			" discharged to Duty " 19	
			" wounded 1	
			Authority granted for Capt Scott & Capt Wishart to wear the badge of rank of a Major while in command of a section of a field ambulance. Promulgated in RO from 1st January 1918	A.

Army Form C. 2118.

WAR DIARY
or
INTELLIGENCE SUMMARY.
(Erase heading not required.)

Instructions regarding War Diaries and Intelligence Summaries are contained in F. S. Regs., Part II. and the Staff Manual respectively. Title pages will be prepared in manuscript.

187

Place	Date	Hour	Summary of Events and Information	Remarks and references to Appendices
WARATAH CAMP	15th March		Patients admitted to Rest Camp 11	a
do	16 March		" evacuated 7	a
do	17"		" to duty 10.	a
do	18"		Patients { admitted 20 / Evacuated 10 / duty 14	a
do	19"		Patients { admitted 32 / evacuated 9 / duty 9	a
do	20"		Patients { admitted 18 / evacuated 11 / duty --	a
do	21"		Patients { admitted 30 / evacuated 76 / duty --	a
			Patients { admitted 32 / evacuated 70 / duty 16	a
			Patients { admitted 53 / evacuated 8 / duty 5	a

Army Form C. 2118.

WAR DIARY
or
INTELLIGENCE SUMMARY.
(Erase heading not required.)

Instructions regarding War Diaries and Intelligence Summaries are contained in F.S. Regs., Part II. and the Staff Manual respectively. Title pages will be prepared in manuscript.

/88

Place	Date	Hour	Summary of Events and Information	Remarks and references to Appendices
WARATAH CAMP	22 March		Under instructions received from A.D.M.S. 37 Division holding parties were sent by 48th Field Ambulance to take over Blue Relay points from No 1, No 2, & No 3 New Zealand Field Ambulances at HAAZEBROUCK, CAESTRE & HONDGHEM respectively. Holding parties consisting of an N.C.O. & two men at each relay.	Bge HAZEBROUCK to HAZEBROUCK
	23 March		NCOs of 48 Field Ambulance attached for duty with 49th Field Ambulance (Sanitation) inspection of trenches, manure, latrines etc	
	24 "		No 1, No 2 & No 3 New Zealand field ambulances left the STAPLE district today and were taken over by 48th Field Ambulance under orders by Division h.q.	

Army Form C. 2118.

WAR DIARY
or
INTELLIGENCE SUMMARY.
(Erase heading not required.)

Place	Date	Hour	Summary of Events and Information	Remarks and references to Appendices
WARATAH CAMP	25th March			
	26th March		Instructions received tonight from ADMS 37 Division attaching 142nd Field Ambulance to the 112th Brigade for the demand now to the STAPLE area near HAZEBROUCK.	HAZEBROUCK, FRANCE
	27th March		Under Brigade orders 112th Brigade the whole of the transport of the 140 Field Ambulance C'as mechanical transport with 25 NCO's & men marched at 10 AM from WARATAH CAMP to CAESTRE under the command of Major Scott. RAMC.	Belgium

Army Form C. 2118.

WAR DIARY
or
INTELLIGENCE SUMMARY.
(Erase heading not required.)

Place	Date	Hour	Summary of Events and Information	Remarks and references to Appendices
WARATAH CAMP	27th March		In compliance with instructions received from ADMS 37 Division the 227 patients in the Rest Camp were all evacuated to day to 37 C.C.S. today	C
CAESTRE	28th		The whole field ambulance moved today to CAESTRE under instructions from 112th Brigade, move being completed at 7 pm today.	Beg an MARCOP- OUT C
			48th field Ambulance and transport returned to station by 6.25 am today for an unknown destination. Motor Ambulances began to proceed by road under command of O.C. 37 Div Motor Transport company.	
			Under orders ADMS 37 Div 48th field Ambulance is attached to 112th Brigade and will move and act in connection with the Brigade under g O.C. 112th Brigade.	C

WAR DIARY
or
INTELLIGENCE SUMMARY.

(Erase heading not required.)

Army Form C. 2118.

Place	Date	Hour	Summary of Events and Information	Remarks and references to Appendices
CAESTRE	29 March		Field Ambulance ordered to entrain at CAESTRE today by 6.25 a.m. Entraining of the unit completed by 5.30 a.m. Train departed at 6.15 a.m. from CAESTRE and arrived at MONDICOURT at 6 p.m. 29/3/18. 48th Field Ambulance detrained at MONDICOURT and Personnel were conveyed by motor lorry under direction from H.Q. 112th Brigade to TOUTENCOURT, arriving there at midnight. Transport of the unit marched by road to TOUTENCOURT. Personnel accommodated in barns for the night.	LENS 1/100,000
TOUTENCOURT	30 March		Personnel and transport of 48th Field Ambulance moved by M.T. today at 11.30 a.m. from TOUTENCOURT to AUTHIE via TOUTENCOURT to AUTHIE. Personnel accommodated in billets at AUTHIE.	

CONFIDENTIAL

WAR DIARY

of 48th Field Ambulance,
from 1st April 1918 to 30th April 1918.

VOLUME 33.

Vol. 133
Page 193

Army Form C. 2118.

WAR DIARY
or
INTELLIGENCE SUMMARY.
(Erase heading not required.)

Place	Date	Hour	Summary of Events and Information	Remarks and references to Appendices
AUTHIE	April 1st		General situation. 8th Field Ambulance is attached to 112th Brigade. 112th Brigade is holding the line in front of Bosqueroir village. (L.4, 5 + c.) (L.9 a + b) (L.7 + 8 - a + b) (K.12 a + b) Map reference Sheet 57 D (N.E)	LENS 1/100,000 57d N.E.
			Medical Posts.	
			Right Battalion. 1st Essex Regt. R.A.P. (K.d.5.3) 8 stretcher bearers.	
			Centre Battalion. 6th Bedfords. R.A.P. (L.1.d.5.2) 8 stretcher bearers.	
			Left Battalion. 13th Royal Fusiliers R.A.P. (L.3.a.5.6) 8 stretcher bearers.	
			Relay Stretcher post at edge of Bois de Riez (L.1.b.5.5) 8 stretcher bearers.	
			Collecting Post for artillery (E.30.6.2.7) 4 stretcher bearers.	
			No 1. Brosnet (Relay Post.) (F.25.a.9.8) 8 " "	
			No 2. " (E.24.b.9.2) 8 " "	
			A.D.S. (E.9.d.9.8) 2 Medical Officers & a first aid dresser.	C.

Army Form C. 2118.

WAR DIARY
or
INTELLIGENCE SUMMARY.

(Erase heading not required.)

Place	Date	Hour	Summary of Events and Information	Remarks and references to Appendices
AUTHIE	April 1st		Car & Horse Ambulance Stand posted in BIEN VILLERS (E.8.6.9.9.), wounded evacuated from transports along BUCQUOY – ESSARTS – HANNESCAMPS road by wheeled stretchers. from A.D.S. at HANNESCAMPS to M.D.S. (49th F.A.) at LA COUCHIE. Evacuation is by ambulance cars and horse ambulance. Orders received today at 6 p.m. to remove holywater of 148th Field Ambulance & Horselines from AUTHIE to COUIN. Col Meyer RAMC was wounded at 4 pm today by HE Shell fragment in the chest and evacuated N over from 1/4 HANNESCAMPS A.D.S. to LA COUCHIE.	57th d NE
COUIN	April 2nd		Head quarters 148th Field Ambulance & Horse lines now at COUIN in BIVOUACS & TENTS. 42 Sick & wounded evacuated through ADS. HANNESCAMP to M.D.S. La Couchie in 24 hours.	

Place	Date	Hour	Summary of Events and Information	Remarks and references to Appendices
CouiN	April 3rd		A.D.S. at HANNESCAMP clears all sick and wounded from 10th Inf. Bde. of the BIENVILLERS. ESSARTS. BUCQUOY Road. A large proportion of the wounded are artillery men and from units in the back area. Many casualties occur along the road owing to night shells, motor and ammunition convoys suffering heavily.	57d NE
do.	April 4th		Main Dressing Station transferred to SOUASTRE. (49.⁼A)	
	April 5th		Severe fighting this morning in front of BIEZ Wood & FONKVILLERS. 63rd Brigade very heavily engaged and attacking enemy line. Enemy attacked today north of BUCQUOY on front held by 42nd Div. Ret. to retire a short distance to 42nd Division. Ret to retire a short distance to and front of 112th Brigade was withdrawn in consequence to the suburbs of BUCQUOY. M.O/c 13th R.F. falling back from BUCQUOY to A.D.S. HANNESCAMP. no Sick RAP. transferred.	

WAR DIARY or INTELLIGENCE SUMMARY

Army Form C. 2118.

Place	Date	Hour	Summary of Events and Information	Remarks and references to Appendices
COUIN	April	6th	On the month of the severe fighting on April 5th, BUCQUOY VILLAGE lost about 250 casualties passed through A.D.S. HANNESCAMP by 9 a.m. 6/4/18 and were evacuated to M.D.S. at SOUASTRE. A large proportion of the casualties were to MUSTARD GAS. The ground is infected with MUSTARD-GAS especially in the neighbourhood of shell-holes as told by men appear to have gassed from small doses unrecognised at the time. Low countries specially affected. Gas masks were not worn or take. Mustard gas was not suspected.	
COUIN		8th	A considerable number of curing TRENCH FEET have passed through the unit especially from 1st ESSEX Regt. The weather has been very cold and wet and our trenches are largely improved since we had the drainage were constantly flooded with water.	

WAR DIARY or INTELLIGENCE SUMMARY

Army Form C. 2118

Place	Date	Hour	Summary of Events and Information	Remarks and references to Appendices
COUIN	April 9th		Sgt ASHWOOD RAMC has been attached to H.Q. 112 Brigade at RETTEMOY FARM in order to supervise the provision of gargling & trench feet treatment. Men with early signs of trench feet report to this NCO who arranges that each man shall wash his feet in warm water, provides them with Boric Ointment when dry, and these put on their own & clean socks. Any cases showing signs of oedema or inflammation are referred to the medical Officer of their battalion.	G —
COUIN	April 10th		The A.D.S. at HANNESCAMPS owing to the very limited accommodation there has been withdrawn to BIEN VILLERS where considered convenient in its duties for the wounded. The two cellars at HANNESCAMPS are used as relay points for parties along the BIENVILLERS ESSARTS Road.	

WAR DIARY
or
INTELLIGENCE SUMMARY
(Erase heading not required.)

Army Form C. 2118

198.

Place	Date	Hour	Summary of Events and Information	Remarks and references to Appendices
Couin	April 12th		Instructions received from A.D.M.S. 37 Division that A.D.S at Bienvillers with bearer posts along Bienvillers – Essart road to be handed over to Field Ambulance of 62nd Division at present stationed in Bienvillers. 48th Field Ambulance bearers to be withdrawn from the left of the Divisional front and transferred to the right of the Divisional front with A.D.S. at Sailly-au-Bois.	SHEET 57 D N.E.
do	April 13th		Above change completed today. Major Scott & Lieut GRAVES returned with all bearers from Bienvillers sector to H.Q. 48th F.A. at Couin. Major Wishart & Lieut Maxeiner opened A.D.S. with a tent subdivision in Sailly-au-Bois, to clear wounded from Hebertune. Bearer posts held today by R.A.P.s (3) in 50 Field Ambulance under Lieut GUNN.	

WAR DIARY
or
INTELLIGENCE SUMMARY

Army Form C. 2118

Place	Date	Hour	Summary of Events and Information	Remarks and references to Appendices
COUIN	April 1/16		Present situation 9 to 8th Field Ambulance. Headquarters at COUIN with Divisional Rest Station J.I.b.5.8. A.D.S. at SAILLY. J.18.a.6.6. with one tram subdivision in reserve at SAILLY. 3 Regimental Aid Posts in HÉBUTERNE. K.9.b.5.1. K.9.b.6.1. K.8.b.8.1. Bearer relay posts. K.9.b.4.4. " " K.9.c.1.7. (3 squads / 5 squads) K.13.b.8.6. " " J.18.b.5.4. Bearer relay post with wheel stretcher carriage at BAYENCOURT. J.Ka.3.9 3 Motor Ambulance Wagons stationed at BAYENCOURT & M.D.S. Wounded evacuated from A.D.S. SAILLY via BAYENCOURT to M.D.S. SOUASTRE. 49.F.A	Sheet 57 D. N.E.

Place	Date	Hour	Summary of Events and Information	Remarks and references to Appendices
COUIN	April 15		Orders received from A.D.M.S. 37 Div. that 8th Field Ambulance to relieve 1/2nd East Lancs F.A. Ambulance on the line on 16/17. 1/2nd E.L. by 1/2nd East Lancs F.A. Ambulance on relief to take over billets at AUTIE ST LEDGER occupied by 1/1st East Lancs Field Ambulance.	SHEET 57. ONE
do	April 16		Advance party sent today from 1/2nd East Lancs F.A. to take over A.D.S. at SAILLY-AU-BOIS and present relay posts from A.D.S. to HEBUTERNE sector of the line. Advance party sent today from 48th F.A. to AUTIE-ST LEDGER to take over billets occupied by 1/1st East Lancs F.A. Advance party of 1/1st East Lancs F.A. arrived today at COUIN to take over Camp and Billets occupied by 48th F.A. at COUIN.	

WAR DIARY or INTELLIGENCE SUMMARY

(Erase heading not required.)

Army Form C. 2118

Place	Date	Hour	Summary of Events and Information	Remarks and references to Appendices
AUTHIE St LEDGER	April 17th		The following moves were completed today by noon. O.C. 1/2nd East Lanc. F.A. 42 Div. took over A.D.S. SAILLY-AU-BOIS and all hand-over papers to during HEBUTERNE sector of the line from 1/8th F.A. 37 Div. O.C. 1/1st East Lanc F.A. 43 Div. took over Billets of 48 F.A. at COUIN O.C. 48th F.A. took over billets occupied by 1/1st East Lanc F.A. at AUTHIE at LEDGER.	A SHEET 57.D.N.E 1/20,000
do	18th		48th Field Ambulance attached to 112th Inf Brigade for purposes 112th Infantry Brigade in IV Corps Reserve has been detailed to hold Red line of recovery from west end of HOUVENCOURT 0.5 to central through BOIS - du - VARNIMONT to J.14 central Major Scott in command of dex Bevin Divisions and C section has taken over . Head qrs 48 F.A. at AUTHIE-St-LEDGER with two sub-divisions of A.F.B. section	

WAR DIARY
or
INTELLIGENCE SUMMARY
(Erase heading not required.)

Army Form C. 2118

202

Place	Date	Hour	Summary of Events and Information	Remarks and references to Appendices
AUTIES St LEGER	April 19		112th Brigade in Corps Reserve. Cars for evacuation carried on Field Ambulances Cars daily to C.C.S. at DOUILENS.	
			Sedan cars of 1st Army tested in General Patton's ward on marked dial the average 16 cwt cars and on marked dial	
			to AUTIE 37 Div. Bath for Hutchinsons & Uny Ralph battalions clothing disinfected in Shark disinfector erected.	
do.	April 20		Orders received from DDMS IV Corps. through ADMS 37 Div. that any car must to taken to prevent break downs 1 ambulance	*
			car to hand to supply 1 spare part.	
do.	21		R.A.M.C. order N°85. 37 Div. received. 28th Field Ambulance to relieve 2/2 West Riding Field Ambulance stationed at SOUASTRE.	ee

WAR DIARY or INTELLIGENCE SUMMARY

Army Form C. 2118

Place	Date	Hour	Summary of Events and Information	Remarks and references to Appendices
AUTIE ST LEGER.	April 23		Advance party sent from 48th Field Ambulance to 2½ West Riding F.A. preparatory to taking over the Main Dressing Station SOUASTRE. 37th Div. relieving the 62nd Division in the line north of BUCQUOY. A.D.S. stationed at BIENVILLERS au BOIS, relay posts along BIENVILLERS ESSARTS Road.	
SOUASTRE	April 24		48th Field Ambulance took over M.D.S. in School Room SOUASTRE at 2 pm today, and transport lines at HENU. 2/2 West Riding F.A. took over Billets occupied by  48th F.A. at AUTIE ST LEGER.	
Do	25		Walking Wounded and stretcher cases received at School Room which is fitted up as a Main Dressing Station. Walking Sick numbering about 100 a day are seen at the CHURCH Room close by which is fitted up for the purpose.	

WAR DIARY
or
INTELLIGENCE SUMMARY

Army Form C. 2118

Place	Date	Hour	Summary of Events and Information	Remarks and references to Appendices
SOUASTRE	April 26		M.D.S. is cleared by 21 M.A.C. cars being stationed at SOUASTRE for the purpose. Evacuation is from M.D.S. to DOULLENS 3 Can. Stat. Hosp. at 45 P.C.S. 3 & 9 the large ambulance cars belonging to 1/8 F.A. are attached to 4 & 9th F.A. clearing cars from A.D.S. to M.D.S. The CORPS (V) Rest station is at AUTIE. Limited accommodation. Divisional Rest Station (50 F.A.) at PAS.	
SOUASTRE	April 27		Capt. GRAVES RAMC evacuated sick today. P.U.O. 64 S.C.C.S. The Divisional Front astride ESSARTS — BUCQUOY road has been quiet except for artillery fire since 24/4/15 and only a few wounded have passed through the M.D.S. each day. There have been a fair number of slam [?] apart from the Division them have been	

WAR DIARY
or
INTELLIGENCE SUMMARY

Army Form C. 2118

Place	Date	Hour	Summary of Events and Information	Remarks and references to Appendices
SOUASTRE	April 27		No characteristic physical signs and the majority of these appear to be cases of Influenza.	
do	April 29		Since taking over the M.D.S. SOUASTRE on 24/4/18 158 sick 78 wounded } have passed through the Dressing Station giving a daily average of 26 sick and 13 wounded, about 75% Shrivon cases an from 37 Div. and 25% from other formations. Lt. Scott U.S.M.O.R.S. proceeded today to take temporary medical charge of 13 A.B. was at HILL RAMC. evacuated sick.	ee
SOUASTRE	April 30		Strength of 148th Field Ambulance. 6 Officers — 2 detached 174 O.R. RAMC 35 " Horse Transport (A.T.) 13 " Motor Transport (A.T.)	

Charles McG Lt/Col RAMC
148/FA
30/4/18

CONFIDENTIAL.

WAR DIARY

for
48th Field Ambulance
from
1st May 1918 to 31st May 1918.

Volume 34.

VOLUME 34

WAR DIARY
or
INTELLIGENCE SUMMARY
(Erase heading not required.)

Army Form C. 2118

Page 206

Place	Date	Hour	Summary of Events and Information	Remarks and references to Appendices
SOUASTRE	MAY 1st		48th Field Ambulance Main Dressing Station at SOUASTRE receiving cases from (A.D.S. + 9th F.A.) at BIENVILLERS. All cases unlikely to be fit for duty within 7 days evacuated to C.C.S. (46) or Can. St. Hosp. (3) DOULLENS, by 21. M.A.C. Cases likely to be fit for duty within a week to IV Corps Rest-Station AUTIE v 37 Div Rest Station. at PAS. (50th F.A.) The Dressing Station was inspected today by the D.M.S. III Army Maj. General. Murray Irwin. EVACUATION STATE { sick 48 wounded 11	57 D ME c
SOUASTRE	May 2nd		A room in this Dressing Station has been set aside for the men Officers suffering from diarrhoea, and likely to be fit for duty within 24 hours. These can on only detained and not admitted on the Field Ambulance Books. EVACUATION STATE { sick 40 wounded 29	c

WAR DIARY
or
INTELLIGENCE SUMMARY

(Erase heading not required.)

Army Form C. 2118

Place	Date	Hour	Summary of Events and Information	Remarks and references to Appendices
SOUASTRE	May 3rd		EVACUATION STATE { sick 30, wounded 6	57 to M.E
			A number of mild gas cases are being evacuated daily, yellow cross showing symp: vomiting, mild conjunctivitis, and felling of general weakness. no signs of any skin inflammation. These cases appear to result from digging dug-outs etc in shelled area and to be due to inhalation of which gas impregnated ground.	
do	May 4th		EVACUATION STATE { sick 31, wounded 19. Main cause of sick 20/6	
do	May 5th		EVACUATION STATE { sick 36, wounded 9	

WAR DIARY or INTELLIGENCE SUMMARY

Army Form C. 2118

Place	Date	Hour	Summary of Events and Information	Remarks and references to Appendices
SOUASTRE	May 6th		EVACUATION STATE { sick 38, wounded 10 The village of SOUASTRE was shelled today from 6pm to 7pm with shrapnel and H.E. shells. About 12 shells bursting in and village. 2 Army Service horses slightly wounded by shrapnel but not evacuated.	Sheet 57D NE
do	May 7th		EVACUATION STATE { sick 40, wounded 16 Capt. MASON. R.A.M.C. T.C. & Capt. RAYMOND R.A.M.C. reported for duty with 48th Field Ambulance. Notice received today that Lt Scott US M.O.R.C. wishes shortly to revert for service with the American Army. From about 6.30pm today until midnight vicinity of M.O.S. SOUASTRE was shelled at ½ hour intervals with high velocity shells. (S.9)	
do	May 8th		EVACUATION STATE { sick 50, wounded 66 The 13th A.B. today attacked on a narrow front north of mill of the cornailles & captured 2 German S.O.R.s at 2pm artillery preparation and capture later in the afternoon from enemy artillery fire and around at M.D.S. from 7 pm onwards to midnight.	

WAR DIARY or INTELLIGENCE SUMMARY

Army Form C. 2118

Place	Date	Hour	Summary of Events and Information	Remarks and references to Appendices
SOUASTRE	May 9		EVACUATIONS { sick 36, wounded 91 (includes 57 NYD gas cases) 51 Cases of NYD gas poisoning passed through the Dressing Station today, clinic symptoms being Headache, vomiting, abdominal colic, dry throat, tingling sensation in arms & legs, some cases with dyspnoea. Two Bristish 18 pndr shells are said to have burst near the water famish gas shells. The probability was however of apparent poisoning from drinking contaminated water and the case is being investigated.	C.
	May 10		EVACUATIONS { sick 22, wounded 5. 3 more cases of NYD gas poisoning were admitted today. Stated vomiting, abdominal colic, tingling in arms & legs. own acknowledged drinking the water from shell hole water.	C.

WAR DIARY or INTELLIGENCE SUMMARY

Army Form C. 2118

No. 210

Place	Date	Hour	Summary of Events and Information	Remarks and references to Appendices
SOUASTRE	May 11th		EVACUATIONS { sick 26, wounded 8 } On QUIVIERS About 7 pm today the enemy commenced a prolonged gas bombardment, using a mixture of "green" and yellow cross gas shells for the purpose.	
	May 12th		Cases of gas shell poisoning began to arrive at the M.D.S. SOUASTRE in large numbers about 1 am today. The majority of the cases were suffering from severe gastric irritation and all the cases vomited bile stained fluid. A few also suffered from diarrhoea. There was some irritation of the eyes and the men complained of severe colic in the abdomen. 1085 gas poisoning cases passed through the M.D.S. between 1 am and 6 pm today. The cases coming down later showed more a distinct poisoning from yellow cross gas. Eyes very inflamed, then slight burns and blisters appeared and irritation of skin. Breathing injected. Breathing ...... inhaled, clothes changed when necessary	

WAR DIARY
or
INTELLIGENCE SUMMARY
(Erase heading not required.)

Army Form C. 2118

Place	Date	Hour	Summary of Events and Information	Remarks and references to Appendices
SOMASTRE	12th May		Evacuation { sick 13 { wounded 1201 (mostly mustard gas shell poisoning)	
SOUASTRE	May 13		Lt Scott. U.S:M.O.R.C. left # 8th Field ambulance today under orders to join the International Section of the American Expeditionary force. Capt. Raymond RAMS proceeded today to take interim charge of 13th Rifle Brigade vice Lt Scott. U.S.M.O.R.C. About 160 cases of gas shell poisoning (Mustard gas) passed through the M.D.S. today. Most of the cases were slight and exhibited only injection of the eyes and some laryngeal catarrh. They were mostly cases from the gas shelling at Fonquevillers. no GW's. 11. 12th May. Evacuation { sick 15 { wounded 62	

WAR DIARY or INTELLIGENCE SUMMARY

Army Form C. 2118

Place	Date	Hour	Summary of Events and Information	Remarks and references to Appendices
SOUASTRE	May 14th		Evacuation { sick 18 / wounded 17	
			A few shell cases of Mustard gas shell passing evacuated today. All my wells out from FOUQUEVILLERS area.	G
	May 15th		Evacuation { sick # 36 / wounded # 13	
			Order No 86 received from A.D.M.S. 37. Div. 48th Field Ambulance at (M.D.S. SOUASTRE) to be relieved by 2/1 West Riding Field Ambulance on 17th May relay to be complete by 5 p.m. 17.5.18.	G
	May 16th		Evacuation { sick 14 / wounded 24	
			The villages of HENU and the environs of the 48th 7.A. transport lines were bombed by enemy aircraft last night. S.y East ROR was killed by a bomb-aeroplane on the Chev. and 2 O.R. wounded	G

WAR DIARY or INTELLIGENCE SUMMARY

Army Form C. 2118

Place	Date	Hour	Summary of Events and Information	Remarks and references to Appendices
SOUASTRE	17 May		Evacuation sick and wounded { Sick 13, wounded 21 }	57/D
MARIEUX			The M.D.S. in billet houses at SOUASTRE was handed over today to 48 Field Ambulance. 2/1 Wesh Riding Field Ambulance. Regt. und. hosp. lines at HENU. The Camp at MARIEUX 1.P.2.2.2. at present under construction by First Camp was taken over by 48 Field Ambulance from 2/1 W.R.F.A. No patients in the camp and being only partly completed. In Niessen Huts at Marquees. There will be accommodation for 250 patients. — Capt Clarke M.C. arrived posted this new Corps Wash in Aupe River. 48th Field Ambulance is attached to 112 Brigade for defence purposes.	
MARIEUX	18 May		No patients admitted into the River Camp, all personnel employed in building huts roofs walls around the tents preparing lining in bivouacs.	

Place	Date	Hour	Summary of Events and Information	Remarks and references to Appendices
MARIEUX	19th May		The IV Corps rest station was opened for patients today. Cook house, ablution room & latrines etc not yet complete but every effort being made for further completion. Admissions. 11 sick. Evacuations. Lieut GARRET. & Lt BARDAL R.A.M.C. joined the unit today.	
	20 May		Admissions. 18 sick. one H. wounded. Capt A W RAYMOND Esq. posted to Medical charge 13th RB	
	21.		Admissions 23 sick. Women 6 completed. Missen hub in the Rest Camp can't accommodating 12 patients. 2 men Niesen huts and big frame field units for the remainder of the patients in Camp. In 20 small hospital marquees.	
	22		Admissions 28 sick and 4 to 48 feet ambulances today in connection with a practice defence of the Millencourt-Bresle Brigade at LOUVENCOURT the Bearer sub-division of the 2nd ASS A walk. together marched from MARIEUX at 9am to VAUCHELLES, where an A.D.S. was formed. Such medical kit front to R.A.P. O.C. joining up shortly. Bearers are regarded as brought officers...	

WAR DIARY or INTELLIGENCE SUMMARY

Army Form C. 2118

Place	Date	Hour	Summary of Events and Information	Remarks and references to Appendices
MARIEUX	May 23		Sick admissions to IV Corps Aust F Stat'n 25. Four days praytice Trench 23-26. wet continuous Every morning the wet muddy big groundsheet for me lashes during his tent.	
	24		Sick admissions 30. In view to protect the patients in the Rest Camp from Bomb the floor of tent lift but + mosquito nets hung up to a depth of 2½ feet.	
	25		Sick admissions 25. A great garden Run has been commenced in the high ground through sea Days set the hours have Planks next in place were Placed on tumbery.	
	26		Sick admissions 23. For the accommodation of patients & staff in from patients 23 young Platinums with materials dug largely obtained from the 13 M.C.S. and will in a wooden rail. 18 inches off the ground	

WAR DIARY or INTELLIGENCE SUMMARY

Army Form C. 2118

Place	Date	Hour	Summary of Events and Information	Remarks and references to Appendices
MARIEUX	May 27		Sick admissions 20 to IV Corps Rest Station. Shelling & suspected hostile aircraft in evening, long range gun Ft Ypolem daily. No pbulls returned. Been falling about the vicinity of MARIEUX	
	28		Sick admissions 32. Afternoon received shock in aeroplane & going for use against full alarms and gasgreen was sounded. Into use. Cendo 9 patients leaving continued serving the wound A7&W.	
	29		Sick admission 15. Art group to the Venir patter completed with talks for skin cases (visitation & improper)	
	30		Sick admission 21. Information received from A.D.M.S. 37 Division that D.A.C. 37 Div. was moving to ORVILLE and unit would be ready to hand over IV Corps Rest Station at that date.	
	31		Patients in the Rest Camp 31.5.18 = 180.	

Strength full
Officers 8
O.R. 173 } 232
A.S.C. H.T. 38
A.S.C. M.T. 13

[Confidential.]

95/36
140/3076

COMMITTEE FOR THE
MEDICAL HISTORY OF THE WAR
Date 7 AUG 1918

War Diary
of
48th Field Ambulance
from
1st June 1918 to 30th June '18.

Volume 35.

WAR DIARY
or
INTELLIGENCE SUMMARY

Army Form C. 2118

VOLUME 35 0893

Place	Date	Hour	Summary of Events and Information	Remarks and references to Appendices
MARIEUX	June 1st		48th Field Ambulance stationed at MARIEUX and forming IV Corps Rest Station. Cases in Rest Station 175 sick & W. Cases in Rest Station 189 sick and wounded.	AMIENS see 17
do	2nd		Capt Clarke R.A.M.C.(T) proceeded today to 29 Div under instruction received from A.D.M.S. 37 Div.	
do	June 3rd		37 Div R.A.M.C. orders received today for 48th F.A. to hand over Camp at MARIEUX to 2/2 N.Z. F.A. and Return 1/3 Elane F.A. at N.Z.F.A. on 7 inst. Cases in Rest Station 189 sick & wounded.	
do	4th		Telegram received at 1.30 pm today ordering unit to be ready to move on 5th June with 112th Inf Brigade. O.C. 2/2 N.Z.F.A. invited to Camp this afternoon. Orders to be issued later.	
do	5th		Telegram received from A.D.M.S. 37 Div. G.O.C. 112 Inf will march tonight after dark, orders follow. 6.10 pm MARIEUX tonight at 8.30 pm. Lt Barrett in command with Horse transport marched from MARIEUX returned from 112th Brigade.	

WAR DIARY or INTELLIGENCE SUMMARY

Army Form C. 2118

Place	Date	Hour	Summary of Events and Information	Remarks and references to Appendices
MARIEUX	June 5th		Under instructions received from A.D.M.S. 37 Div. 48th Field Ambulance handed over the charge of the IV Corps Rest Station to 2/2 New Zealand Field Ambulance handing over was completed today at 10 a.m. Personnel & Motor transport of 48th Field Ambulance marched from MARIEUX at 8.30 p.m. Tonight and entrained in Motor lorries on the VAUCHELLES — LOUVENCOURT road at a point 500 yards west of LOUVENCOURT. Together with the other units of 112th Inf. Brigade. Motor Bus convoy then proceeded at 10 p.m. by road to the west of AMIENS.	Annex 17 a
BREVIL les MOLLIENS	June 6th	6 a.m.	48th Field Ambulance personnel arrived at BREVIL les MOLLIENS with 112th Infantry Brigade in Barns in the villages 6.6.18. Personnel of 48th Field Ambulance attached arm now in H. Army. XXII Corps. 112th Inf. 13th M.Y. at DISSY.	a

Army Form C. 2118.

WAR DIARY
or
INTELLIGENCE SUMMARY.
(Erase heading not required.)

Places	Date	Hour	Summary of Events and Information	Remarks and references to Appendices
DREUIL lès MOLLIENS	July 7th		A small dressing station for troops of 112th Brigade has been opened in the village of DREUIL lès MOLLIENS by 48th Field Ambulance.	AMIENS 17
	8th		112th Brigade Hqs started at Chateau DISSY CROUY. Sick evacuated to No 5 C.C.S. CROUY.	
	9th		Two officers & 4 O.R. sent in an ambulance car to examine roads where its started along the ridge running south from AMIENS. along DURY St SAUFLIEU and Orders received from A.D.M.S. 112th Brigade for 48th Field Ambulance to be ready to move on 1½ hours notice. Enemy attack south of Montdidier commenced at 4:30 a.m. this morning.	
DREUIL lès MOLLIENS	10th		Under orders received from 112th Brigade, 48th Field Ambulance marching from DREUIL lès MOLLIENS to BRIQUEMESNIL to BRIQUEMESNIL at 9 am this morning. Buses embussed on BRIQUEMESNIL — FERRIERES Road. Buses proceeded to CONTY ave. and Billeted in L'HORTOY South of AMIENS. arriving at 11 pm.	

WAR DIARY
or
INTELLIGENCE SUMMARY.

(Erase heading not required.)

Army Form C. 2118.

Place	Date	Hour	Summary of Events and Information	Remarks and references to Appendices
L'HORTOY	11th		Village school used as a Dressing Station. Battalions in two large Barns. 112th Brigade Dressing Station at FLERS.	Amiens 1/100,000 17
do.	12th		Officers visited roads and villages in forward area and with 9 mention of Field Ambulances. Main Field Ambulance Dressing Station at ESSERTAUX. JUMEL road.	
do.	13th		Sent new rumour from 112th W. Brigade — 48th Field Ambulance to reach Convoy N from L'HORTOY to St FUSCIEN area. Detailed orders to follow. 10.30 pm 48th Field Ambulance marched by road from L'HORTOY to VERS.	ce
VERS	14th		Field Ambulance arrived in billets at VERS at 5 am this morning. Hospital located in three local factories.	

Army Form C. 2118.

WAR DIARY
or
INTELLIGENCE SUMMARY.
(Erase heading not required.)

Place	Date	Hour	Summary of Events and Information	Remarks and references to Appendices
VERS	15th		Instructions received from 112th Brigade situated at St FUSCIEN	AMIENS 17.
			all commanding units to reconnoitre roads out through AVRE in region of CAGNY & BOVES. 112th bg Brigade to be ready to defend second	
			positions across the AVRE in case of attack by enemy. Patients admitted 9 evacuated to CCS 18.	
do	16th		Instructions received from A.D.M.S. 37 Div. OC 48th Fd Ambulance to select proposed site for A.D.S. in CAGNY.	
			site proposed in Convent in CAGNY in case of active operations across the AVRE. Patients admitted 4 — evacuated to CCS 4	
Vers	17th		Whilst in Reserve the Personnel of 48th Field Ambulance are engaged in daily training. An experimental march of Fd Amb from VERS to proposed site of A.D.S. at CAGNY was undertaken today. The teams marched the distance within 2 hours. Patients admitted 1 evacuated to CCS 3	

Army Form C. 2118.

WAR DIARY
or
INTELLIGENCE SUMMARY.
(Erase heading not required.)

Instructions regarding War Diaries and Intelligence Summaries are contained in F. S. Regs., Part II. and the Staff Manual respectively. Title pages will be prepared in manuscript.

Place	Date	Hour	Summary of Events and Information	Remarks and references to Appendices
VERS	18th June		Orders received today. Unit to be prepared for marching orders. No Divisional number. Patient admitted 9.	AMIENS a.17 1/100,00
VERS.	19th		Evacuated to C.C.S. Information received that 37 Div. was being transported from 4th to 3rd Army. from XXII Corps to IV Corps. Billeting N.C.O. sent this morning to look at billets. Personnel	a.
do.	20th		Transport & Field Ambulance marched today from VERS at 7AM under Brigade Orders 112. Personnel & F.A. marched at 2 am to entrain at CREUSE.	a.
CREUSE.	21.		Personnel in billets in CREUSE. Paraded at 2.30am marched to LOEUILLY Station and entrained at 7 AM. Arrived at AUTHIEULE at 1 pm. marched from AUTHIEULE to TERRA NESNIL arriving at 2.30 pm	a.

WAR DIARY
or
INTELLIGENCE SUMMARY.

Army Form C. 2118.

Place	Date	Hour	Summary of Events and Information	Remarks and references to Appendices
TERRAMESNIL	22 June		No Hospital accommodation - sick of 112th Brigade collected and evacuated to C.C.S. at GEAZANCOURT.	a
	23.		Capt MORTON RAMC posted to permanent medical charge of 9th Staffords	a
	24.		Orders received today for 48th Field Ambulance to proceed to PAS on 25 June and relieve 2/3 West Riding F.A. 62 Division	a
PAS	25		Personnel of 48th Field Ambulance transferred to PAS today under arrangements made by 112th Brigade. Rest Camp in tents and huts for 90 patients taken over from 2/3 West Riding Field Ambulance. 61 patients left in Hospital by 2/3 W.R.(F.A.) and taken over by 48th F.A. Admitted to Field Ambulance. 8.	a

Army Form C. 2118.

WAR DIARY
or
INTELLIGENCE SUMMARY.
(Erase heading not required.)

= 27/6 =

Place	Date	Hour	Summary of Events and Information	Remarks and references to Appendices
P.A.S	26th		Rest Camp divided into two main divisions one for Pyrexia cases and the other for I.C.T and Scabies cases. Rest Spray baths have been put up and all patients with to gets up are treated daily. Admissions to Rest Camp 54.	e
	27th		Accommodation of the Rest Camp has been increased by the erection of 3 marquee tents. 9 + 8th F.A. and 3 marquee tents. 9 + 50 F.A. together with all other available bell tents. Admissions to Rest Camp 40	e
	28th		The majority I admission to Rest Camp are for Pyrexia which is never permanent. Serum is used in typhus, chief symptoms are Headache, Pyrexia, injected Eye, cough, recovery after 4 or 5 days with some weakness. Admissions to rest camp 53	e

Army Form C. 2118.

WAR DIARY
or
INTELLIGENCE SUMMARY.
(Erase heading not required.)

Title pages — 275 —

Place	Date	Hour	Summary of Events and Information	Remarks and references to Appendices
C.A.S.	29		Lieut Bardal RAMC posted to medical charge of 37th Div Wing. Admissions to Rest Camp. 87.	A 57.° C
C.A.S.	30		Lieut Garrett RAMC posted to temporary medical charge of 123 Brigade F.A. Admissions to Rest Camp 99. Field Ambulance was inspected today by D.M.S. 3rd Army. Since 25th June to today 2,12 cases of Influenza have been admitted. Strength and Ration Return 7. — O.R. 191. — M.T. 35 — M.T. 13 — Clarke Lieut Colonel O.C. 48th Field Ambulance 30/6/18	C

CONFIDENTIAL.

War Diary
of
48th Field Ambulance.
From 1st July 1918
to 31st July. 1918.

Volume 36.

Army Form C. 2118.

WAR DIARY
or
INTELLIGENCE SUMMARY.

VOLUME - 36 - 226.

Place	Date	Hour	Summary of Events and Information	Remarks and references to Appendices
PAS	1st July		Billet No 3 in PAS with accommodation for 50. OR has been given to the Rest Camp for use of personnel F.A. Barns occupied by personnel are now used for patients.	"
do	2nd July		Admissions to Field Ambulance 92. Remaining in Hospital 142 patients (Influenza) + other patients 161 - 234 Total Influenza 96 / 292	"
do	3rd July		Patients admitted 46 " " " 212 - 281	"
do	4th July		" 28 " " " 218 - 280	"
do	5th July		Lieut D.G. Garrett R.A.M.C. to transport today for duty with A.D.M.S. 39th Division Influenza admitted 32 Influenza remaining 161 - Influenza remaining 219	"

Army Form C. 2118.

WAR DIARY
or
INTELLIGENCE SUMMARY.
(Erase heading not required.)

Page 227

Place	Date	Hour	Summary of Events and Information	Remarks and references to Appendices
P A S	July 6th		Influenza Patients. Admitted 37. Total influenza in Hospital 144.	c.
do	July 7.		Total patients in Hospital 237. Lieut A.M. Macdonald RAMC U.S.A. posted for duty with 48th Field Ambulance. Influenza { admitted 37, remaining 173 } Total in Hospital 233.	c.
	8.		Influenza { admitted 30, remaining 143 } Total in Hospital 226	c.
	9.		Influenza { admitted 35, remaining 152 } " " " 220	E.A.F. Colwell RAMC posted 45 8 F.A. Lt Q..... NE Walsh RAMC posted 48 FA 9/7/13
	10.		Influenza { admitted 14, remaining 116 } " " " 166	c.
			Lieut Bartel RAMC proceeded today to report for duty with ADMS 39 Div. Capt Green RAMC transferred for duty as MO. 13th R.F.	c.

Army Form C. 2118.

WAR DIARY
or
INTELLIGENCE SUMMARY.
(Erase heading not required.)

Page 228.

Place	Date	Hour	Summary of Events and Information	Remarks and references to Appendices
P.A.S.	July 11th		Influenza { admissions 16 Total in Hospital 140 remaining 89	
do	July 12		Influenza { admissions 19 Total patients in Hospital 141 remaining 60	
do	July 13		Influenza { admissions 17 Total patients in Hospital 132 remaining 53	Rear Station fev. 9 Officers S/37 Ors Opened in P.A.S. Yesterday 14/7/18
do	14		Influenza { admissions 30 Total " " " 183 remaining 76	
do	15		Influenza { admissions 19 Total " " " 197 remaining 83	
do	16		Influenza { admissions 30 Total " " " 193 remaining 89	
do	17		Influenza { admissions 22 Total " " " 158 remaining 81	

Army Form C. 2118.

WAR DIARY
or
INTELLIGENCE SUMMARY.
(Erase heading not required.)

Page 229.

Instructions regarding War Diaries and Intelligence Summaries are contained in F. S. Regs., Part II. and the Staff Manual respectively. Title pages will be prepared in manuscript.

Place	Date	Hour	Summary of Events and Information	Remarks and references to Appendices
PAS	July 18		admissions 31 Total patients in Hospital	143.
			remaining 69	
do	July 19		admissions 17 Total patients in Hospital	133.
			remaining 66	
do	July 20		admissions 10 Total patients in Hospital	134.
			remaining 63	
do	21.		admissions 11 Total " " "	129
			remaining 62	
do	22		admissions 17 Total " " "	134
			remaining 69	
do	23		admissions 5 Total " " "	143
			remaining 52 Capt R.S. Stewart RAMC (T.) posted to 2/8th Field Ambulance	

Army Form C. 2118.

WAR DIARY
or
INTELLIGENCE SUMMARY.
(Erase heading not required.)

Page 230.

Place	Date	Hour	Summary of Events and Information	Remarks and references to Appendices
PA'S	July 24		Capt Bruce A.M.C. relieved Lt McDonald U.S.M.O.R.C as M.O.Ic 37 Div Wing	
			hyspag { admissions 5. Total in Hospital 142.	
			remaining 52.	
do.	July 25		Lieut McDonald M.O.R.C U.S.A. transferred to Base Hospital No 9. A.E.F. 25.7.18.	
			hyspag { admissions 18 Total patients in Hospital 131.	
			remaining 71.	
do.	July 26		Total admissions 41 remaining in Hospital 132	
do	July 27		admissions 31 " " " 120	
do	July 28		admissions 33 " " " 107	

Army Form C. 2118.

WAR DIARY
or
INTELLIGENCE SUMMARY.

(Erase heading not required.)

Page - 23/=

Instructions regarding War Diaries and Intelligence Summaries are contained in F. S. Regs., Part II. and the Staff Manual respectively. Title pages will be prepared in manuscript.

Place	Date	Hour	Summary of Events and Information	Remarks and references to Appendices
P.A.S.	July 29.		Admission to Rest Camp 33. remaining in Hospital 117	—
do.	30.		admission to Rest Camp 33 remaining in Hospital 119	—
do.	31.		Lt Cummings. U.S. M.O.R.C. posted to 48th Field Ambulance today. Admissions to Rest Camp. 27. remaining in Hospital 107. The epidemic of influenza which commenced towards end of June 1918 and accounted for the large number of cases in the Rest Camp during the early part of July 18th has almost completely subsided now. During the month of July 488 cases of influenza were admitted from the 37 Divison. Total admissions for influenza during Month of July 672. Strength of Unit. Officers 17. M.O. + 1 Q.M. M.O.R. 176 RAMC 35. A.S.C. 12. M.T.	—
do	31.		C Clark Lt Col Reeve O.C. 48 Field ambulance	

Confidential.

War Diary

of

48th Field Ambulance

from

1st August 1918 to 31st Augt. 1918.

Volume 37.

Army Form C. 2118.

WAR DIARY
or
INTELLIGENCE SUMMARY.
(Erase heading not required.)

Volume 37 Seqs 232

Place	Date	Hour	Summary of Events and Information	Remarks and references to Appendices
PAS	Aug 1st		Capt Drew RAMC proceeded to Takh in exchange of 37 Div RE today vice Capt Watson RAMC.	
"	2		Admissions 20. evacuations to C.C.S. 5.	
"	3		" 21 " C.C.S. 3.	
"	4		" 27 " C.C.S. 10.	
"	5		" 18 " C.C.S. 5.	
"	6		" 26 " C.C.S. 4.	
"	7		" 18 " C.C.S. 5.	
"			" 17 " C.C.S. 4.	
			Two small Hospital tents 20 beds have been set aside for drawing cases, thus bring 30 ct admissions for drawing each day from the Divisions	

Army Form C. 2118.

WAR DIARY
or
INTELLIGENCE SUMMARY.
(Erase heading not required.)

Page 233

Place	Date	Hour	Summary of Events and Information	Remarks and references to Appendices
P.A.S.	7. Aug.		Rectal cultivations or taken from all suspicious cases and motos are sent to 13th Mob. Lab. for examination. There have been a few cases of protozoan dysentery (Flexner) detected in this way. All cases of Dysentery & Clinical Dysentery are evacuated to No. 21. C.C.S. / 37 Div Rest Station	
"	8"		Admission 13. evacuated to C.C.S. 5.	"
"	9"		" 17. " C.C.S. 3.	"
"	10.		" 20. " C.C.S. 2.	"
"	11.		" 12. " C.C.S. 2.	"
"	12.		" 23. " C.C.S. 3.	"
"			D.M.S. III Army + D.D.M.S. IV Corps visited 48th F.A. 16 bdey.	"

Army Form C. 2118.

WAR DIARY
or
INTELLIGENCE SUMMARY.
(Erase heading not required.)

Page 23d

Instructions regarding War Diaries and Intelligence Summaries are contained in F. S. Regs., Part II. and the Staff Manual respectively. Title pages will be prepared in manuscript.

Place	Date	Hour	Summary of Events and Information	Remarks and references to Appendices
P.A.S	13th Aug		1st Lt S. L. McKinny U.S.M.O.R.C. posted to 48th F.A. today. Admission to Rest Station. 20. Evacuated to C.C.S 3.	3
"	14 Aug		Lieut Caldwell have proceeded today to attack company 13th K.R.R.C. vice Capt Rutherford to base. medical charge.	3
"	15 Aug		Patients admitted to Div. Rest Stn 23 discharged to C.C.S. 4.	3
"	16		" " " " " 21 " " " 4	
"	17		" " " " " 22 " " " 2	
"	18		" " " " " 28 " " " 4	
"	19		" " " " " 17 " " " 3	
"	20		" " " " " 41 " " " 3	
"			Our Brant Subdivision under Command Major Scott proceeded today to camp temporarily under Command 1 O.C. 5D. F.A.	3

Army Form C. 2118.

WAR DIARY
or
INTELLIGENCE SUMMARY.
(Erase heading not required.)

Army Form No. 235

Place	Date	Hour	Summary of Events and Information	Remarks and references to Appendices
PAS.	21st Aug.		Patrols wounded to Div Rec Station 5. discharged to C.C.S. 61. 1st Lt McKinney + 2 clerks posted to 29 C.C.S. 48th Field Ambulance transferred to HENU today. map reference 1 camp. D.13.d. Sheet 57.D.	
HENU.	22. Aug.		Lt. Cumming U.S.M.O.R.C. posted to May Scott for temporary duty with 50. F.A. at ESSARTS. #19.c. Sheet 57.D	
BIENVILLERS	23. Aug.		48th Field Ambulance transferred today to BIENVILLERS to form walking wounded Station at E.9.A.19. Sheet 57.D. 760 walking wounded passed through the Dressing Station at Bienvillers today and were evacuated on the lorries of 149th Field Ambulance	
BUCQUOY	24th Aug.		48th Field Ambulance transferred to F.26.c.7.7. one tent subdivision under May Scott to A.D.S. G.2. B.3.9.	

D. D. & L. London, E.C.
(A8004) Wt. W4771/M2731. 750,000 5/17 Sch. 53 Forms/C2118/14

Army Form C. 2118.

WAR DIARY
or
INTELLIGENCE SUMMARY.
(Erase heading not required.)

Page 236

Place	Date	Hour	Summary of Events and Information	Remarks and references to Appendices
BUCQUOY	Aug 25		Under instructions received from ADMS 37 Div 48th Field Ambulance opened a Main Dressing Station for 37 Div at 12 noon today at F.26.c.7.7. Patients being accommodated in tents and under tarpaulins. Walking wounded evacuated to GEZAINCOURT by empty lorries passing down BUCQUOY-ESSARTS road. Lying cases by MAC cars to DOULLENS. 80 cars transported to C.C.S. admitted 82 cases.	
"	Aug 26		Main Dressing Station admitted 59 cases. 58 cars transport to C.C.S.	
"	Aug 27		admitted 15 cases. 6 cars transport to car. Walking wounded from today transport to rail head at PUISIEUX. L20a.0.95. BUCQUOY continuing work.	

Army Form C. 2118.

WAR DIARY
or
INTELLIGENCE SUMMARY.
(Erase heading not required.)

Pages 237

Place	Date	Hour	Summary of Events and Information	Remarks and references to Appendices
BUCQUOY	Aug. 28.		Patients admitted 33. Evacuated to C.C.S. 20.	
"	Aug 29		" 20. " C.C.S. 9.	
"	Aug 30.		" 17. " C.C.S. 18.	
"	Aug 31		" 16. " C.C.S. 7.	
			48th Field Ambulance started at F.26.c.7.7. acting as Main Dressing Station for 37th Div. the division on present time in Reserve.	
			Strength 9 Off. F.A. Br + 9 ftn 1. Medical Units 7. ASC H.T. 35 R.A.M.C. O.R. 184. " M.T. 13	

Clarke Lieut

Confidential

War Diary
of
48th Field Ambulance
from
1st Sept 1918
to
30th Sept 1918

Volume 38

138 /

Army Form C. 2118.

WAR DIARY
or
INTELLIGENCE SUMMARY.
(Erase heading not required.)

VOL 38.

Place	Date	Hour	Summary of Events and Information	Remarks and references to Appendices
BUCQUOY F26.c.7.7	Sept 1st		48th Field Ambulance motor cars met Bucquoy and acting as MAIN Dressing Station for 37th Div. in Return light cars of sickness evacuated to Div Reception camp HENU & Walking cases sick and wounded to PUISIEUX railway station, stretcher and sitting cases by M.A.C. cars to GEZAINCOURT. Patients admitted 14. evacuated to C.C.S. 11.	
"	Sept 2nd		Patients admitted 23. evacuated to C.C.S. 17.	a
ACHIET-LE-GRAND	Sept 3		Under instructions received from A.D.M.S. 37 Div 48th Field Ambulance was transferred from Bucquoy today to ACHIET-LE-GRAND Sheet 57.c G.9. 6.5.0. Patients admitted 29. transferred to C.C.S. 31. 48th Field Amb. detailed to form a Div. Rest Station at ACHIET-LE-GRAND	a

Army Form C. 2118.

WAR DIARY
or
INTELLIGENCE SUMMARY.
(Erase heading not required.)

139

Place	Date	Hour	Summary of Events and Information	Remarks and references to Appendices
ACHIET LE-GRAND	Sept 4		Under instructions received from ADMS C. Sector 28th F.A. was transferred to FREMICOURT about 57° 1.19 centrals under the command of Major Wishart. Two Bearer subdivisions and 3. MAC amb. Cars were sent for duty with 50th Field Ambulance. Patients admitted 16 Evacuations out CCS 6.	a
	5 Sept		" 27 " "	a
	6 Sept		" 34 " C.C.S. 9/2 A Special Ward has been established in the Rest Camp for dysentery cases. Evacuations cars are examined by medical staff which is sent for evacuation to 13. M.A.Lab. GAZAIN COURT.	a

Army Form C. 2118.

WAR DIARY
or
INTELLIGENCE SUMMARY.
(Erase heading not required.)

Instructions regarding War Diaries and Intelligence Summaries are contained in F. S. Regs., Part II. and the Staff Manual respectively. Title pages will be prepared in manuscript.

Place	Date	Hour	Summary of Events and Information	Remarks and references to Appendices
ACHIET LE GRAND	Sept 7.		Rest Camp at Achiet le GRAND. Patients admitted 31 evacuated to C.C.S 9	ee
"	8		" 26 " " 14	ee
"	9		" 35 " " 6	ee
"	10		" 9 " " 5	ee
"	11.		Under instructions received from ADMS 37 Div. O.C. 2/8 field ambulance removed his quarters from ACHIET le GRAND. today and tomorrow until O Section 9 & 8" field ambulance at FREMICOURT in reserve in case a Walking Wounded Station was required at FREMICOURT	ee
"	12		Patients admitted 27 evacuated to C.C.S 6	
"	"		" 20 " " 12	
"	13.		Over tent subdivision of 2/8" field ambulance (C section) Two Officers and Transport, posted to 34 C.C.S. GREVILLERS S. For Villiers duty. Patients admitted 18 evacuated to C.C.S. 5.	ee

Army Form C. 2118.

WAR DIARY
or
INTELLIGENCE SUMMARY.
(Erase heading not required.)

Instructions regarding War Diaries and Intelligence Summaries are contained in F. S. Regs., Part II. and the Staff Manual respectively. Title pages will be prepared in manuscript.

Place	Date	Hour	Summary of Events and Information	Remarks and references to Appendices
ACHIET LE GRAND	Sept 14		A & B Field Ambulance Stations A & B at ACHIET LE GRAND. Mayor Wishart & transport of C section returned to ACHIET LE GRAND from FREMICOURT yesterday. Headquarters 9 FA at ACHIET LE GRAND. Patients evacuated 24.	
"	15th		evacuated to C.C.S. 5	
"	16th		26 evacuated to C.C.S. 9. Major WISHART, R.A.M.C. evacuated to 58 C.C.S GRENVILLERS suffering from dysentery. Sgt Sebastian states that he returned Major Wishart during partum of a minimum attack of dysentery. Patient admitted 111. evacuated to C.C.S. 12.	
"	17th		Lt Cummings M.O.R.C. (U.S.A) (prototype) duty with C-ration 48th F.A. at 34 C.E.S. Patient admitted 2. Evacuated to C.C.S. 10.	

Army Form C. 2118.

WAR DIARY
or
INTELLIGENCE SUMMARY.

(Erase heading not required.)

Place	Date	Hour	Summary of Events and Information	Remarks and references to Appendices
ACHIET LE GRAND	Sept 18		Under instructions received from A.D.M.S. 37 Division the REST CAMP of 37 Div was transferred today from the Brickfields ACHIET le GRAND to LOGEAST WOOD. Patients admitted 19. Evacuated to C.C.S. 5.	
LOGEAST WOOD	19		Patients admitted 8. Evacuated to C.C.S. 4.	
do	20		Patients admitted 4. Transferred to C.C.S. 3. Capt MASON R.A.M.C. (temporary attached) having completed his temporary absence of duty as acting D.A.D.M.S. to 37 Div. (Major Gibbons, on leave) Lt. Cawdron R.A.M.C. returned this unit and reported for premium medical charge of 13th K.R.R. Regt	
do	21		Patients admitted 4. Transferred to C.C.S. 3. " " " 3 " " C.C.S. 5.	

WAR DIARY or INTELLIGENCE SUMMARY.

Army Form C. 2118.

Place	Date	Hour	Summary of Events and Information	Remarks and references to Appendices
LOG-EAST WOOD.	Sept 22		REST Camp. Patients admitted 13. Transport to C.C.S. 13	
	23		Units instructions received from A.D.M.S. REST Camp at LOG-EAST WOOD was handed over by F.A. today. 148 Field Ambulance moved today into tents on our side in BAPAUME - ALBERT MH & cookhouse in LE BARQUE. Patients admitted into transport to C.C.S. nil.	
	24		48th Field Ambulance at rest in dugouts along BAPAUME - ALBERT road north of Butti. di Warlencourt. Patients admitted 6, evacuated to C.C.S. 1	
	25		A small party of 20 men was sent today to take over 12 empty Niessen huts on L.31, along BANCOURT - HAPLINCOURT R. Patients admitted 4, evacuated to C.C.S. 1.	

WAR DIARY or INTELLIGENCE SUMMARY.

Army Form C. 2118.

Place	Date	Hour	Summary of Events and Information	Remarks and references to Appendices
LE BARQUE	26 Sept.		Field Ambulance with transport 2/ Sick of 112 & 111 Brigades collected daily in Motor Ambulance wagons. Patients ½ admitted 1 evacuated to CCS	ox
"	27 Sept.		Patients 13 admitted " " evacuated to CCS	
"	28 Sept.		" 6 " 2 "	ox
"	29 Sept.		Under instructions received from ADMS the 48th Field Ambulance moved today by road from Le BARQUE to BANCOURT. Patients admitted 5. Transferred to 4.1	
METZ	30 Sept.		Under instructions received from ADMS 48th Field Ambulance moved today to METZ en COUTURE from BANCOURT. to the civil occupied by 14 Field Ambulance. S.Bn as A.O.S. Patients admitted 519. discharge to O.C.S. 2.	

Army Form C. 2118.

WAR DIARY
or
INTELLIGENCE SUMMARY.
(Erase heading not required.)

Place	Date	Hour	Summary of Events and Information	Remarks and references to Appendices
METZ EN COUTURE sheet 57.c.	Sept 30		No enemy posts taken out from 14th Field Ambulance gunmen in what is called now BAINTEAUX. 111th Brigade still in reserve to own front. No heart squads attached to each battalion R.A.P. 112th Brigade in support, two heart squads attached to each Battalion aid post. Strength unit. Officers 8 R.A.M.C. O.R. 182 A.S.C. H.T. 35 A.S.C. M.T. 13	57.c.
			Clark W/Col Commdt 43 Field Ambulance O.C. 30/9/18	

CONFIDENTIAL

WAR DIARY
of
48th FIELD AMBULANCE
FROM 1st OCTOBER 1918
TO 31st OCTOBER 1918

VOLUME 39.

Army Form C. 2118.

Page 146
VOLUME 29

WAR DIARY
or
INTELLIGENCE SUMMARY.
(Erase heading not required.)

Place	Date	Hour	Summary of Events and Information	Remarks and references to Appendices
GOUZEAUCOURT.	Oct 1st		48th Field Ambulance moved today from METZ-EN-COUTURE to GOUZEAUCOURT and opened an Advanced Dressing Station in a ruined building on the CAMBRAI-PERONNE Road at Q.36.d.5-9. CAMBRAI Sheet 57. Bearer Officer and car loading post on battalions at R.21.d.a.m. Aid posts R.22.e.5.2. 10 R.F. R.27.b.1.5. 13 R.B. Cars evacuate to M.D.S. at METZ-EN-COUTURE through CAMBRAI, PERONNE R. FINS along CAMBRAI, PERONNE R.	
"	Oct 2nd		One battalion of 111th Brigade in the line along the canal near BANTEUX this morning and increased to a two battalion front today.	

Army Form C. 2118.

WAR DIARY
or
INTELLIGENCE SUMMARY.
(Erase heading not required.)

Place	Date	Hour	Summary of Events and Information	Remarks and references to Appendices
GOUZEAUCOURT	Oct 3		A.D.S. in GOUZEAUCOURT enlarged by clearing rubbish and bricks out of ruined buildings and roofing them with corrugated iron. Walking Wounded Post established across the road at: Q.36.b.3.1. Lt Brackney. Transferred for duty to 50th Field Ambulance	
do.	Oct 4		Information received that the Corps Walking Wounded Collecting Post was being moved from ROYAULCOURT to GOUZEAUCOURT. Q.35.d.9.3.	
do	Oct 5th		A general attack this morning on BANTEUX Brigade established crossings over BANTEUX — VAUCELLES front line about 2500 yards east of their present line. Ambulance cars loading post established at Pont de la GRENOUILLERE near VAUCELLES clearing to A.D.S. at GOUZEAUCOURT.	

Army Form C. 2118.

WAR DIARY
or
INTELLIGENCE SUMMARY.
(Erase heading not required.)

148

Instructions regarding War Diaries and Intelligence Summaries are contained in F. S. Regs., Part II. and the Staff Manual respectively. Title pages will be prepared in manuscript.

Place	Date	Hour	Summary of Events and Information	Remarks and references to Appendices
GOUZEAUCOURT	6th		A.D.S. was moved today from GOUZEAUCOURT to Pont d.2 GRENOUILLERE. M20.a.8.3. the site of a German Dressing station being taken for the purpose, together with the cellar of this station building.	
VAUCELLES	7th		General situation quiet, very few cases passing through the A.D.S.	
VAUCELLES	8th		At 4.30 am this morning there was a general attack by three & fourth Armies on the Hindenburg line. marked progress was immediately made. During the evening the A.D.S. was advanced from the Pont de 2 GRENOUILLERE with the village of VAUCELLES. Capt Davidson R.A.M.C. posted to 48th July Ambulance and reported to Lt. Col. Thompson midway between 9/13th R.F. via Capt GRAVES wounded sick.	

D. D. & L., London, E.C. (A8604) Wt. W1771/M231 750,000 5/17 Sch. 52 Forms/C2118/14

149

WAR DIARY or INTELLIGENCE SUMMARY

Army Form C. 2118.

Places	Date	Hour	Summary of Events and Information	Remarks and references to Appendices
VAUCELLES	Oct 9th		Owing to the retreat of the enemy the A.D.S. moved from VAUCELLES (M15c.9.2) to ESNES. (H34c.95.45)	
ESNES			The village school being taken for an A.D.S. Our holding post situated at HOUCOURT (H.36.6.7.3) Capt Davidson RAMC evacuated wounded, and Lt Mitchell U.S.M.C. was posted as medical officer in temporary charge 9/13 R.F.	
CAUDRY	Oct 16th		Enemy retreat continuing A.D.S. advanced today to CAUDRY. (L30c.0.4) an empty lace factory being utilised for this purpose. Capt Trudgold posted to 1/1 & 48 F A Coy	

Army Form C. 2118.

150

WAR DIARY
or
INTELLIGENCE SUMMARY.

(Erase heading not required.)

Instructions regarding War Diaries and Intelligence Summaries are contained in F. S. Regs., Part II. and the Staff Manual respectively. Title pages will be prepared in manuscript.

Place	Date	Hour	Summary of Events and Information	Remarks and references to Appendices
CAUDRY.	Nov. 11th		Enemy retreating. A.D.S. advanced today to an emp^y factory in BEAUMONT. J.21.6.95.6b. Car loading post in VIESLY. J.4. central.	Sheet 57.B.
BEAUMONT	6N 12th		The 37 Div was relieved this evening by 5th Division. The A.D.S at BEAUMONT being handed out to 15th Field Ambulance at 1830 hrs. The Ambulance car of the 37 Division remained until midnight to assist in evacuation of the wounded.	

Army Form C. 2118.

WAR DIARY
or
INTELLIGENCE SUMMARY.
(Erase heading not required.)

Place	Date	Hour	Summary of Events and Information	Remarks and references to Appendices
CAUDRY	Oct 13th		37th Division at rest out of the line. 63rd & 112th Brigades in CAUDRY. 111th Brigade at LIGNY. The 48th Field Ambulance moved into an empty factory in CAUDRY today at (1.18 a central) the site of a previous German Hospital.	
CAUDRY	Oct 14		The large factory situated in CAUDRY at 1.18 a central appears to have been in the course of preparation for a German Casualty Clearing Hospital, as there are several hundred iron and wood frame trestles with a great number of parts of trestles not yet put together	

151

Army Form C. 2118.

WAR DIARY
or
INTELLIGENCE SUMMARY.
(Erase heading not required.)

152

Place	Date	Hour	Summary of Events and Information	Remarks and references to Appendices
CAUDRY	Oct. 15.		The Factory Building occupied by the Field Ambulance is being cleaned out. The returning Germans have made it a practice to stable their horses in all ground floor rooms, even recent hospital wards are being used as any duty not mainly staff	
do	2V/16.		An examination of the motor material left over in the Buildings left behind by the German rear about 600 paper bandages and 600 packets of paper tissue substitute for wool. numerous wooden splints and bottles of serum were also found. These have been placed in a crate and directed to D.M.S. III Army for War Museum of Medicine.	

Army Form C. 2118.

WAR DIARY
or
INTELLIGENCE SUMMARY.
(Erase heading not required.)

153

Instructions regarding War Diaries and Intelligence Summaries are contained in F. S. Regs., Part II. and the Staff Manual respectively. Title pages will be prepared in manuscript.

Place	Date	Hour	Summary of Events and Information	Remarks and references to Appendices
CAUDRY	Oct 17		48th Field Ambulance in billets near 1.18 & centred 37th Division resting in billets out of the line. CAUDRY is shelled by enemy HV gun at frequent intervals several casualties have occurred amongst the civilian population as well as amongst the troops billeted in the town	
	Oct 18			
	19th		A selection of German splints, dressings, bandages, oxygen cylinder etc. under sent today in a Regt: crate to ADMS Third Army for the National War Museum	
	25th		G.O.C. 37th Division ordered 48th Field Ambulance today and inspected the Hospital site and billets. General attack commenced this morning 5th Div in the line, 37 Div in support. Prisoners in Corps Cage inspected by interns and injections given by Maj Mason.	

Army Form C. 2118.

WAR DIARY
or
INTELLIGENCE SUMMARY.
(Erase heading not required.)

154

Place	Date	Hour	Summary of Events and Information	Remarks and references to Appendices
CAUDRY.	Oct. 21st		General attack progressing well. 5th Div. have captured BEAURAIN. Several hundred prisoners have passed through the Corps Cage at CAUDRY.	
	Oct 22nd		ADMS 37 Div. & OC 48FA inspected VIESLY today for M.D.S. etc.	
VIESLY	Oct 23rd		48th Field Ambulance moved today at 05.00 hrs from CAUDRY to VIESLY. M.D.S. established in the CHATEAU the RC church, for stretcher cases. A Walking Wounded station was established across the road in the village school house. A blacksmith shop and a large store were used to take RCth accommodation. 50 stretcher cases + 200 walking wounded. M.D.S commenced to function at 14.00 hrs. 37 Div. arrived 5 km in line this morning. 10:00 h.	

Army Form C. 2118.

WAR DIARY
or
INTELLIGENCE SUMMARY.

(Erase heading not required.)

Instructions regarding War Diaries and Intelligence Summaries are contained in F.S. Regs., Part II. and the Staff Manual respectively. Title pages will be prepared in manuscript.

155

Place	Date	Hour	Summary of Events and Information	Remarks and references to Appendices
VIESLY	Oct 24th		Stretchers and blankets taken on from Field Ambulance	
			5 Div at BETHENCOURT. 5 Div. M.D.S.	
			A.D.S. +9th Field Ambulance at BRIASTRE. Admissions 26. 5T	
			M.D.S. 48th " " VIESLY sick 57 wounded	
			Evacuations 14. 5T	
VIESLY	Oct 25		Attack by 37th Division progressing. New Zealand Division on left flank. 21st Div. on right flank.	
			VENDIGIES + NEUVILLE VENDIGIES occupied up by 57 B. (F 7 antr)	
			Admissions sick 30. wounded 10.0.	
			Evacuations 15. 98.	
			The Germans are covering their retreat by fire shelling of recently occupied Tys in with high Explosion shells and gas shells of Br. YELLOW + GREEN Cross amm.	"

WAR DIARY
or
INTELLIGENCE SUMMARY.

Army Form C. 2118.

156

Place	Date	Hour	Summary of Events and Information	Remarks and references to Appendices
VIESLY	Nov 26		Advance continued. BEAUDIGNIES + GHISSIGNIES occupied outskirts of LE QUESNOY reached on western side. (VALENCIENNES MAP)	C
			admissions 41 sick 41 wounded	
			Evacuated 30 sick 40 wounded	
			of the 48" Field Ambulance one ambulance car driver was on trek was evacuated wounded which had also been evacuated suffering from yellow cross gas poisoning. A boy's member of stretcher cases had to be evacuated by night along a hand shelled road & in addition two dug-outs occupied by teams were struck by bursting gas shells which scattered a considerable quantity of earth into them during raid.	
do	Nov 27		No attack by 37th Div today	a
			admissions 27 sick 55 wounded	
			evacuations 20 53	

WAR DIARY or INTELLIGENCE SUMMARY.

Army Form C. 2118.

Place	Date	Hour	Summary of Events and Information	Remarks and references to Appendices
do	Oct 28		No attack by 37th Division today. Wounded Sick 23 34 Evacuations Capt SHEENAN RAMC (TC) & Lieut SLEIGH R.N reported for duty, the former was evacuated sick to the 50th Field Ambulance. Lieut Col G. CLARKE DSO RAMC proceeded on leave. Major S. SCOTT took over temporary command of the Ambulance, was evacuated. Diagnosed Passed (? female) (shell) W. General situation very quiet.	SS
do	Oct 29		No attack by 37th Division today. Wounded Sick 36 33 Evacuations Situation still very quiet.	SS
do	Oct 30		Situation unchanged. Wounded Sick 25 14 Evacuations	SS
do	Oct 31		Situation unchanged. Wounded Sick 19 21 Evacuations A site at the Convent in SOLESMES was reconnoitred with the view to a new Dressing Station. It was decided to send up the following morning an advance party on...	SS

Army Form C. 2118.

WAR DIARY
or
INTELLIGENCE SUMMARY.
(Erase heading not required.)

-158-

Place	Date	Hour	Summary of Events and Information	Remarks and references to Appendices
Vicoly	31st Oct		Strength of Unit on October 31st 1915	
			Officers 9	
			R.A.M.C. (Other ranks) 174	
			M.T. 13	
			A.S.C. 35	
			S. Scott	
			Major RAMC T	
			A/OC 46th Field Ambulance	

CONFIDENTIAL

WAR DIARY
OF
48th FIELD AMBULANCE
FROM
1st TO 30th NOVR- 1918.

VOLUME 40.

48 F.A.

VOLUME 40. Page 159

Army Form C. 2118.

WAR DIARY or INTELLIGENCE SUMMARY.

Place	Date	Hour	Summary of Events and Information	Remarks and references to Appendices
VIESLY	Nov 1		The unit is still manning the Main Dressing Station for the Division. There are no active operations taking place on this front so that the casualties coming through are very few. Sich —16 } for 24 hours Wounded —30 } Capt. SHEEHAN R.A.M.C. was posted for duty (H.q. 4th North Staffordshire Regiment) An advance party under Major MASON R.A.M.C. was sent to the front at SOLESMES (E.1.9.7.2) Sheet 57 B with the view to preparing it for a Main Dressing Station	S.S.
VIESLY	Nov 2		No change in situation. Casualties Wounded 8 } for 24 hours Sich 30 }	S.S.
SOLESMES	Nov 3		The unit moved to-day to SOLESMES to-gh over the tramways which the Advance Party had previously prepared. The attack is being carried on across now. Holding Party was left behind at VIESLY to hold the billets. Capt GRAIG R.A.M.C. 50th Field Ambulance reported for duty, as a reinforcement during the operations. Casualties Wounded 8 } for 24 hours Sich 41 }	
SOLESMES	Nov 4		Attack started this morning at 0530 hours. The 17th Division were on the right and the New Zealand Division on the left of the Division. The 113th Brigade made the initial attack which they had captured their objectives then the 112th Brigade passed through them	

WAR DIARY or INTELLIGENCE SUMMARY

Army Form C. 2118.

Place	Date	Hour	Summary of Events and Information	Remarks and references to Appendices
SOLESMES (continued)	Nov 4		49th Field Ambulance are running the line with the Bus loading Post at BEAUDIGNIES & A.D.S. at SALESCHES, clearing from thence to M.D.S. at SOLESMES. The arrangements at the Main Dressing Station worked well, at one time in the late afternoon we had 80 shelter cases & 100 walking wounded waiting to be cleared which the M.A.C. were not apparently able to do at once, but they were all under shelter & were fed. The C.C.S. were not always able to return blankets & stretchers in exchange for those sent down in this way it is calculated we lost 200 blankets & about 60 stretchers in the afternoon. Casualties passed through M.D.S. up to 6 p.m. Wounded 49 Sick 49	
SOLESMES	Nov 5		The Main Dressing Station closed down at 06.30 hrs, the function being taken on by the A.D.S. at SALESCHES under the charge of the 49th Field Ambulance until such time as the Main Dressing Station is established by the 5th Division, the 14th Division operation relieving our men in the line this morning. The M.D.S. were cleared of all patients by 0630 hours, 34th Division 14th Division Prisoners of War. Casualties 344 215 152 It was particularly noticeable how our badly wounded the majority of them Prisoners of War were most of them from	CS

WAR DIARY
or
INTELLIGENCE SUMMARY.

Army Form C. 2118.

Place	Date	Hour	Summary of Events and Information	Remarks and references to Appendices
SOLESMES	Nov 6th		Still fine. In the early morning the unit vacated by the new Headquarters of the 49th Field Ambulance villers shut in nosing sick collected from the 111th Inf. Bde (such who are also stationed in the village	S.S
BEAUVAIN	Nov 7th		Sick collected from units in village & despatched to 50th Field Ambulance at BRIASTRE. Capt. W.R. Wyeth R.A.M.C reported for duty after sick leave in England. Unit moved to BEAU over to Divisional Rest Station situated at S.S	S.S
BEAURAIN	Nov 8th		BRIASTRE from the 50th Field Ambulance. A conference at the A.D.M.S. office was attended in the afternoon, subjects being (1) the Prophylactic treatment of Venereal disease in the Army (2) Recent epidemics. Capt. Eaves R.A.M.C reported to the unit for duty having been discharged from hospital.	S.S
BRIASTRE	Nov 9th		Running Divisional Rest Station, all cases of Pyrexia are being sent to C.C.S owing to the dangerous epidemic of Influenza & lack of proper facilities for treatment at the D.R.S. The accommodation for patients of which is about 150. Lieut MITCHELL S. U.S.M.O.R.C. took over the permanent medical charge of the 13th Royal Fusiliers	S.S

Army Form C. 2118.

WAR DIARY
or
INTELLIGENCE SUMMARY.
(Erase heading not required.)

No. 2

Place	Date	Hour	Summary of Events and Information	Remarks and references to Appendices
BRIASTRE	Nov 10th		A special evacuation of 40 patients & G.C.S. at SOLESMES was settled for in the morning, this was carried out. 37th Division Admissions 23. Evacuated to C.C.S. 53.	S.S
BRIASTRE	Nov 11th		37th Division concentrated in GAUDRY & BETHENCOURT. An Armistice was proclaimed. An announc. between the firing of Allied troops firing to cease at 1100 hours. 37th Division Admissions 25. Evacuated to C.C.S. 13.	S.S
BRIASTRE	Nov 12th		37th Division Admissions 6. Evacuations to C.C.S. 6.	S.C
BRIASTRE	Nov 13th		8 other Ranks proceeded from this unit to form a detachment from 49th Field Ambulance to form a representative party from the 37th Division under the command of Major G. Nicholson RAMC in the ceremonial presentation by the G.O.C. Commander at GAUDRY. 37th Division Admissions 4. Evacuations 1.	S.S
BRIASTRE	Nov 14th		Lieut GUMMINGS R.O.R.C. & 1st sub-division returned to duty from 21 C.C.S. where they had been on loan. 37th Division Admissions 1. Evacuations 1.	S.S

Army Form C. 2118.

WAR DIARY
or
INTELLIGENCE SUMMARY.
(Erase heading not required.)

No. 163

Instructions regarding War Diaries and Intelligence Summaries are contained in F. S. Regs., Part II. and the Staff Manual respectively. Title pages will be prepared in manuscript.

Place	Date	Hour	Summary of Events and Information	Remarks and references to Appendices
BRIASTRE	Oct 15		48th Field Ambulance in CHATEAU BRIASTRE. Journey not station for the Division. H.Q. of 37 Div. Oct 11 to Felleu	
do	16		CAUDRY. 37 Division resting in Felleu	
do	17		Rest Station. Patient admission 12	
			Evacuation 12 to trains	
			" " admissions	
			Evacuations sick 3	
			Surgeon It. SLEIGH. R.N. transferred for duty to IX Corps.	
do	18		Rest station. Admissions	
			Canadian CCS 1.	
			Inspection of 48th Field Ambulance by ADMS 37 Div, 10 Royal Fusiliers	
			Capt GRAVES. M.C. transferred to MDS	

Army Form C. 2118.

WAR DIARY
or
INTELLIGENCE SUMMARY.

(Erase heading not required.)

Place	Date	Hour	Summary of Events and Information	Remarks and references to Appendices
Bruah	Nov 19th		Rest Station { admissions 1 evacuations 1 }	
	Nov 20th		Rest Station { admissions 7 evacuations nil }	
	Nov 21st		48th Field Ambulance opened Coy at BETHENCOURT by G.O.C. 112th Brigade. Rest Station { admissions 1 evacuations nil }	
"	Nov 22nd		Commandant paid S/ 37 Div. by G.O.C. 37 Div at CAPPRY 48 FA, 49 FA, 50 FA hospital for sick by pass under command ADMS. Col Mophing CMG DSO Rest Station admissions 5 evacuations nil	

Army Form C. 2118.

WAR DIARY
or
INTELLIGENCE SUMMARY.
(Erase heading not required.)

165

Place	Date	Hour	Summary of Events and Information	Remarks and references to Appendices
BRIASTRE	Nov 23		R.a.P Station { admissions nil { Evacuations 2.	
"	Nov 24		" { admissions nil { Evacuations nil	
"	Nov 25		" { admissions 3 { Evacuations nil	
"	Nov 26		" { admissions 3 { Christening nil { admissions 2 { Evacuations 1.	
"	Nov 27		Under instructions from A.D.M.S. 37 Division on Medical Officer was sent today to SOLESMES to visit BRITISH P.O.W's lately visited there inspecting returning British Prisoners of War from Germany. British improved in the O form of SOLESMES Railway Station 5% cases. Numbers of British men in mown of unknown though known by campo and Railway Station. 200 to 300 various.	

WAR DIARY
or
INTELLIGENCE SUMMARY

Army Form C. 2118.

Place	Date	Hour	Summary of Events and Information	Remarks and references to Appendices
BRIASTRE	Nov 28		An Aeroplane both dropped Christmas cheer &	
			Xmas Chronical. Also the unit made the following exchanges	
			Churchy & Papers — Min. of les — Ant.	
			Shorthand — German — ENGLISH	
			French	
			Arithmetic — Bookkeeping — English literature	
			Rest Station { atr mins 1	
	Nov 29		" " { enanitis 2	
			{ abrasions 1	
			{ Gastritis 1	
			{ abrasions 3	
			{ Incidents 2	
	Nov 30		Major Mason proceed today for duty with ADMS	
			Lieut Cummings U.S.M.C. posted for temporary duty in MDS & Travels	
			Strength 4 Stret Ambulance HT 35	
			officers 6 OR (RAMC) 167 ASC. MT. 12	

O Clark Major
OC 2/1/1 Fd Amb
30/11/18

[CONFIDENTIAL]

War Diary

of

48th Field Ambulance

from

1st Dec. 1918 to 31st Dec. 1918.

Volume 41.

VOLUME H

Army Form C. 2118.

WAR DIARY
or
INTELLIGENCE SUMMARY.
(Erase heading not required.)

Page 167.

Place	Date	Hour	Summary of Events and Information	Remarks and references to Appendices
BRIASTRE	Dec 1st		48th Field Ambulance at BRIASTRE CHATEAU. Lt Col Smith in charge of the 37th Divisional Hospital. Patients { admitted 12 { Evac to C.C.S. 3	
do	Dec 2nd		Patients { admitted 2 { evac troops n.l.	
do	Dec 3rd		Patients { admitted 12 { Evac to C.C.S. 1	
do	Dec 4th		Patients { admitted 5 { Evac to CCS 1	
do	Dec 5th		Patients { admitting 9 { evacuations 6. An advance party of AD of M Ambulance, 1 Tent subdivision with transport complete, proceeded today to BAVAI to open a rest station, a crossroads amount of function attaining it for the rest station together with 20 personnel proceed from BRIASTRE to BAVAI by lorries.	

Army Form C. 2118.

WAR DIARY
or
INTELLIGENCE SUMMARY.
(Erase heading not required.)

Instructions regarding War Diaries and Intelligence Summaries are contained in F. S. Regs., Part II. and the Staff Manual respectively. Title pages will be prepared in manuscript.

Place	Date	Hour	Summary of Events and Information	Remarks and references to Appendices
BRIASTRE	Dec 6th	6.	Capt Brady & RAMC proceeded today to BAVAI to take charge of Rest Station there. Rest Station Briastre { Patients admitted 4 { Evacuated CCS 3	
BAVAI.	Dec 7th		48th Field Ambulance together with 43 patients in the Divisional Rest Station proceeded to BAVAI today personnel & patients travelling in lorries, transport by road. Rest Station { admitted 11 Patients. { Evac to CCS 10	
BAVAI.	Dec 8		Rest station situated in a German military Hospital building in BAVAI at junction of Mons & Maubeuge Rds. Capt Brady RAMC posted to temporary medical charge 13 R.I.F. 8th Brigade. U.S.M.C. rejoined 48th F.A. from " Lt Cunningham. Rest Station. Patients { admitted 5 { Evac CCS 8	

(A8004) Wt. W1771/M2931 739,000 5/17 Sch. 52 Forms/C2118/14
D. D. & L., London, E.C.

Army Form C. 2118.

WAR DIARY
or
INTELLIGENCE SUMMARY.
(Erase heading not required.)

169.

Place	Date	Hour	Summary of Events and Information	Remarks and references to Appendices
BAVAI	Dec 9th		Patients { admitted 7 { Evac to CCS 2	
do	Dec 10		Patients { admitted 12 { Evac CCS 6	
do	Dec 11th		Divisional Education scheme working well in the various trades and classes having been formed of the following subjects. FRENCH. GERMAN. Bookkeeping. Shorthand. Chemistry + Physics. DRAWING. ARITHMETIC. Classes in each subject enough for three hours work. Patients admitted 13 - sending 2 to CCS 3. Patients admitted 14 = discharged to CCS. nil	
do	Dec 12th		Patients admitted 14 = discharged to CCS. nil	

WAR DIARY or INTELLIGENCE SUMMARY.

Army Form C. 2118.

Place	Date	Hour	Summary of Events and Information	Remarks and references to Appendices
BAVAI.	Dec. 13.		Major Scott RAMP evacuated today to 58 CCS suffering from NYD (Dysentery). Patients adm. 21. discharged to CCS nil.	
			Patients admitted 21 discharged 6 CCS nil.	
			Col. Morphew DSO CMG proceeded on Home leave. Lt Col R Clarke DSO (2nd in command) took over ADMS in the absence.	
do	Dec 14		Patients admitted 19 discharged 17. Transport now 74 O.R.	
			" " 19	1 Appx.
			" discharged 17 CCS	
BAVAI.	Dec/14		37 Div. commenced moving today from area near BAVAI to area north of CHARLEROI. 111th Brigade to about [?]. 48" Field Ambulance to about 111 Brigade on the march & moved area. Two tent subdivisions of 48/17A C.F. attached at BAVAI under Capt Wishart to form Rest Station for Divisionary Baggage ?? and one tent subdivision under Major Nixon to follow 111th Brigade on the march and clear sick.	

Army Form C. 2118.

WAR DIARY
or
INTELLIGENCE SUMMARY.
(Erase heading not required.)

Instructions regarding War Diaries and Intelligence Summaries are contained in F. S. Regs., Part II. and the Staff Manual respectively. Title pages will be prepared in manuscript.

VALENCIENNES

Place	Date	Hour	Summary of Events and Information	Remarks and references to Appendices
BAVAI	Dec 14		Rest Station. Patients admitted 11. 111th Brigade marched today from WARGNIES RRE to HERGIES. Two horsed and two motor ambulance wagons attached to the Brigade for chest - sick	
BAVAI	Dec 15		111th Infantry Brigade marched today from HERGIES to LOUVROIL. Patients admitted to Rest Station 15 — discharged to duty 1.	
BAVAI	Dec 16		111th Inf. Brigade marched today from LOUVROIL to JEUMONT. Patients admitted to Rest Station at BAVAI 4 — discharged to C.C.S. 1. Capt. RAYMOND R.A.M.C relieved Major RASON R.A.M.C. from command of section marching with the 111th Inf. Brigade. R.S.M. ELLIS rejoined for duty.	S.C.
BAVAI	Dec 17		111th Inf. Brigade rested today. Admissions 15 — discharged to C.C.S. 4	C.S
BAVAI	Dec 18		111th Inf. Brigade resumed the march & marched to VELLEREILLE - LES - BRAYEUX. Admissions 5 — discharged to C.C.S. 3.	S.S

Army Form C. 2118.

WAR DIARY
or
INTELLIGENCE SUMMARY.
(Erase heading not required.)

Place	Date	Hour	Summary of Events and Information	Remarks and references to Appendices
BAVAI	Dec	19th	111th Inf Brigade marched to AUDERLIES. Major MASON & Capt WISHART left the unit & proceed to War Office London for demobilisation. Capt MAGIRGAN M.C. RAMC R.O. I/c RAMC R.O. I/c 13th Herts Regt (Capt RAYMOND) M.C. RAMC R.O. I/c 13th Rifle Brigade are recalled to the Field Ambulance to replace them. Admissions 9. Evacuated to C.C.S. 8.	S.S
LODELINSART	Dec	20	111th Inf Brigade reached their billeting area. 45th Fd Amb are stationed in LODELINSART Hdqrs transferred to LODELINSART, all the personnel are billeted in civilian houses. Admissions 8. Evacuated to C.C.S. 5.	S.S
LODELINSART	Dec	21	Brigade Rest Station formed in an empty café. Admissions 5. Evacuated to C.C.S. 7.	C.C
LODELINSART	Dec	22	Time spent in cleaning up, formation of canteen, reading room, recreation room etc. Admissions 4. Evacuated to C.C.S. 1.	S.S
LODELINSART	Dec	23	Admissions 2. Evacuated to C.C.S. 3.	S.S
LODELINSART	Dec	24	Admissions 3. Evacuated to C.C.S. 2.	S.S
LODELINSART	Dec	25	In the evening a dinner was given to the men then dinner consisted of Turkey, ham, plum pudding from the funds of the canteen; beer & cigarettes being held in the Village Concert Hall. A dinner of Roast Beef, Plum Pudding was given to the patients. Admissions 2. Evacuated to C.C.S. 1.	S.C
LODELINSART	Dec	26	Remainder of personnel from BAVAI reported at LODELINSART. Admissions 5. Evacuated to C.C.S. 1.	S.S

Army Form C. 2118.

WAR DIARY
or
INTELLIGENCE SUMMARY.
(Erase heading not required.)

Instructions regarding War Diaries and Intelligence Summaries are contained in F.S. Regs., Part II. and the Staff Manual respectively. Title pages will be prepared in manuscript.

Place	Date	Hour	Summary of Events and Information	Remarks and references to Appendices
LODELINSART	Dec 27th		Remainder of transport arrived from BAVAI having spent 2 days on the road attending the intervening night at BINCHES, they were under the command of Lieut CUMMINGS MORC. VS. Admissions 5. Evacuations 3.	S.S.
LODELINSART	Dec 28		Admissions 4. Evacuations 2.	S.S.
LODELINSART	Dec 29		Building for our Rest Station reconnoitred in LODELINSART. Admissions 2. Evacuations nil.	S.S.
LODELINSART	Dec 30		Admissions 3. Evacuations 1.	S.S.
LODELINSART	Dec 31		Admissions 2. Evacuations to C.C.S. 1. In the evening a Regimental Dance was run by the field Ambulance, civilians were invited by invitation. Effective strength of Unit. Officers 5. R.A.M.C personnel 158. A.S.C. (H.T.) 28. A.S.C. (M.T.) 12. Total 656 H cos 5/188 men.	S.S.

S. Scott
Maj R.A.M.C.
A/O.C. 46th Field Ambulance
R.A.M.C.

Confidential

War Diary

of

48th Field Ambulance

from

1st to 31st January

1919

Volume 42

Army Form C. 2118.

WAR DIARY
or
INTELLIGENCE SUMMARY.
(Erase heading not required.)

Place	Date	Hour	Summary of Events and Information	Remarks and references to Appendices
LODELINSART	Jan 1st		New Year's Day – The Rest Station was transferred from the Café in the Rue Yserie to a house in the Rue Reurchival, which has a capacity for 30 beds. Admissions to hospital.	S.S.
"	Jan 2nd		Authority received from A.D.M.S. to draw beds from the 42nd & 23rd Division at CHARLEROI up to the number of 150 as at present unit.	S.S.
"	Jan 3rd		Admissions to hospital. Evacuations to H.G.S. Received by train from 34th Divisional M.T. Coy 6 rugs, 2 mattresses & curtains. Rest Station equipped. Admissions to hospital. Evacuations to C.C.S.	S.S
"	Jan 4th		R.A.M.C. Order No 137 received by which all the medical officers in 15 Division are grouped in the Field Ambulances, this field ambulance has the Medical Sanitary Care of the 111th 2nd Brigade Group then the 9th North Staffs, 34th Machine Gun Company, 34th Divisional M.T. Coys & 2 Coys Vols Working Party sent to Gosselies to clean up & prepare a school which has been chosen for the new Divisional Rest Station. Lieut GIBBS R.A.M.C. O.C. 60 Sanitors Section & personnel reported to this unit & under orders from A.D.M.S. are attached for rations.	S.S
"	Jan 5th		Capt. TREADGOLD R.A.M.C. and 13th Royal Fusiliers reported for duty. Admissions to hospital. Evacuations to C.C.S.	
"	Jan 6th		In the morning the hospital & transport lines were inspected by the G.O.C. 34th Division. In the evening a very successful dance was held in the hall in the Central	S.S

Army Form C. 2118.

WAR DIARY
or
INTELLIGENCE SUMMARY.
(Erase heading not required.)

Instructions regarding War Diaries and Intelligence Summaries are contained in F. S. Regs., Part II. and the Staff Manual respectively. Title pages will be prepared in manuscript.

Place	Date	Hour	Summary of Events and Information	Remarks and references to Appendices
LOBELINSART (cont)	Jan 6th	6th	Square: Admissions to hospital 4. Evacuations to C.C.S. 4	S.S
	Jan 7th		Admissions to hospital 4. Evacuations to C.C.S. 1	S.C
	Jan 8th	6th	Admissions to hospital 3. Evacuations to C.C.S. 2	
	Jan 9th	9th	Admissions to hospital 8. Evacuations to C.C.S. 5	S.S
			The patients from the 111th Brigade were allotted to #8 Fd Amb., then sent onwards to C.C.S. or returned to their Lodgment. 12. Rue de RENDOSSEVAL where a small hospital exists. 20 patients has been established. Serious patients are treated in this Hospital.	J. W. Hackett
	Jan 10th		Investigation of the Personnel of the unit to proceed for demobilization. Army sent to the IV Corps Collecting Camp in CHARLEROI. up to date from Jan 1st 1919. 4 Ryders [illegible] and 3 men (O.R.) have been demobilised.	
	Jan 11th	11th	Admissions to hospital 16. Evacuations to C.C.S. 12.	
	Jan 12	12	Admissions " " 19. " " 15.	
	Jan 13	13	Admissions " " 7. " " 2.	
			Admissions " " 8. " " 2.	C.L.

Army Form C. 2118.

WAR DIARY
or
INTELLIGENCE SUMMARY.
(Erase heading not required.)

176

Place	Date	Hour	Summary of Events and Information	Remarks and references to Appendices
LODELINSART	Jan 14th		Admissions 10. Evacuations to C.C.S. 8	
	Jan 15th		" 14. " 12.	
	" 16th		" 3. " 5.	
			A Conference was held today at the ADMS office with reference to the reorganization of Field Ambulances. According to the new organization a Field Ambulance will consist of two sections commanded by a Lt.Col. with a Major as 2nd in command. Total strength 8 officers 162 Rank & personnel 25 att. H.T. H.S. 13 MT H.S.	
			Instructions were issued for the return to medical stores (ISADMS.) all medical equipment of C section. Instructions with reference to the disposal of the ordinary horse wagons and animals of C section to be issued later. Cl-	
	16th		Admissions 3. Evacuations 5.	

Army Form C. 2118.

WAR DIARY
or
INTELLIGENCE SUMMARY.
(Erase heading not required.)

Instructions regarding War Diaries and Intelligence Summaries are contained in F. S. Regs., Part II. and the Staff Manual respectively. Title pages will be prepared in manuscript.

Place	Date	Hour	Summary of Events and Information	Remarks and references to Appendices
LODELINSART	Jan 17		Admissions to Hospital 6 Evacuations to CCS 7	c
	18		admissions 1 " " 2	c
			4 other Ranks belonging to 7th unit were discharged today	
	19		admissions 7 evacuations to CCS 6	
	20		admissions 1 " CCS 1	
	21		admissions 6 " CCS 6	
	22		admissions 5 " CCS 6	
	23		admissions 6 " CCS 5	
			10 Other ranks of this unit were discharged today. The personnel of the unit are billeted in the houses of LODELINSART those were being fixed in a house. Beds with sheets are provided and the Belgian inhabitants hun down everything possible to make the men feel as comfortable as possible.	c

Army Form C. 2118.

WAR DIARY
or
INTELLIGENCE SUMMARY.

(Erase heading not required.)

178

Place	Date	Hour	Summary of Events and Information	Remarks and references to Appendices
LODELINSART	Jan 24th		Admissions to Hospital 3 evacuated to C.C.S. 1.	
	Jan 25th		Admissions to Hospital 4 evacuated to C.C.S. 3. The serious patients in the Hospital at LODELINSART were transferred today to the new Hospital at GOSSELIES where full length baths have been installed and better facilities exist for the treatment of skin diseases. 11.0.R) were demobilised today	a
	Jan 26th		Admissions to Hospital 4 evacuations to C.C.S. 2.	
	Jan 27th		Admissions to Hospital 5 C.C.S. 1. 6 (O.R.) were demobilised yesterday. All the remaining patients in the Hospital at LODELINSART were transferred today to GOSSELIES. Capt McLagan RAMC acting officer in charge of the Hospital at LODELINSART.	a
	Jan 28th		Admissions to Hospital at GOSSELIES 3. Admissions 4 evacuation to C.C.S. 3.	a

Army Form C. 2118.

WAR DIARY
or
INTELLIGENCE SUMMARY.
(Erase heading not required.)

179

Place	Date	Hour	Summary of Events and Information	Remarks and references to Appendices
LODELINSART	Jan 29th		Admissions to Hospital 3. Evacuations to C.C.S. 4. Owing to the shortage of personnel amongst the A.S.C. H.T. considerable difficulty is experienced in running the transport and cars of Motor horses and mules. ASC. H.T. 12 RAMC personnel has been detailed to report daily to the Senior M.O. for stable duty.	
"	Jan 30th		Admissions to Hospital 0. Evacuations to C.C.S. 5. So much sickness for the personnel of this has been attained by holding but owing to the hard frost of railways any repairs has been stopped. A weekly dance has been organised for the personnel of the unit each man turning daily by rotation.	
"	Jan 31st		Strength of the unit Officers 7/8. RAMC 118. RASC.MT. 24 RAMC MT. 12 —— 161	[signature]

70 & 8 Field Ambulances.

Army Form C. 2118

WAR DIARY
or
INTELLIGENCE SUMMARY.
(Erase heading not required.)

Place	Date	Hour	Summary of Events and Information	Remarks and references to Appendices
LODELINSART	Feb 1st		General situation of the unit. Headquarters of the #8 Field Ambulance at LODELINSART, together with ambulance cars. Horse lines of the unit one mile away at LODELINSART railway station. Divisional Rest Station at GOSSELIES in the school next to the Hotel de Ville Gosselies. 19 patients in Hospital today with 1 admission. Demobilization of the unit in progress.	c.
do	Feb 2nd		Patients admissions 2 to duty 2 remaining in Hospital 17. evacuations 3. Four men of the unit demobilized today.	c.
do	Feb 3		Patients admissions 7 to duty 1 remaining in Hospital 14. evacuations 4. according to orders received 3 men will be demobilized from the unit over day [?] in every three days.	c.

Army Form C. 2118.

WAR DIARY
or
INTELLIGENCE SUMMARY.
(Erase heading not required.)

Place	Date	Hour	Summary of Events and Information	Remarks and references to Appendices
Lodelinsart	Feb 4		Patients:- admitted 2 Evacuees 3 } remaining in Hospital 16. The general health of the Division is very good except for a few cases of influenza: everyone feels the cold can be treated in the surrounding area. A certain number however develops symptoms of signs of lung infection and require evacuation to CCS.	G.
Lodelinsart	5.		Patients:- admitted 5 to duty 1 } remaining in Hospital 15 Evac. NYPS 2 There was 9 other units demolished today.	G.

Army Form C. 2118.

WAR DIARY
or
INTELLIGENCE SUMMARY.
(Erase heading not required.)

Instructions regarding War Diaries and Intelligence Summaries are contained in F. S. Regs., Part II. and the Staff Manual respectively. Title pages will be prepared in manuscript.

Place	Date	Hour	Summary of Events and Information	Remarks and references to Appendices
Lodelinsart	5/6			
			Patients	
			admitted 1 } remaining in Hospital 17.	
			Evacuated 1 }	
	7"		The weather has become very cold with hard frost to count number of cases of influenza and pyrexia on the increase due possibly to the men remaining in tents more in pneumo weather	c
do.			Patients admitted 5	
			to duty 1 } remaining in Hospital 17.	a
			Evacuated to C.C.S. 3	
do.	8"		Patients admitted 8	
			to duty 2 } remaining in hospital 18.	c
			Evacuated to C.C.S. 3	
			Three men deserted to-day from the unit.	

Army Form C. 2118.

WAR DIARY
or
INTELLIGENCE SUMMARY.
(Erase heading not required.)

Place	Date	Hour	Summary of Events and Information	Remarks and references to Appendices
LODELINSART.	Feb 9th		Patients in Hospital 21 admitted 3. To duty 1, to C.C.S. 2.	
	Feb 10th		Patients in Hospital 22 — admitted 3 — to duty 1 — to CCS 2.	
	Feb 11th		Patients in Hospital 22 — " 4 — " 1 — " 4. Three R.A.M.C. personnel admitted today	
	" 12		Patients " 21 — " 4 — " 3 — " 1. one N.C.O. admitted today	
	" 13		Patients " 21 — " 8 — " 1 — " 8.	
	" 14		Patients " 20 — " 7 — " 2 — " 1. Three men R.A.M.C. admitted today	
	" 15		Patients " 24 — " 10 — " 0 — " 6.	
	" 16		Patients " 28 — " 3 — " 3 — " 0. No'cases admitted also 3. O.R. admitted to-day	
	" 17		Patients " 28 — " 3 — " 5 — " 1. 3.O.R. R.A.M.C. had been admitted today.	
			The general distribution of the Division remains the same. (CE) HQ & Div. 63rd Brigade MELLET area. 112th Brigade & Divisional Artillery in GOSSELIES. 111th Brigade in JUMET area. in RANSART area.	
			Owing to the progress of demobilization each brigade commands now of not more than the strength of a battalion. The health of the division troops remains good in April 67	

Army Form C. 2118.

WAR DIARY
or
INTELLIGENCE SUMMARY.
(Erase heading not required.)

Instructions regarding War Diaries and Intelligence Summaries are contained in F.S. Regs., Part II. and the Staff Manual respectively. Title pages will be prepared in manuscript.

Place	Date	Hour	Summary of Events and Information	Remarks and references to Appendices
LODELINSART	July 17.		The great prevalence of influenza amongst the civil population. The influenza was shown a marked tendency to affect the boys with varying degrees of broncho-pneumonia. Several cases is with any marked the number of cases occurring in the Brigade at minimum more than 2 or 3 a week. The early treatment was provided in each unit in consulta with the Landrat and Post. For several battalions an out used to any post estates. Colonel Gran has been taken out and in full charge under. Of the men contracting the disease the majority take no prophylactic measures before exposure to infection in part? and treatment seems possibly.	&
	July 18.		Patients in hospital 25. admitted 7 total. O. evacuated to Cm 8. 3 heavy draught horses marked for evacuation everywhere own own to CHARLEROI station this morning	&

Army Form C. 2118.

WAR DIARY
or
INTELLIGENCE SUMMARY.
(Erase heading not required.)

Instructions regarding War Diaries and Intelligence Summaries are contained in F.S. Regs., Part II. and the Staff Manual respectively. Title pages will be prepared in manuscript.

Place	Date	Hour	Summary of Events and Information	Remarks and references to Appendices
Lodelinsart.	Feb 19	9	Patients in Hospital 24 / admitted 2 / totals 2 / to C.C.S. 1.	
	20		Patients " " 23 " " 8 " 3 " C.C.S. 6.	
			Col. J. McCARTHY R.A.M.C. took over the duties of A.D.M.S. 34th Division. Col MORPHEW D.S.O leaving to become D.D.M.S. Corps.	Adm. O.R. Dumfries 5th day
			Patients in Hospital 23 / admitted 2 / totals 3 / to C.C.S. 1.	
Gosselies	21		Headquarters of Field Ambulance moved to Gosselies, Gun + transport still remains at Lodelinsart.	
	22		Patients in Hospital 21 Admitted 12 Evacuated to C.C.G.S. 5	
"	23		Patients in Hospital 25 Admitted 4 Evacuated to C.C.S. 6	
"	24		Lieut Col GLARKE D.S.O. R.A.M.C proceeded on ordinary leave to England, Major S. SCOTT taking on command of the Field Ambulance	
			Patients in Hospital 23 Admitted 4 Evacuated to C.C.S. 3	
	25		C.H.D. horses Class Y were sent away 8 day, evacuation of personnel still proceeding at the rate of 3 O.Rs every 3rd day.	
			Patients in Hospital 23 Admitted 4 Evacuated to C.G.S 8	
"	26		Orders received that owing to the Influenza prevalent in this area, all Rioting Entertainments were to be forbidden	
			Patients in Hospital 22 Admitted 5 Evacuated to C.C.S. 6	
			Orders received that Capt G.W. TREADGOLD R.A.M.C. attached to 13th K.R.R.C who are leaving the division for the Rhine	
"	24th		Patients in Hospital 22 Admitted 6 Evacuated to C.C.S. 2	

Army Form C. 2118.

WAR DIARY
or
INTELLIGENCE SUMMARY.
(Erase heading not required.)

Instructions regarding War Diaries and Intelligence Summaries are contained in F. S. Regs., Part II. and the Staff Manual respectively. Title pages will be prepared in manuscript.

Place	Date	Hour	Summary of Events and Information	Remarks and references to Appendices
Gouchie	Feb	28th	Patients in hospital 23 Admitted 1 Evacuated 6 C.C.S. 1	
			Strength of Unit at End of month	
			Officers 6	
			Rank & file 84	
			A.S.C. (M.T. & H.T.) 28	
			Total 118	
				C. Scott
				Major RAMC T
				A/O.C. 45th Fd Amb.

Army Form C. 2118.

WAR DIARY or INTELLIGENCE SUMMARY.

Vol 44

Place	Date	Hour	Summary of Events and Information	Remarks and references to Appendices
GOSSELIES	March 1st		The Ambulance still remains dug in between Gosselies & Jodelinsart the Hd.Qrs. & Hospital being at GOSSELIES, at LODELINSART there is the 9F15 Stores, Transport with bayonets of the personnel. At 0800 hrs a day Summer Time came into action, the clock being advanced one hour	
"	March 2		Remaining in hospital. Admissions 1 to C.C.S. 5	
"	March 3		Remaining in hospital. Admissions 2 to C.C.S. 3	
"			Demobilisation still proceeds at the old rate, that is 2 or 3 every 3rd day. Admissions 2 to C.C.S. 3	
"	March 4		Remaining in hospital. Lieut CUMMINGS M.C. U.S.A. was sent for temporary duty to day with 1/5 4th Army Concentration Camp during the temporary absence on leave of Capt SHEEHAN.	
	March 5		Remaining in hospital. Admissions 4 to C.C.S. 2	
			Food reinforcements were received to day, all 1914 or 15 men from 1st Convalescent Camp.	
	March 6th		Remaining in hospital. Admissions 1 to C.C.S. 1	
	March 7th		Remaining in hospital. Admissions 3 to C.C.S. 3	
	March 8th		Remaining in hospital. Admissions 3 to C.C.S. — 1	
			Capt RAYMOND R.A.M.C. SR. was invalided to hospital to day suffering from a fracture of the lower end of the Tibula accidentally received. Admissions 3 to C.C.S. 1	
	March 9th		Remaining in hospital. Admissions — to C.C.S. 1	
	March 10th		Remaining in hospital. Admissions 4 to C.C.S. 1	
	March 11th		Remaining in hospital. Admissions 6 to C.C.S. —	
			The Hdqrs moved to day, 2nd Division went to-day, three leaving only 2 Divisions	

Army Form C. 2118.

WAR DIARY
or
INTELLIGENCE SUMMARY.
(Erase heading not required.)

Instructions regarding War Diaries and Intelligence Summaries are contained in F.S. Regs., Part II. and the Staff Manual respectively. Title pages will be prepared in manuscript.

Place	Date	Hour	Summary of Events and Information	Remarks and references to Appendices
Gozeelees	March 11th		10 inches. Admissions to hospital 4 Runners	
"	March 12th		Admissions to hospital 3 Runners 40 6.6.S. 3	
	March 13th		Admissions to hospital 2 Runners 40 6.6.S. 2 Lt Col Clarke D.S.O. R.A.M.C. returned from leave & day 0 & resumed command of 4 field Ambulance	
	March 14th		Field Ambulance equipment checked by G/098 and intents prepared for all articles deficient intents taken not to be contracted to DADMS until further orders. Patients admitted 9. evacuated to C.C.S. 9	Clarke Warren
	March 15th		Medical Panniers in the A.I.D. Posts of Battalions in 111th Brigade checked and intents prepared for minimum when addressed. Patients admitted 7 evacuated to CCS 7	a
	March 16th		Headquarters of 48th Field Ambulance under Command of O.C. unit Kepelus with the Divisions at Etaples. in East Moyen-Gozelies. Home time. Motor ambulance Car Jarry & Epidermal notes at Estalwurs admonished and by Int withour. Epidermal in address of Mag Scott in leave by order issued by O.C. 48th Field Ambulance at gozelies Patients admitted 2 evacuated to CCS nil	a

Army Form C. 2118.

Army Form C. 2118.

WAR DIARY
or
INTELLIGENCE SUMMARY.
(Erase heading not required.)

Instructions regarding War Diaries and Intelligence Summaries are contained in F. S. Regs., Part II. and the Staff Manual respectively. Title pages will be prepared in manuscript.

Place	Date	Hour	Summary of Events and Information	Remarks and references to Appendices
March 17th Gouzeaucourt			Usual instructions received from A.D.M.S. 37th Div. Prisoner of War Camp was inspected on RANSART CHATEAU today by O.C. 48th Field Ambulance and report submitted. The clothing, bedding etc. of all prisoners in the camp were disinfected in the "Thresh Disinfector". Patients admitted 11. evacuated to CCS 5.	
	March 18th		Patients admitted 7. evacuated to CCS 6.	
	March 19th		List of all supplies received & kit prepared for submission to 37th Div. HQrs. Patients admitted 7. evacuated to CCS 7.	
	March 20th		All vehicles in the former cart taken to the exhibition ground. Overhaul and painted under grant provided by the Division. Patients admitted 9. evacuated to CCS 8.	
	March 21st		Cheques for £8..15.- out of Canteen funds sent to Cassell's Publishers London for 70 copies of "The Golden Horseshoe". Each member of the unit actively with the unit on 21st March to have 2/6 spent on copy. Published price 3/6. To be sent to mens home address. Patients admitted 9. evacuated to CCS 6.	
	March 22nd		Our Sgt Stor for boiling water handed over to Prisoner of War Camp RANSART CHATEAU for boiling all water before drinking. Evacuated to CCS 4. Patients admitted 4.	

Army Form C. 2118.

WAR DIARY
or
INTELLIGENCE SUMMARY.

(Erase heading not required.)

Instructions regarding War Diaries and Intelligence Summaries are contained in F. S. Regs., Part II. and the Staff Manual respectively. Title pages will be prepared in manuscript.

Place	Date	Hour	Summary of Events and Information	Remarks and references to Appendices
Gomeries	March 23.		Patients admitted 4. evacuated to C.C.S. 1.	
Gomeries	March 24.		Under instructions received from ADMS 37 Div Capt McGregor rcr proceeded today for duty with No 57 C.C.S. CHARLEROI and no March 9/1 strength unit. Patients 3 admitted. 3 evacuated to C.C.S.	
do	March 25.		Instructions received today for holding ready to be submitted to DADOS 37. Div. to complete equipment of ambulance according to new. G.1098. on a 2 section basis. Patients admitted 4 evacuated to C.C.S 2	
do	March 26th		DMS letter received today stating that order 9 i fully understood would consist of 1 medical officer in command and a ?? remaining medical officers to be warned for any duties in ?? departure of cadre for England. Patients 7 admitted 2 evacuated to C.C.S	

Army Form C. 2118.

WAR DIARY
or
INTELLIGENCE SUMMARY.
(Erase heading not required.)

Instructions regarding War Diaries and Intelligence Summaries are contained in F. S. Regs., Part II. and the Staff Manual respectively. Title pages will be prepared in manuscript.

Place	Date	Hour	Summary of Events and Information	Remarks and references to Appendices
Gondia	March 27		The main cause of sickness in the Division at present is venereal disease. The men here at the dictated on the danger of infection and the value of early treatment and prophylactic measures. The amount of venereal disease has been known taken in proportion and many appear to have come under the influence of alcohol at the time. Patients 3 admitted 1 evacuated to CCS	a
Gondia	March 28		Patients 4 admitted 1 evacuated to CCS	
do	March 29		Patients 8 admitted 5 evacuated to CCS very few cases of infantry admitted principally venereal cases and sickness.	a
do	March 30		Patients admitted 3. evacuated to CCS 5. Some Horse Artillery evacuated to Bhusa by train today been 10 miles still held unit.	a
do	March 31		Patients admitted 3. evacuated to CCS 3. Strength of unit RAMC officers 4. other ranks 39. SC other ranks 24	a

Clarke Lt/Col RAMC
O.C. 48th Field Amb.

140/3550

April 1919

COMMITTEE FOR MP
17 JUL 1919

Vol. 45

Army Form C. 2118.

WAR DIARY
or
INTELLIGENCE SUMMARY.
(Erase heading not required.)

Instructions regarding War Diaries and Intelligence Summaries are contained in F. S. Regs., Part II. and the Staff Manual respectively. Title pages will be prepared in manuscript.

Place	Date	Hour	Summary of Events and Information	Remarks and references to Appendices
GOSSELIES	April 1st		49th Field Ambulance stationed at Gosselies in the solid building and forming the Station for the Cadre units of the 37th Division now located in JUMET. Amongst 9 admissions are 5 of slight catarrh with temperature lasting a few days (2 or 3) reason of recurrence very few men avail themselves of the truly obvious means on April 1. 9 trains admitted to this unit.	
			Patients admitted to evacuated to C. C. S. 3	
	April 2nd		Patients admitted 3 " " " cas. 3	Staff
	3rd		" " 8 " " " cas. 4	"
	4th		" " 3 " " " cas. 3	"
	5th		" " 2 " " " cas. 2	"
			With reference to the medical equipment of battalions and units in the 37th Division the information has been received from ADMS that the personnel will not be completed or dismantled. It has a full kit of uniform will be placed in each payment before the Cadre proceeds to England.	

Army Form C. 2118.

WAR DIARY
or
INTELLIGENCE SUMMARY.
(Erase heading not required.)

Instructions regarding War Diaries and Intelligence Summaries are contained in F.S. Regs., Part II. and the Staff Manual respectively. Title pages will be prepared in manuscript.

Place	Date	Hour	Summary of Events and Information	Remarks and references to Appendices
Gosselies	April 7		Patients admitted 1 evacuated by rail	
		7/8	" " 1 " " 6	
		9	" " 3 " " 2	
			Angush group.	
	April 11	10ᵃᵐ	Instructions received today that 48th Field Ambulance takes with it warning to Antwerp about 14th & 16th April, with 6th 63rd Infantry	
			Surgical Evacuation at School Building, Gosselies closed today, for the admission of patients, all patients in the Hospital today were marked for Light duty or transfers to C.C.S. Chatham.	
			Instructions received today to hand over GLENCORSE on all wheel and packages to 48th Field Ambulance.	
	April 12		Two mules belonging to 48th Field Ambulance were handed over to the IV Corps Heavy Artillery today on complains with instructions received from A.D.M.S. 37 Div.	

D. D. & L., London, E.C.
(A8001) Wt. W2771/M2031 750,000 5/17 Sch. 53 Forms/C2118/14

Army Form C. 2118.

WAR DIARY
or
INTELLIGENCE SUMMARY.
(Erase heading not required.)

Instructions regarding War Diaries and Intelligence Summaries are contained in F. S. Regs., Part II. and the Staff Manual respectively. Title pages will be prepared in manuscript.

Place	Date	Hour	Summary of Events and Information	Remarks and references to Appendices
Gosselies	April 12"		The G/1093 instruction sent with for Ch. Field Ambulance with all diffiencies in equipment of Field Ambulances was completed. Church Parade - 10th Corps troops parade to DAROS 37 Div. for inspection and when 37 m Div'D Instructs to complete sent of equipment and number strengths were also submitted to stages 37 Div.	
do.	April 14"		Instructions received from D.M.S. 4 Army that Lt Col C. Clarke R.A.M.C. would receive order instructions to proceed to Army J. on the Rhine.	
do.	April 15"		Instructions received from D.M.S. 2 Div to truvy aunt Caden 4 Major Kerr R.A.M.C. roome with unit take the cadre to GLENCORSE, SCOTLAND.	
do.	April 16"		A/D.D.M.S. cadre to load wagons on train at CHARLEROI at 09.00 hrs. Train leaves for ANTWERP at 17.00 hrs. 16/4/19.	

D. D. & L., London, E.C.
(A8001) Wt. W1771/M2031 750,000 5/17 Sch. 52 Forms/C2.10/14

Army Form C. 2118.

WAR DIARY
or
INTELLIGENCE SUMMARY.
(Erase heading not required.)

Place	Date	Hour	Summary of Events and Information	Remarks and references to Appendices
Antwerp	April 17"		After an eventful journey complete Cadre reached Antwerp were accommodated in the Staging Camp then embarked on the S.S. "AJAX" in the evening for Southampton. Cadre strength:- 2 Officers 56 Other ranks. S Scott Trayner Major T O/C 48th Fd Ambulance Cadre	

www.ingramcontent.com/pod-product-compliance
Lightning Source LLC
Chambersburg PA
CBHW080835010526
44114CB00017B/2314